Reading the Bible with Its Writers

"The question of how we interpret Scripture—and interpret it we must—is a centuries-old challenge and will continue to be so, no doubt, until Jesus returns. Steve Burnhope's excellent new book, *Reading the Bible with Its Writers*, takes a deceptively simple yet richly suggestive approach to this complex issue. Burnhope invites us to take the big themes of the Bible as our first and most important interpretive key, then consider genre and its implications as the second. Rather than reaching for our favorite 'proof texts,' this way of reading the biblical texts honors both their human and divine origins and challenges us again to think carefully about what it means to call them 'the Word of God.'"

—**Neal Swettenham**, founding senior pastor, Melton Vineyard Church

"To be an evangelical is to engage the Bible seriously. Steve Burnhope supports this vision by helping us read the Bible with the grain, attending to its key themes and different genres. In this way he helps us attend to the process of interpretation. There are always disputes about interpretation, and I have some here as well, but Burnhope rightly focuses on hearing God's voice so that we respond with our 'yes' to live in a flourishing relationship with him."

—**Ben C. Blackwell**, principal, Westminster Theological Centre, Cheltenham

"This book is the key to unlocking your understanding of the Bible in ways you've always hoped for: designed to be accessible, concise, and practical, making it easy for everyone to read and interpret the whole Bible. Steve expertly moves us beyond dry facts and proof-texting to discover the truth and life-giving power of Scripture. Discover what the Bible said and why, to hear its message for today."

—**Jason Swan Clark**, director of the London Centre for Spiritual Direction

"Steve Burnhope's writing exemplifies the timeless adage that true understanding is the key to clear and simple explanation. In his latest book, *Reading the Bible with Its Writers*, he once again speaks directly to the thoughtful Christian, inviting readers to engage deeply with the what, why, and how of the Bible's original authors. Steve encourages us to move beyond isolated texts and explore the overarching story and broader themes woven throughout scripture. This book is an invaluable resource for any Bible reader but is particularly beneficial for pastors and those, like me, who have the privilege of preaching and teaching regularly."

—**David Graham**, lead pastor, Southcourt Baptist Church, Aylesbury

"Steve is a rare breed, in that he can take challenging, complex theological concepts, and communicate them, not only in an articulate and clear way, but in a pastoral way as well. There is such a need for pastoral wisdom in the outworking of theological truth and I am grateful that Steve has stepped into that space with *Reading the Bible with Its Writers*, and I highly recommend both it—and Steve—to you."

—**Henry Cross**, senior pastor, Rock and Redeemer Vineyard Church, Dunstable

Reading the Bible with Its Writers

*What They Were Saying,
Why They Said It,
How They Said It*

Stephen Burnhope

 CASCADE *Books* · Eugene, Oregon

READING THE BIBLE WITH ITS WRITERS
What They Were Saying, Why They Said It, How They Said It

Copyright © 2025 Stephen Burnhope. All rights reserved. Except for brief quotations in critical publications or reviews, no part of this book may be reproduced in any manner without prior written permission from the publisher. Write: Permissions, Wipf and Stock Publishers, 199 W. 8th Ave., Suite 3, Eugene, OR 97401.

Cascade Books
An Imprint of Wipf and Stock Publishers
199 W. 8th Ave., Suite 3
Eugene, OR 97401

www.wipfandstock.com

PAPERBACK ISBN: 979-8-3852-2836-2
HARDCOVER ISBN: 979-8-3852-2837-9
EBOOK ISBN: 979-8-3852-2838-6

Cataloguing-in-Publication data:

Names: Burnhope, Stephen [author].

Title: Reading the Bible with its writers : what they were saying, why they said it, how they said it / by Stephen Burnhope.

Description: Eugene, OR: Cascade Books, 2025 | Includes bibliographical references.

Identifiers: ISBN 979-8-3852-2836-2 (paperback) | ISBN 979-8-3852-2837-9 (hardcover) | ISBN 979-8-3852-2838-6 (ebook)

Subjects: LCSH: Bible—Study and teaching. | Bible—Hermeneutics. | Bible as literature.

Classification: BS600.2 B87 2025 (paperback) | BS600.2 (ebook)

VERSION NUMBER 02/27/25

All Scripture quotations, unless otherwise indicated, are taken from the Holy Bible, New International Version®, NIV®. Copyright ©1973, 1978, 1984, 2011 by Biblica, Inc.™ Used by permission of Zondervan. All rights reserved worldwide. www.zondervan.com. The "NIV" and "New International Version" are trademarks registered in the United States Patent and Trademark Office by Biblica, Inc.™

Scripture quotations marked NIrV are taken from the Holy Bible, New International Reader's Version®, NIrV® Copyright © 1995, 1996, 1998, 2014 by Biblica, Inc.™ Used by permission of Zondervan. All rights reserved worldwide. www.zondervan.com. The "NIrV" and "New International Reader's Version" are trademarks registered in the United States Patent and Trademark Office by Biblica, Inc.™

Scripture quotations marked NASB are taken from the (NASB®) New American Standard Bible®, Copyright © 1960, 1971, 1977, 1995, 2020 by The Lockman Foundation. Used by permission. All rights reserved. lockman.org.

Scripture quotations marked NLT are taken from the *Holy Bible*, New Living Translation, copyright © 1996, 2004, 2015 by Tyndale House Foundation. Used by permission of Tyndale House Publishers, Inc., Carol Stream, Illinois 60188. All rights reserved.

Scripture quotations marked NRSV are taken from the New Revised Standard Version Bible, copyright © 1989 National Council of the Churches of Christ in the United States of America. Used by permission. All rights reserved worldwide.

Scripture quotations marked ESV are from The ESV® Bible (The Holy Bible, English Standard Version®), © 2001 by Crossway, a publishing ministry of Good News Publishers. Used by permission. All rights reserved.

Scripture quotations marked MSG are taken from THE MESSAGE, copyright © 1993, 2002, 2018 by Eugene H. Peterson. Used by permission of NavPress. All rights reserved. Represented by Tyndale House Publishers, Inc.

Scripture quotations marked J. B. Phillips are taken from The New Testament in Modern English, copyright © 1958, 1959, 1960 J. B. Phillips and 1947, 1952, 1955, 1957 The Macmillan Company, New York. Used by permission. All rights reserved.

Contents

Author's Preface | ix

General Introduction | 1

Part I—What They Were Saying and Why: The Big Themes

Introduction | 21

1. Creation and New Creation | 25
2. Relationship with God | 45
3. Covenant | 62
4. The Nature and Character of God | 84
5. Justice, Righteousness, and Shalom | 94
6. A People of God | 112
7. The Enemies of God | 124
8. Messiah | 135
9. The Kingdom of God | 143

Part II—How They Said It: The Genres

Introduction | 155

1. Narrative/History | 163
2. Commandments | 171
3. Parables | 177

4. Exaggeration/Hyperbole | 182
5. Letters | 185
6. Wisdom | 193
7. Poetry, Song, and Lament | 204
8. Prophecy and Apocalyptic | 210

Bibliography | 221

Author's Preface

THIS IS A BOOK about theology—but don't let that put you off! The reality is that we all *have* theology and we all *do* theology, because we all have thoughts about God and the things of God that we express through words. The only question is where we're getting them from—and, of course, whether they're any good or not. Theology is not an optional extra for "the really keen ones."

Theology done well is what enables us to "make sense" of things in the Christian life. And, of course, vice versa—theology done badly is what causes things not to make sense (whether that's to us or to our friends). Either way, there is no "theology-free" option of just reading the Bible and believing the Bible, however sincerely that may be intended.

A well-known characterization of theology is "faith seeking understanding" (*fides quaerens intellectum*), credited to Anselm, the eleventh-century archbishop of Canterbury, though originating in a similar phrase attributed to Augustine several centuries earlier. Note that faith is not *the alternative* to understanding; they are not in competition. This both/and (rather than either/or) approach is helpful in framing the book's objective, which is to empower Christians who begin from a position of faith but want to add understanding to that faith.

Although the book stands alone, it can be thought of as a companion volume to *How to Read the Bible Well*,[1] which signposts the style and approach in this present book. Here I have been able to make available material that could not be included in its predecessor without it

1. Burnhope, *How to Read the Bible Well*.

becoming unmanageable, size-wise. It allows me to say more on subjects that were addressed only briefly, and to respond to questions raised in seminars and conversations since its publication.

Both books are directed at thoughtful Christians—pastors, students, and lay people alike—who have a desire to think better and more deeply theologically. This target audience is not well served right now. The typical offerings in the popular Christian world tend toward devotional material (which is fine so far as it goes) while the material available from the academic world is insufficiently accessible—it's either too complex, too specialized, too lacking in obvious application, or readers simply don't know where to start (or with which authors to start). My aim is to provide good theological thinking written in an easy-to-read, accessible way.

Notice that I include pastors in the mix of target readers. Many pastors I know are very conscious of having had little or no opportunity to engage in formal academic theological training—especially when it comes to responding to their congregants' big questions (if not also their own big questions). In some cases, it's not so much no training as what they did have being many years ago. For those in that position, I hope my books offer something of an accessible "crash course," allied to practical pastoral relevance, for minimal outlay.

I also hope that along with its predecessor the book will be of value for faculty members to recommend to their students as a primer for hermeneutics,[2] and especially for those training for Christian ministry.

The book is consciously structured in bite-sized pieces. The reader can easily pick it up and put it down (dip in and dip out), without losing continuity. It is not necessary to read the book sequentially.

For those who may be interested in the technicalities of these things, the book reflects a combination of biblical theology and systematic theology. To speak of *biblical* theology can appear to be granting it a higher status compared to the less-spiritual sounding *systematic* theology—the implication being that "biblical" must mean "closer to the Bible." The reality, however, is that these disciplines overlap, especially when practiced in an evangelical context; neither is intrinsically more honoring of Scripture nor more concerned for Scripture. We could say that biblical theology seeks to identify the "what" in Scripture, while systematic theology seeks both to organize that "what" and to address the "therefores"—the

---

2. Hermeneutics is the technical term for "biblical interpretation," often used to speak of the principles and approaches applied to interpreting the Bible: how we go about it.

implications and applications for the church's beliefs and practices today. Biblical theology is concerned to identify texts and their meaning; systematic theology asks what we are to do with those texts and their meaning. Systematics has been particularly known for collating scriptural teaching for the purpose of framing beliefs. For example, drafting or revising a church's statement of faith is a systematic theological exercise.

Neither discipline stands alone and separate, however. The overlap between the two—especially for evangelicals, with our customary emphasis on the centrality of Scripture—is such that it's unhelpful to posit a sharp distinction between them; they complement rather than compete. Both are concerned for good hermeneutics to determine texts' original meanings (then) and their contemporary relevance (now). We might even say that it's not possible to be doing one without the other (or at least, that one without the other will come up short in some sense).

Already we have had cause to reference "evangelical," which has become an increasingly contested word, largely because in the United States it has acquired a distinct sociopolitical identity linked to a version of "Christian nationalism" that is especially associated with the Republican Party and a particular form of cultural as well as religious conservatism. Here, however, we will be using the term only to speak of those streams within organized Christianity that manifestly align their beliefs and practice with the four core features of popular evangelicalism identified by the British historian David Bebbington:

1. "Biblicism"—affirming the central importance of Scripture as the Word of God;

2. "Activism"—being actively engaged in the work of the kingdom: "doing," not just believing;

3. "Conversionism"—the need for individuals to come into a personal relationship with God through Jesus; and

4. "Crucicentrism"—the central place of the cross in making that relationship possible.[3]

Some have contested Bebbington's list, usually to expand upon it rather than reject it,[4] but it remains a useful description of the movement's core

---

3. Commonly known as the "Bebbington Quadrilateral": Bebbington, *Evangelicalism*, 1.

4. Alister McGrath, for example, proposes an expanded six points, in *Evangelicalism*. Personally, I would add "Conservatism" as a persistently visible feature (certainly

characteristics from an irreducible minimum perspective, if not from a maximal (or even, ideal) perspective.[5] Personally, I am entirely happy to identify as an evangelical who affirms Bebbington's four criteria, though, as you might expect from any theologian worth their salt, I would offer my own take on each of those features if we were treating the subject in any depth (and I would beg to differ from some of the elements that the word "evangelical" has recently been taken to embrace and require).

A certain amount of repetition will be found within the book. This is not the result of careless editing! Rather, it's to enable chapters and sections to be read on a stand-alone basis without the reader needing to recall things said elsewhere. Another contributing factor is the overlapping nature of some of the themes, especially in Part I, where (for example) it is impossible to separate God's relational purposes in the creation story (chapter 1) from his nature and character (chapter 2), and in turn, not to see the covenantal journey embedded in Scripture as the natural outworking (chapter 3).

It remains only to thank everyone who has in some way contributed to this book's publication. Naturally, I begin with my thanks to the lovely people at Wipf and Stock, and most especially to my wonderful editor, Dr. Robin Parry, now for the third time of asking; surely the very epitome of fortitude. And to Andrew Jacobs, my copy editor. Thank you for your most excellent wisdom, insights, and advice. I would also like to thank my endorsers for their kind words, and those who kindly reviewed and proofread the book in manuscript form. Naturally, any failings and weaknesses in the finished product are entirely down to me.

---

religious conservatism, but usually cultural conservatism as well—with these often commingled in practice, without the distinction being recognized). I would also add "Experiential Pietism," and ideally swap "Christocentrism" for "Crucicentrism," because of the former's broader scope.

5. It's important to remember that Bebbington is seeking to define evangelicalism as it is generally encountered, rather than promoting a view on what it ought to be.

General Introduction

WHEN A FRIEND RECOMMENDS a book they've just read—or for that matter, a movie they've just watched—the first question that normally springs to mind is, what's it all about? A simple enough question, you would think; but in the case of the Bible it's not one that's so easily answered.

Though we speak of the Bible as a book, it's really a collection of books: a compendium, contributed to by many different people over a long period of time. In that sense, it's more like a small library. The individual works that comprise it were first recognized as special in their own right—formative in some way in relation to life and faith—by our forebears.

In the first instance, this took place within a people of God called Israel, concerning the books that Christians speak of as the Old Testament or Hebrew Bible, which Jewish people call the Tanakh.[1] The composition of this collection was essentially already determined by the first century CE, at the time of Jesus and the early church. In due course, a further group of books came together under the auspices of the early church fathers in the first few centuries CE, a collection that Christians now call the New Testament. Those same church fathers, taking their lead from the early church, continued to recognize the special significance of the Hebrew Bible alongside the New Testament. The two groups together Christians now know in combination as "the Bible."

---

1. Tanakh is an acronym derived from the names of the three divisions of the Hebrew Bible: *Torah* (Instruction, or Law, also called the Pentateuch), *Nevi' im* (the Prophets), and *Ketuvim* (the Writings). See Kuiper, "Tanakh."

Precisely how the Old and New Testaments came together—what determined which writings were included and which were left out—is an interesting historical question for another time. Suffice to say that Christian tradition, building on Jewish tradition preceding it, has handed down to us the Bible as we know it. We could spend time speculating on the boundaries of the canon (whether certain apocryphal books might have been included) but we are where we are: we need to trust the decisions made by our forebears that have been recognized for nigh on two thousand years. Or put differently, we have enough to be working with in relation to the books that *are* in the canon, and nothing material is gained by speculating around the edges.

Yet none of this helps answer that starting question: What's the Bible all about? To which the answer is both simple and complex. In its simplest form, we might say that it's the story of God and people, within an overarching story of God and creation. It presents a supernatural personified being who is the one, true God (over and above other so-called gods and supernatural beings) and the relationship of that God with people across several millennia.

The story begins as an explanation, in easily assimilated picture language form, originally passed down as oral tradition, of how things began, and then where they began to go wrong. Soon enough, a divine plan appears for how God will in due course right those wrongs. It begins with God choosing a couple (Abraham and Sarah) from whom will emerge over many generations an extended family that will become a nation, ultimately known as Israel. Before the first book (Genesis) has even finished, the plot takes a detour to mainly focus thereafter on that one nation and its relationship with God, who becomes known as "the God of Israel." The nation is unilaterally chosen to be a people with whom he has a special and enduring relationship. The remainder of the Old Testament is, in short, that story unfolding and outworking, with its ups and downs, triumphs and disasters, successes and failures. A key theme is the unshakable faithfulness of God juxtaposed with the patchy and inconsistent faithfulness of his people in response.

In the prophetic portions of the Old Testament, we see the foreshadowing of a time to come when God will directly intervene in the affairs not just of the nation of Israel but of all nations, reaching out not just to Jewish people but to all people—gentiles (non-Jews) included. What, precisely, this direct intervention or reaching out will involve—and when it will happen—is far less clear. There are promises and hints framed mostly in values-centered goals rather than specific actions, but sufficient to encourage God's people that there is a divine master plan which in his own good time he will fulfill, a plan that will embrace the whole world. This reaches its zenith with the coming of Jesus—Son of God and Son of Man.

Having begun as the story of all people, before being channeled into a story of one people, it now returns to being the story of all people. The inclusion of the gentiles into the people of God is a direct consequence of the incarnation, life, death, and resurrection of Jesus and the sending of the Holy Spirit that follows. The one true God now becomes more clearly framed as trinity: one God in three persons.

The New Testament is the story of Jesus (told from four overlapping perspectives that we know as Matthew, Mark, Luke, and John) together with the writings of early church leaders to groups of Jesus-followers in cities in the Roman Empire of the Mediterranean world, as they tried to work out what all this meant: the consequences of the coming of Jesus and the inclusion of the gentiles. Prominent among those writers is Paul, a faithful Jewish believer who received a divine calling to take the message of Jesus to the gentile world: a message of invitation into the people of God on terms that were distinct from those that prevailed for Jewish people. Included within those writings (rather as was the case in the Old Testament) are similarly prophetic portions foreshadowing a time to come when God will once more directly intervene in the affairs of this world, to complete the divine plan centered on Jesus, finally righting all wrongs, in a renewed creation.

So that is one way of answering the question of what the Bible is all about. And while we could use some alternative language and frame some things differently, it's not wrong so far as it goes. But of course, there is more that needs to be said. What's been said so far is only one element. The complication, if you will, is that the Bible is more than a story—more than even a very important story. We also know it as "the word of God"—generally with a capital "W." So what does that phrase mean? A few moments' thought will tell us it's far from self-evident, not least because there is also a sense in which the Bible is the words of people, at least in the first instance. The Bible is not written in the first person, and even on the occasions that statements are presented to us as that, they come through people speaking on God's behalf.

No serious biblical scholar thinks of the Bible as divine dictation per se, so there is an enigmatic interaction that we cannot avoid between the Bible as the words of people and the Bible as the word of God (I will follow academic convention—no capital letter—to avoid unwittingly conflating it with the Word of God spoken of in John 1 and 1 John—the second person of the Trinity; the Bible is not divine in any corresponding sense).

The Nature of the Bible as "the Word of God"

Surprisingly, perhaps, the Bible says very little about itself in terms of its nature and it never actually speaks of itself as the word of God. The concept that this extra-biblical phrase seeks to reflect for Christians is that the Bible is a unique text in literature. We believe it to be "inspired" by God, per 2 Tim 3:16,[2] and to hold a unique position in mediating the things of God to us. We therefore want to be faithful to that when we read it.

Second Timothy 3:16 is important as the only direct biblical reference to the nature of Scripture. But that simply takes us to another question: what, exactly, divine inspiration means—what it "does" to the text.[3] It's easy to assume that the involvement in its production of a God who is outside of time means that everything in the Bible "must be" speaking timelessly. In other words, that it must be saying the exact same thing to people, now, that it was saying to people, then—or at least, it should be applied the same way as often as conceivably possible; "biblical truths" for then must still be biblical truths for now.[4]

And yet, we all know that this is far too simplistic—an easy example would be many of the Old Testament commandments. Once we realize that not everything from then is directly applicable to now—it cannot all be copied and pasted—we see that we have a job to do. Yes, Scripture is inspired throughout, but that does not mean that what it is saying is "timeless" in every instance.[5] Yes, of course the Bible *has* timeless content,

---

2. Technically, the writer was speaking here of what we call the Old Testament, but it is not unreasonable from a Christian faith perspective to extend that principle to the whole of Scripture as we now have it.

3. Some take "inspired" to be synonymous with "inerrant" or "infallible" and conjoin it with the Bible's implicit (divine) authority. We are at liberty to believe those things about it, but none come directly from the notion of "inspired" or "God-breathed," which remains enigmatic, perhaps intentionally so.

4. This gives rise to some complexities when it comes to applying the (timeless) authority of Scripture—a quality that evangelical statements of faith typically affirm.

5. It is certainly not intending to offer timeless truths when it comes to matters of science—biology, cosmology, and anthropology.

but it is *not all* timeless content, and even that which *is* timeless comes to us in the first instance in a time-bound, context-specific wrapper. Everything in the Bible meant something to people then, before it ever means something to us now—if we ignore its first meaning we are in danger of getting today's meaning wrong. Determining the relationship of the "then" to the "now" in ways that are faithful to God's intentions for the text is the interpreter's challenge.

The hazards of unwittingly reading the Bible anachronistically are exacerbated by us calling it "the word of God." I am not suggesting we retire the term, but we all need to think carefully—and not take for granted—what we understand by it.

Of course there is a sense in which the Holy Spirit who inspired Scripture is also a "writer," metaphorically speaking, so we need to be reading it with him, listening for his voice in the text. But we shouldn't be too quick to leap to that. Let's first make sure that we're understanding how the human writer saw and understood things.

The relationship between the humanity and the divinity in the text is not straightforward; it's something to grapple with. There is a tendency for Christians to attribute a very high element of divinity to the text and a correspondingly low element of humanity—not quite equating the word of God with the *words* of God in all instances, but not far short in practice.

In fairness, of course, the same tendency occurs with the person of Jesus. In both cases, the default position seems to be to allow only so much humanity to come through as is deemed to be unavoidable, for fear of diminishing the divinity and thus undermining the standing of the word of God—written or incarnate, as the case may be. The contribution of Scripture's divine author in what's said is emphasized (God's degree of control over what was written), while the contribution of the human authors is diminished (to avert any suggestion of human flaws having crept in). I don't suggest that this is intentional. It's more unwitting, led by a desire to uphold the standing of Scripture as our supreme authority for beliefs and practice.

For the avoidance of doubt, let me stress that we are not questioning *whether* the Bible is the word of God but rather *what we mean* by that phrase. We're not questioning its centrality for Christian faith, but simply asking how being something called the word of God "works" in practice. We're thinking through God's part in its composition alongside the human writers' part and how those impact the nature of the Bible we have in our hands (or on our handheld devices) today, in which the critical factor is *God's intentions* for the nature and function of the text and how he intends us to engage with it.[6]

In practice, I suspect most Christians make their judgments on whether a scriptural imperative is context free (and hence, to be followed today) or context specific (to be ignored, or at least marginalized) on the basis of whether they can see what it's saying "working well" in our world. Such judgments may be made in good faith, but the subjectivity involved is rather obvious. It's also clearly allowing the contemporary culture to take a lead role—which will understandably make many Christians uneasy. To simply reject any texts that don't translate well to our world and society today cannot be an across-the-board response; but nor should insisting on them all the more stridently, when they're making no sense to our audience, be treated as a badge of honor. We need (a) to be really sure that we are reading and applying those texts correctly for today, as God would have us do, and (b) to be conscious of the negative impact on our mission to draw people into relationship with Jesus through the gospel when things that we are insisting upon as "biblical" come across as simply inconceivable. If we're experiencing that negative impact in our mission, then it's very likely we should be seriously rethinking things, because we must be absolutely sure that it's worth it—that whatever it is *matters so much to God* that it doesn't matter how many people fail to come to faith because of it.

More About "Then" and "Now"

One of the characteristics of the Christian world that has emerged in the past century or so is the proliferation of Bible translations.[7] Not that long ago, for all practical purposes we had just the one—the seventeenth-century King James Version (or KJV). It was *the* Bible. One could say, "The Bible says," and that was that. But now the first question is, "Which Bible says? Which version?" Every Christian is now aware not only that there is something called biblical interpretation but also that it's unavoidable. *In itself, of course, translation is an act of interpretation.*

---

6. One of the main goals for *How to Read the Bible Well* was to help us begin to grapple with these kinds of issues about the Bible, not least because it's our perceptions about its nature that lead directly to our application: what it's "for," what we are to do with it.

7. Over sixty versions are available to compare on biblegateway.com, for instance.

And yes, translators (and their publishing houses) have prior doctrinal commitments that their translations will reflect.

An abundance of translations has also democratized biblical interpretation, insofar as we no longer need the KJV's archaic English decoded for us. Except for uber-traditionalist "KJV-only" advocates—who cling to that ancient translation for cultural reasons rather than scholarly reasons—the newer translations from the better academic resources that are now available help us to avoid misunderstandings of meaning based on some of the KJV's now-redundant olde English. If anything our problem today is that we have too many versions available, offering too many takes on a text's meaning. Just click on the "Other Translations" button beside a verse on biblegateway.com and you'll see what I mean. The temptation now is to pick the version that we like best! But the point is made that, just as there is no "theology-free" option of just reading the Bible and believing it, so too there is no "interpretation-free" option.

The availability of contemporary translations in our native languages unquestionably makes the ancient world text more accessible for today's readers. And to the extent it encourages Bible reading, that's definitely a good thing. We want to close the gap between the biblical writers and ourselves. We want the inspired text to speak to people and for its relevance to be clear in our world today. And yet, closing the gap can also be problematic. Rewriting the text into what are perceived to be comparable contemporary phrases and expressions—especially in a paraphrase—can lead people to read what they're reading as if it was written directly to them, today. We can miss the original context, in other words, which is an essential ingredient for reading the Bible and its meaning well.

The Epistles are a good example. These were occasional letters written to specific groups of early Christians for particular reasons. In every case, there was a context and an audience to whom the letter was addressed. There were reasons for the letter's content, often addressing local questions and issues, with localized answers and emphases. The writers were not consciously writing theology textbooks for all times and places. The letters were not written to us in the first instance; we are eavesdroppers on their conversations.

All biblical truths are true, but they're not all timeless truths (just as all biblical promises are true, but they're not all true for us right now). We need the Holy Spirit's guidance to wisely discern in community whether a writer is making a timeless and universally applicable truth statement or a time-bound and locally applicable truth statement. Both are "true" in their respective senses, but they are not to be applied in the same way. The writer may be referencing something as a *norm* (something that was customarily the case—if not taken for granted—in the context into which he was writing) or prescribing something as *normative* (something that should always be the case, in all contexts, with the authority of the divine author standing behind it). This is where wisdom comes in; we need to hear the divine voice in and through the text and discern that which was culturally situated and culturally conditioned from that which God intends to be culture free and universal.

This alerts us to the need, before we do anything else with a text—and especially before we seek to apply it to ourselves today—to establish as best we can what the writer was intending to say to his audience at the time. Equally importantly, we need to ask *why* he was saying it. Then we are in a position to move to the quite separate, distinct question of what it might be saying to us, now, in our context. But if we skip that crucial first step, we are in serious danger of reading the Bible anachronistically.

To ask such questions in no way undermines or challenges the inspired nature of what the biblical writers wrote. It's simply recognizing that "inspired" is not a synonym for "context free" or "culture free"—both context and culture are embedded in inspired Scripture.

Beyond the particular local factors in a place and time—in first-century Galilee, Jerusalem, Corinth, Ephesus, or wherever—the differences between our world and the biblical world are huge; the ways people thought then, how they lived then, and how they understood things then, compared to today, could scarcely be greater.

A well-known announcement on the London Underground (the "Tube") is "Mind the gap!"—warning travelers of the risk of falling between the platform edge and train when boarding and alighting. As Bible readers, and especially as interpreters, we ignore the gap between then and now at our peril. Contemporary versions of the Bible are not always our friend in this, especially when they "update" things for us. This is all the more true of paraphrases, where the "updating" can all too easily cause people to read Scripture as if it was a contemporary text (and interpret it accordingly). Taking full and proper account of the "gap" is part of understanding what the writer was intending to say, what he meant by what he said, and why he was saying it.

Notwithstanding the perils of inappropriately *collapsing* the gap between then and now, we do of course need to *bridge* that gap. This does not mean simply rejecting anything that the biblical writers said then—or *appear* to have been saying then, which is not always the same thing—if it fails to comport with how people think today. That is emphatically *not* how to read Scripture, not least because of its dual authorship. The role of the Holy Spirit inspiring the text elevates it beyond just "how people thought then." Our challenge as biblical readers and interpreters (we are never only the former) is to discern what divine inspiration "does" to the text in communicating the things of God to us in our day and our world—in other words, how inspiration "works" in relation to the gap.

This is by no means always straightforward: all Scripture was written *by* people—and addressed *to* people—who lived in what we would now call an ancient world context (obviously they didn't think of it as "the ancient world" at the time!). The writers and their audiences shared broadly the same perspective on "the way things are and are supposed to be." This applies to all manner of aspects of life and human knowledge, whether it's (what we would now call) politics, government, religion, science (biology, cosmology, health, medicine), social structures, ethics, and morals. They saw the world in the light of a common worldview, as we call it, with an accompanying metanarrative (an overarching explanatory story about how life is).[8] Hence, if we are to grasp what they were "saying" we need to begin from the same point.

The Challenges for Us as Readers

We cannot talk about the Bible as a text without also saying some important things about the reader when he or she approaches the text. None of us comes to the Bible without a base of existing knowledge and opinions—things we already know to be the case, or believe to be the case, rightly or wrongly—that form the lenses through which we read the Bible and perceive what it's saying. We call these "presuppositions," or "preconceptions." They are not a bad thing per se; they are unavoidable. We all have them. The problem comes when we're unaware that we have them, and what they are, such that we're unable to see how they're influencing our ideas about meaning. That does not mean there are not good presuppositions and bad presuppositions—again, it depends what they are! But either way, we need to reckon with them. No one approaches the Bible

---

8. See Burnhope, *How to Read the Bible Well*, chapter 5, "How the Biblical Writers Saw Their World (and Why That Matters to Us)."

as if our prior knowledge and opinions on all things biblical have been wiped clean prior to each reading.[9]

The first step is therefore to be aware of our presuppositions. These are typically indicated when we take for granted that something "obviously," "must be," or "can't be" the case. *Usually, that's a presupposition talking.* The second step is being willing to have a genuinely open mind as to whether some of our presuppositions may be less well founded than we thought.

I think there are three key questions that impact how we read the Bible and how we believe we should apply what we read. Those are:

1. What is the nature of the Bible?
2. What is God like?
3. What things are most (and least) important to him?

How we answer each of those questions affects how we read the Bible and what we believe God is saying to us through the Bible. They will also determine—number three in particular—how we treat people based upon the Bible. These need to be questions to which we give considerable attention, because if we get the nature of the Bible wrong, we will get God wrong. If we get God wrong, we will miss what's most important to him. If we miss what's most important to him, we will be majoring on minor things (or even irrelevant things). All of which will mean we are misreading the Bible, misusing its "authority," and, consequently, misreading God and misrepresenting him to the church and the world. All of which will be damaging to the gospel in people finding God and damaging to people in their relationship with God. This is a self-evidently downward and destructive spiral, so it's important to think these things through and get them right.

The Shortcomings in "the Bible Says" Plus a Verse

It would be tempting to say that the answers to those key questions are simply "what the Bible says." This is an admirable faith-based response

---

9. Other influences will play a part too, such as our cultural context, social and family context, age, sex, ethnicity, economic situation, educational background, whether life has been good or life has been hard, its joys and its tragedies—past and present. No one reads from a neutral "objective" position uninfluenced by those things and nor are we supposed to.

and no doubt intended sincerely. But we can never just say, "The Bible says"—or even, its more authoritative-sounding cousin, "The Bible clearly teaches"—without adding a Bible verse to that phrase, with an implied interpretation and consequent application that we think comes as part of the package, things we take to be intrinsic. This approach to "what the Bible teaches" is called prooftexting and it's extremely common in everyday Christianity.[10]

Strictly speaking, a Bible verse teaches nothing in and of itself, especially when extracted from its context and deployed stand-alone. There is no such thing as uninterpreted Scripture, whether that's in its meaning or its application.

Let's take a verse we mentioned a moment ago. Second Timothy 3:16 in the NIV says, "All Scripture is *God-breathed.*"[11] What does that enigmatic phrase mean? Scripture itself doesn't tell us (either there or elsewhere).[12] Some translators say it means "breathed *into*" in the sense of Gen 2:7 and John 20:22, where the same Greek word appears (in the case of the former, that's in the Septuagint, the Greek translation of the Hebrew Old Testament that was in widespread use in the Second Temple period and is often the version quoted in the New Testament). However, the ESV renders it "breathed *out* by God," which perhaps reflects the translators' desire to assert a more pronounced divine role in Scripture's writing, alluding to something closer to "dictation" while formally shunning it, as scholars invariably do. The NRSV, meanwhile, along with several other translations, goes with the more traditional phrase, "All scripture is *inspired* by God."

Reformed conservatives routinely take the phrase to be synonymous with inerrant, or infallible, and affirming of the authority of the Bible (even though none of these are words that Scripture itself uses to speak of itself). I am not here debating the merits of inerrancy or infallibility

---

10. "Prooftexting" is isolating verses from their original contexts and quoting them in a decontextualized way to supposedly substantiate (or "prove") that something the person is saying reflects "biblical truth."

11. The literal meaning of the New Testament Greek word usually translated as "inspired."

12. Aside, that is, from the rather modest claims that the verse then goes on to make: that it's "useful for teaching, rebuking, correcting and training in righteousness." Anyone championing the typically strident language in evangelical statements of faith concerning the nature of Scripture will surely find such apparent modesty ("it's useful") somewhat disappointing and hence in need of supplementation with other ideas (such as infallibility, inerrancy, and authority).

as descriptors of the nature of Scripture—and still less its authoritative status for Christian faith, which I gladly affirm. I'm simply pointing out that it's a very big step to get those ideas, as things that the Bible "clearly teaches," directly from 2 Tim 3:16. Unless, of course, we "already know" from elsewhere (from ideas that we've brought with us to the text) that these are things that Scripture is. It's an interpretation deriving from (and/or substantiating) a doctrinal view.

Even an apparently plain and obvious truth statement such as "God is love" (1 John 4:8, 16) raises the question of what someone means by "love." I am not trying to be clever here; it's a genuine question. At one extreme, some will hear the word in a way that is essentially no more than a wishy-washy, postmodern "God's OK with everything" kind of sentimentality, where God is perceived to be like everyone's favorite grandpa. At the other extreme, some will define God's love as including so many other necessary elements—such as, his wrath toward sin and his demands for righteousness and holiness—that for all practical purposes the plain and obvious meaning of love becomes eviscerated, certainly insofar as it manifests in grace, mercy, and freely granted forgiveness. They will say that it is inappropriate to speak of God's love in isolation from his justice, which then begs another interpretation question: what we mean by "God's justice"! Hence, we might all readily agree that God is love, but what we think Scripture means by that—more importantly, what God has in mind by that—may still vary quite widely. Even with something so apparently simple as "God is love," there is no such thing as uninterpreted Scripture.

This is especially important, of course, when it comes to the "authority" of Scripture—how it is to function "authoritatively" in the life of the believer. Beware of commingling the idea of *the authority of Scripture* with the authority of *someone's interpretations* of Scripture (which, quite naturally, a preacher or Bible teacher will often treat as the same thing!).

The ultimate objective of reading the Bible, studying the Bible, and grasping the nature of the Bible—with its concurrent featuring of divinity and humanity—must surely be to form the very best possible answers to what God is like and what things are most important to him. Continuing to cycle around *those* questions, informed by an increasingly good grasp of Scripture under the guidance of the Holy Spirit, should be our unceasing endeavor, since few questions can be more important. To be clear, understanding the nature of Scripture is always subordinate to understanding the nature of God. Even the best answers to the former are never more than stepping stones to arriving at the best answers to the latter. But how people understand the nature of the Bible (well or badly) will inform how they understand God (well or badly). And vice versa: how they understand God will inform how they understand the Bible. It's a spiral.

Where Academic Theology Fits

For Christians in the evangelical Protestant tradition, in particular, the Bible is at the very heart of Christian faith. The Bible's significance is reflected in its status among the five *solas* (technically, the *solae*) of the Reformation—specifically, *sola scriptura*, or "the Bible alone."[13] A key focus for the Reformers was to liberate the Bible from what they saw as the strictures placed upon it by the medieval Catholic church—they wanted to get it into the hands of the ordinary people in their native language and allow them to read and apply it for themselves under the personal guidance of the Holy Spirit (rather than being told what to think by the Catholic theologians).[14] Scripture "alone" meant to elevate it into an overarching relationship to the traditions and edicts of the institutional church. In this endeavor, the Reformers were of course greatly assisted by the invention of the printing press and the Bible being translated into native languages, without which this democratization of Scripture could not have proceeded.

With this historical background, it is hardly surprising that everyday evangelicalism has had what we might call an "on/off" relationship with academic theology. On the one hand, the contribution of theologians—for example, in writing Bible commentaries that offer helpful background to understanding passages—has been appreciated. On the other hand, there remains a lingering idea that the ordinary Christian should be able

---

13. The five *solas* are *sola scriptura* (Scripture alone), *solus Christus* (Christ alone), *sola fide* (faith alone), *sola gratia* (grace alone), and *soli Deo gloria* (glory to God alone).

14. Reformed folks will quite rightly want to add a rider that when the Reformers asserted "the right of private interpretation of the Scriptures" they did not intend that therefore "anything goes." They will say that the necessity to be interpreting them "correctly" remains. However, that still brings us back to whose interpretations are authoritative, and on which matters. In practice (Protestant statements of faith and confessions of faith are evidence of this) the centralized interpretive authority of the Catholic church has simply been replaced by sundry interpretive authorities of Protestant churches and organizations, just without the excess baggage of medieval Catholicism against which the Reformers were protesting.

to just read the Bible and understand everything they need to without "professional" help—the Holy Spirit alone will suffice to reveal ("speak to them" about) the meaning of a passage; they don't need theologians and biblical scholars to tell them.[15] This is why in some more recently founded church movements theological qualifications are seen as purely optional. Charismatic Christians are, unsurprisingly, particularly prone to such thinking. A powerful blending of two Johannine (proof)texts—1 John 2:27, "The anointing you received from him remains in you, and you do not need anyone to teach you"; and John 16:13, "When he, the Spirit of truth, comes, he will guide you into all the truth"—would appear to prove the point for those who read what those verses are saying that way (as "prooftexts" always do, of course!).

Pitching "heart versus head" (in a "good versus bad" contrast) is profoundly unhelpful. To be blunt, it is no more than crass anti-intellectualism. Jesus' Great Commandment was that we should love the Lord our God with our heart, soul, strength, *and* mind. The mind got a mention for a reason.

In fairness, though, the contributions of academic practitioners are not always helpful for ordinary Christians seeking to work out their personal faith in a simple way. That's because terms such as "theology" and "biblical scholarship" cover a very wide spectrum of approaches and authors—evangelical and nonevangelical, charismatic and noncharismatic, more conservatively minded and more liberally minded, and many other divides. Not all theologians and scholars are even necessarily Christian (as classically defined) and still less are they all evangelical. Not everything produced in the category of academic theology or biblical studies will be seen as helpful for the average Christian.

This skepticism toward formal theological study derives in no small part from the fact that decades ago it was commonly held in evangelical circles—and not without some truth in it—that the easiest way for keen young Christians to lose their faith was to study theology at a "secular" university (in many circles, that thinking still prevails among

---

15. Some might say that this is asking a lot of the Holy Spirit! In relation to the difference between the meaning of a text and the Spirit speaking meaningfully to someone through a text, see Burnhope, *How to Read the Bible Well*, 206–12. The Reformers' belief that the ordinary Christian could read and understand the Bible without professional help is referenced in the Westminster Confession of Faith (1646), 1.7 (Schaff, *Creeds of Christendom*, 604). However, this expressly applies only to "those things that are necessary to be known, believed, and observed for salvation." It was never expected to apply to anything and everything in Scripture.

older evangelicals). Hence, if one really had to study theology, the safest bet was a denominational college that would make sure that only "the right things" were learned. However, the self-evident price to be paid for such safeguarding was teaching students only *what* to think, rather than training them in *how* to think—discouraging them from addressing difficult questions through examining the potential answers from a variety of possible perspectives.[16]

The cost to the church at large is that what may initially appear to work well in producing "safe" cookie-cutter pastors—steeped in "believing only the right things" so far as a denomination is concerned—does *not* work so well in training them to think theologically. The approach stops working when it's stress tested by now former students becoming increasingly aware that the learned-by-rote answers they'd imbibed in their younger years don't always work so well in the outside world, because they'd been shaped and formed in an echo chamber. Telling folks "This is the answer" to such-and-such doesn't work if we have no credible response when people ask why. "Because I say so," or "so-and-so says so," is unlikely to work for very long.

Everyone Is a Theologian

It's easy to assume that when we use the word "theology" we're talking about an academic subject taught in a higher educational context. But as we said in the Preface, the reality is that everyone "has" a theology, and we all "do" theology, because we all have thoughts and ideas about God that we express in words. The very word "theology" derives from two Greek words: *theos*, referring to God, and *logos*, referring to words. There is no "theology-free" way of "just" reading the Bible or being a Christian, even for those untainted by formal study. Theology isn't like a side order on a restaurant menu—an option to select or decline. Theology of some sort is unavoidably part of the Christian life; its presence and its practice are nonnegotiable. The only question is where we're getting our theological ideas from and whether they're any good or not. The same can be said of biblical interpretation: everyone is a Bible interpreter. There is no "interpretation-free" way of just reading it, believing it, and obeying it.

---

16. No doubt neither of these institutional stereotypes fully (or fairly) reflects the reality, then or now, but stereotypes only become stereotypes in the first place because there is some truth in them.

So again, the only question is where we're getting our ideas from and the extent to which they reflect good hermeneutics.

This begs the obvious question of what good theology and good interpretation look like—what do we mean by "good"? It's well known that beauty is in the eye of the beholder, so it will ultimately be for the reader to decide that for themselves. But a sensible place is always to start by asking, "Does this seem to make good sense to me? Does it sit comfortably?" If not, then that's a valid starting point for further inquiry.

A question that might spring to mind at this point might be, "What kind of perspective is *this* book seeking to offer?" in its theological and hermeneutical approach, so that the reader can judge for themselves whether it sounds like it's going to be their kind of thing. In terms of goals and objectives, we are aiming to follow standard principles of biblical interpretation from an evangelical standpoint, with a few small caveats.

The first caveat is that there is no universal list of evangelical interpretive principles. Evangelicalism is a broad term.[17] To illustrate that, Reformed theology would be considered to be squarely within the boundaries of evangelicalism. But not all evangelicals are Reformed in their theology. Calvinism is a branch of Reformed theology, and also identifies itself within evangelicalism—as does its more recent hybrid, neo-Calvinism. But by no means are all evangelicals Calvinists or neo-Calvinists. Arminianism believes the precise opposite to Calvinism on a number of key theological points, but it too would consider itself evangelical. We could say similar things about fundamentalism (indeed, fundamentalists might well say that they are the only "true" evangelicals—that the two terms should be considered synonymous).

Fortunately, evangelicalism—at least when it's framed in terms of Bebbington's quadrilateral of biblicism, activism, conversionism, and crucicentrism—need not be constrained (still less, defined) by any one of those theological systems. But it does mean that in seeking to follow academic best practice in evangelical approaches to Scripture we will inevitably diverge from some perspectives of some streams.

Another caveat is that a particular concern of this book is to try to translate good theology into ways of thinking that postmoderns will be able to recognize. Why? Simply because most of the audience for this book will themselves be postmodern in their thinking. I do not have

---

17. Even when we decouple it from its recent deployment in the media as virtually synonymous with white Christian nationalism and Trump-voting Republicanism and so too, from the cultural conservatism that is often commingled and which (consciously or otherwise) infuses its theological conservatism. For a useful primer on evangelicalism, past and present, see Noll et al., *Evangelicals*.

it as a goal to persuade them that in order to be good Christians acceptable to God they need become modern in their thinking—not least because it's simply not going to happen; all that the endeavor would do is to cause conflict and confusion. At times, this will mean gently and respectfully challenging some evangelical thinking on its accretions from modernity. Not, I stress, because the postmodern worldview is inherently better, but because our mission is *taking place* in that context so we need to *communicate* in that context in ways that *make sense* in that context. The single greatest danger for evangelicals brought up to think in modern terms is unwittingly confusing the worldview of modernity (and the doctrinal formulations that have been influenced by it) with something called a "biblical" worldview.

Does a "biblical" worldview exist? Yes and no. The term must be used with caution, since to the extent it does exist (in the culture free and timeless sense that the phrase implies) it comes to us in Scripture commingled with the ancient world worldview. No worldview—of any era—is intrinsically right, or best. Each has its strengths and weaknesses; each reflects elements of good and bad. We must think critically concerning all of them, modernity's included—*that's the hard one, for older evangelicals.*

Reading the Bible *with Its Writers*

We have needed to say rather a lot by way of background concerning the nature of the Bible and our approach to the Bible, including the necessity of recognizing that there is no theology-free or interpretation-free option—whether that's in relation to something's original meaning or its application today. But what do we mean by the second part of the book's title: reading it "with its writers"? Simply put, it means reading the Bible *with the grain of their thinking*, epitomized in Scripture's "big themes." This sits in contrast to a dehistoricized, decontextualized way of reading verses and passages *against the grain*.

The big themes in Scripture are features that recur throughout Old and New Testaments, pretty much from cover to cover, and which frame the scriptural story. Features that span "soup to nuts"—as my American friends might say—and which provide the big story's explanatory framework.

Already we have said that the Bible as we have it comprises the contributions of a large number of writers, copyists, editors, and redactors over many centuries, before the canon was finalized and brought together.¹⁸ So we might well imagine that those contributions would be theologically diverse, if not inconsistent and even contradictory. Certainly there are elements that *could* be read that way; but I don't think so. Not when the nature of Scripture is properly understood.¹⁹ In fact, I would suggest that the very opposite is the case. We see an astonishing consistency running throughout in relation to the "big themes" of the Bible, to which Part I is devoted.

Familiarity with these themes enriches everything we read. They add depth to our reading-in-context. So much in Scripture takes place against the backdrop of those big themes that we might almost say it's impossible to read the Bible well absent familiarity with them. Through that familiarity, and by reference to them, we are better equipped to find answers to our questions about God and life—including answers to questions that the biblical writers themselves never directly faced.

By that, I do not mean word-searching the Bible for a prooftext to deploy! To the extent that there are verses that appear to offer simple direct answers to simple direct questions—and of course, such verses do exist—we still have to make our usual inquiries. These can be summed up fairly simply as a series of questions to pose to ourselves:

- Are we clear on what the verse or passage was saying (its "meaning") in its original context *and why it was saying it*?
- Is what it was saying then in its original context applicable directly to our context now in the exact same way—*and if so, why*?
- Is the question that the verse or passage was answering then the same question that we're looking for it to answer now?
- In the meaning that we are perceiving, are we taking proper account of the genre? And
- Is interpreting the verse or passage in the way we propose consonant with Scripture elsewhere (and especially when viewed through the lens of Jesus in the Gospels)?

Applying these kinds of tests is our best safeguard against misreading. But I want to add something that is relatively underrecognized but equally important, something that this book is seeking to bring more

---

18. Quite aside from those who participated in the oral tradition that preceded Scripture being written down. Their role in the formulation and transmission of the inspired text deserves a shout-out, too.

19. For more on this, see *How to Read the Bible Well*, 7–41.

prominently into the mix: *taking our bearings for our reading of Scripture from the big themes that permeate it from cover to cover.* That is a far better interpretive approach than taking our bearings from one or more isolated prooftexts!

The big themes permeate Scripture because they permeated the consciousness and worldview of its writers. I would suggest that one of the senses in which the Bible is "inspired" or "God-breathed" is through its infusion with the big themes. Although it's a category error to think of the Bible as inerrant in relation to matters of science—biology, cosmology, and so on; matters that it was never intending to be inerrant about—there is no reason for us not to think of it as inerrant in regard to its big themes. We are well positioned to avoid error ourselves, as readers, if we are reading and interpreting the Bible through the lens of those themes.

Finally, a brief introductory word on Part II of the book, the "how?" question: how the biblical writers went about saying what they said. In other words, the genres or "styles of writing" that they employed.

Genre is the "poor relation" of reading-in-context. For most Bible readers, it's not really on their radar; yet to have that awareness is essential in terms of its impact on meaning. The biblical writers were fully aware of genre and so, too, should we be. To ignore it—and even more so to be reading the text as if it was written in a modern genre—is disrespectful to both the human author and the divine author. They chose their genre for a reason; let's allow them that and work with that.

Genre is an important element of context; and so, too, is the worldview of the ancient world that was shared by the writers and their audiences. In other words, everything that they took to be "obvious" about life, the world around them, and "the way things are." To be reading the Bible well, we need to be taking these contextual factors fully into account. To be properly *literal* involves reading in a way that is fully consonant with the nature of the *literature*.

Many sincere Christians assume that the most faithful way of interpreting a Bible verse is to "take it literally" (at so-called "face value") *wherever that is not impossible.* But this is a category error, not least because what is usually meant by "literal, at face value" is what we assume those English words mean to us, stand-alone, with scant if any reference to their original context. The most faithful way of interpreting a Bible verse is always, always, always what it meant in the minds of its original author and audience: what they understood it was "saying" to them.

PART I

What They Were Saying and Why: The Big Themes

Introduction

THE SECOND WORLD WAR British Prime Minister, Winston Churchill, apparently said that if you put two economists in a room you will get two opinions—unless one of them is Lord Keynes, in which case you'll get three opinions. Had Churchill asked theologians rather than economists, he might have considered this to be an understatement. There's a similar well-known Jewish saying along the lines that if you put four rabbis in a room you will get six or seven opinions.[1]

I'm fairly sure that if we asked a number of theologians to produce their lists of the big themes in the Bible, we would end up with far more opinions person-for-person than either Lord Keynes or an archetypal group of rabbis. There would no doubt be considerable overlap in terms of the content, but not necessarily in the way it was being framed and assembled.

For something to qualify as a "big theme" for our purposes is the extent to which it meets a combination of three principal elements:

---

1. The number of rabbis and opinions varies, depending on who is telling the story, but you get the general idea.

1. It is introduced early in the biblical story;
2. It is evident throughout the story, in both Old and New Testaments, through to its climax and conclusion; and
3. It is theologically significant for the story along the way (in other words, something important would be missing if we ignored it).

By way of example, our list begins with creation; the reason it's a big theme is because it bookends the biblical story from the original creation in Genesis through to a new, renewed, or "saved" creation in Revelation. "The way things were intended to be" and "the way things will one day be" recur through the narrative, along with the obvious questions that God's people were so often feeling the need to ask as to why things are not now as they should be and when and what God was going to do about it. It's interesting in passing that the original creation narrative in Genesis and the new creation narrative in Revelation are both presented in picture language (and so too are many prophetic and apocalyptic passages).

If you're tempted to ask, "Why isn't such-and-such a big theme?" the answer is likely to be either because it falls short in fulfilling one of the aforementioned criteria or because it's included in one of the other themes, subsumed into a broader category. An example would be the theme of "Sin," which comes under "The Enemies of God."

For readers in the UK, one way of picturing these big themes is as the writing running through a stick of seaside rock. For readers elsewhere, you will need to Google it or simply accept that Brits can be a bit weird at times and move on. Nothing of theological significance rides on the metaphor of seaside rock. I was tempted to cite a source for "seaside rock" in a footnote, but good sense prevailed.

One of the exciting things about the presence of these big themes is that despite the Bible being written by over forty different authors—not to mention the contributions of an unknown number of editors, redactors, and copyists who participated in the creation and coming together of the documents that ultimately became our scriptural canon (and many more before them, in the antecedent oral tradition preceding written Scripture as we know it)—the themes are indicative of an amazing continuity from cover to cover within the canonical story. Many would attribute that continuity to the inspiration of the divine author at work behind the scenes, but it also evidences that Scripture's human writers were keenly aware of those themes and of their significance for the story of which they were a part. We also regularly see similar awareness of those themes on the part of the biblical characters whose stories are being narrated.

Big themes are the backdrop to the biblical story all the way through the Bible; they are "there" whether they're mentioned explicitly or not. Sometimes they're "sitting behind" the text and sometimes they're "up-front" in the text. Hence, if we are to read the Bible well, we need to know what those big themes are, and why they're important, so we can see how they shine light on what we're reading—and indeed, shine light on Christian faith.

It's important to recognize that the big themes in the New Testament are the same big themes in the Old Testament, and vice versa. The big themes in the Old Testament were not canceled after Malachi, with new ones taking over in Matthew; there was no "old" set replaced by a "new" set. Indeed, it's the continuity through both Testaments that helps define them as big themes in the first place. One could also say that if Christians generally had a better appreciation for the presence of these themes in the Old Testament, they might not be so habitually dismissive of it. Or at least they might realize that what they are being dismissive about is usually not what the biblical writers (even the New Testament writers) were talking about at the time; hopefully this will become clearer with examples later.

Most importantly, the reason they're big themes in the Bible is because they're big themes in the heart and mind and purposes of God. Since God never changes in his nature and character, and since his plans and goals never change,[2] and since we ourselves are part of the continuing story that Scripture recounts, the big themes in the Bible should be our big themes as well. They should significantly inform how we "do" our Christianity—how we do relationships, how we do church, how we do mission and so on; our theology and practice should be very closely aligned with those big themes.

Faithfulness to the big themes is a really good way for us to think about what it means to be "biblical" in an enduring sense. In other words, asking the Holy Spirit to show us what faithfulness to the big themes looks like for us, in our context, in our world today—recognizing that it will not necessarily look the same as it did for Noah, Moses, Isaiah, or the apostle Paul.

---

2. Which is not to say we never see a localized "change of course" in God's activity (such as with Abraham and Lot in the story of Sodom in Gen 18:23–32) usually in response to relationship.

Instead of asking what it means to be "biblical," a far better question is what it means to be "faithful to the big themes." Not only will that help us to answer questions we're faced with today that simply did not arise in Bible times, but it will also allow us to do a swerve around the problematic adjective "biblical." If the reason they're big themes in the Bible is because they're big themes in the heart and mind of God, then to look at a contemporary question through the lens of the big themes will surely contribute to us hearing what God might be saying to us on it without needing to resort to anachronisms or "prooftexting." Scripture offers us a sourcebook, not a textbook. We're challenged to think through what a faithful application of those themes should look like in our world, not to replicate in a copy-and-paste fashion what potentially similar things looked like in the biblical world.

The big themes serve as "windows" as to how we should look at the rest of Scripture. They provide us with clues as to how we should interpret what it is and isn't saying, not least when it comes to more difficult passages, subjects, and verses. It is highly likely that we will be reading those better if we are allowing the big themes to guide us. There is an often-cited interpretive principle to the effect that we should "allow Scripture to interpret Scripture." And that's right, certainly to a point. Where it's less helpful is that a good deal depends on which Scriptures we've selected, to interpret which other Scriptures; which ones we read in the light of which others. Thinking in terms of the big themes helps us to avoid that dilemma and to be less reliant on selective prooftexts as source material.

— 1 —

Creation and New Creation

THE NAME OF THE first book of the Bible, Genesis, comes from the Greek translation of the Old Testament (the Septuagint, or LXX) in Gen 2:4: "This is the book of the origins (*geneseōs*) of heaven and earth." We find the creation account in the first chapters of Genesis—what happened "in the beginning," as Gen 1:1 begins the narrative.

It's appropriate that our big themes should begin with creation not simply for chronological reasons but because it announces so many other big themes: Genesis is where we are first introduced to them. Creation fulfills a criterion for being a big theme insofar as it is thematically paired, or "bookended," with new creation at the very end of the Bible, in the book of Revelation.

The first thing to grasp is that the creation story is a relational account, not a manufacturing account. It's not answering scientific questions of *how* the universe was "made" in a manufacturing sense.[1] It's answering "who?" questions and "why?" questions.

---

1. Our modern mindset wants to tell us that it "must be" answering those scientific questions. There are two reasons for that: one is because "it's the word of God," so it "must be" timelessly accurate in all things, in science as well as theology (the "*of God*" tag makes it so). The other is that because we live in an Age of Science, we assume it's "obviously" a scientific account because that's what people today expect it to be ("factually accurate"). Whenever we use terms such as "must be" (or "can't be") and "obviously," it's our worldview speaking.

The Hebrew word translated "made"—or "created"—is never used in the Bible in a manufacturing sense, only ever in a "bringing it about" sense. Psalm 51:10 ("Create in me a clean heart, O God") is the same word, but self-evidently the psalmist is not envisaging God performing a heart transplant; rather, it's a heart transformation. Questions of "how?" in a medical or scientific sense are not in view here.

The early chapters of Genesis, including the creation story, are offering us a theological account centered on what the writers saw as important theological truths; they're not a scientific account offering scientific truths. Genesis is certainly offering answers, but only if we ask it the right questions. We are not defending the truth of the Bible—or the inerrancy of the Bible—if we're defending a wrong way of reading it, if we're expecting it to be providing answers that it never intended to, simply because we're reading it through modernity's lenses.

We should not be asking Genesis to answer questions that twenty-first-century readers happen to be interested in just because we live in an Age of Science. Genesis was not writing a science textbook; it was painting an artistic picture, deploying memorable imagery for an oral culture in the same way that so much of the Bible does. Instead, we should be listening for the answers Genesis was offering its original audience, to the questions that it was interested in. Genesis contains no less truth than if it had been a "scientific" or "historical" account in an encyclopedic sense, but its truths are not conveyed that way; they're theological and anthropological truths. Students in the arts and humanities will likely grasp that more easily.

It is disrespectful to the text—more to the point, it's disrespectful to the authors, including the divine author—to insist that it somehow "must be" answering our modern questions, which are mainly to do with "how" things were made. In contrast, the original audience's concerns were all about the "who" and the "why" of creation, and how this "story of origins" informed their understanding of themselves and the way things were in their world. Their backdrop for seeking answers was generations of exile in Babylon and the ever-increasing threat of losing their identity as a nation of God's people called Israel. Whereas our backdrop is things like the big bang theory, evolution, and the age of the earth.

Even though we may know in our heads that the Genesis account is not a modern manufacturing account—that it's not trying to communicate scientific truths as to how the world was made—it's nonetheless very tempting for the modern reader to still want to try to find points of correspondence between what we read in Genesis and what we know scientifically today, to want to try to "reduce the gap" between them. As if finding some small element of correspondence—a few little divine clues, things the human writers could not possibly have known—helps to validate the Bible's authoritative divine status. In other words, finding hints of God's authorial contribution.

A simple example would be wanting to argue that even if the six days are not to be taken "literally" as twenty-four-hour periods, the text is still pointing to six periods of time (building on a principle seemingly found in Ps 90:4, that a day is like a thousand years in God's sight and deploying that as a prooftext). This desire is understandable from a modern perspective, but it's a fool's errand. The more we strain to find modern correspondence, the more the lack of correspondence becomes obvious. We dig our own hole and unwittingly help to validate the very argument—that Genesis is "fake news," scientifically speaking—that we have been trying to undermine. Self-evidently "what happens" each day in the creation account does not fit chronologically with a scientific account of creation. I'm not a scientist by any stretch of the imagination, but even I can see that the authors of Genesis saw no reason to separate the creation of "evening and morning" from any role performed by the sun and the moon in bringing that about. God created evening and morning (the Jewish day was measured from evening to evening) on day one; he created the sun and moon on day four.

Another example would be the various references in Genesis to a flat earth covered by a dome (the sky) behind which waters were held back; rain was understood to occur when God "opened the windows" in the dome for a period (rather like roof windows in a house—see Gen 7 and 8). Trying to make these various references conform to what modern meteorology knows, by arguing that they were intentionally metaphorical, is once again overstretching to no purpose.

A recent survey by the Barna Group carried out in the UK found that 20 percent of respondents thought the church's beliefs were "not compatible with science," while 17 percent thought they were "simplistic."[2] Although Christians are not to blame for all of the negative views expressed toward them (and in fairness, many respondents also had positive things to say: for example, 26 percent of those polled believed that on balance

---

2. World Vision UK, *UK Church in Action*, 13.

the church was "good for the community")³ we have only ourselves to blame for defending the Bible against accusations that ought not to need defending. We need to lay to rest the mistaken idea that in Genesis God was wanting to tell us about "how" the world was made. We need to stop looking for little clues that he may have "hidden in the text" which would "prove" that what Genesis says is consistent with what modern science says, as if that would somehow validate the biblical account as "true." When we do that, we're looking for things that aren't there. Neither the human authors nor the divine author were secretly embedding little scientific clues for twenty-first-century readers to find.

Genesis was not written to explain how the world was made but why it was made and who made it. The creation account is a theological explanation centered in God rather than a cosmological explanation centered in science.

If we're going to read Genesis well—and for that matter everywhere else in the Bible where it also chooses to use "picture language," or poetry, or creative writing, to communicate memorable theological truths—then we have to resist a tendency to assume that "the best" kind of biblical interpretation must always be a "literal" interpretation. Taking everything literally is not by definition taking it more seriously. The best interpretation is not automatically a literal interpretation; rather, it's whatever is most appropriate to the genre—the "style of writing"—that the writer was using. The best interpretation will be the one that follows the rules that they followed, in that kind of writing, at that time. In which process, of course, the divine author was intimately involved behind the scenes. The best reading is one that respects all of that and doesn't try to turn the text into a style of writing that we would use today—and insisting on interpreting it as if it was.

The New Creation as a New Eden?

You may occasionally have come across a preacher referring to the creation account—either expressly or by implication—as describing a state of perfection to which it's our destiny to return in new creation. In other words, that what we call "heaven" will be like Eden was before "the fall" (as it's traditionally called). That's an easy assumption to make; it sounds logical. Except that Genesis never says that creation was perfect, or that

---

3. World Vision UK, *UK Church in Action*, 12.

Eden was perfect, or that anything else was perfect. What it says is that each element that God spoke into being each day was "good," and then the whole package together, once he'd finished that primordial creational activity at the end of day six, was "very good" (Gen 1:31).

It's the influence of Greek philosophical ideas on Western thought that has led to the Hebrew concept of an original "goodness" being replaced by the Neoplatonic concept of an original "perfection" (which the modern reader assumes to be synonymous). The Neoplatonic concept of perfection is problematic because by its very nature it allows for no possibility of becoming. Perfection is a static state. If something is already perfect in those terms then any change must—by definition—be a bad thing; it will be diminishing that existing perfection. But to rule out change is to rule out learning, growing, developing, and maturing.

Accordingly, it's flawed to think of Adam and Eve in the garden as the perfection of what it means to be human to which humanity is destined one day to return—that is not the gospel. The pre-fall garden of Eden is not picturing heaven. We are not destined to be resurrected as Adams and Eves. Or, perhaps more to the point, there is no scriptural evidence suggesting that childlike naïvety and ignorance of right and wrong will be a feature of eternal life.

In the new creation in Revelation, we do not see a return to the heavens and the earth as they were then—"in the beginning"—but the heavens and the earth as they're destined to become. We see everything that was "very good" in the original creation reaching its completion and fulfillment, including the completion and fulfillment of the other big themes in the Bible, once the cosmos has been healed and restored—or, "saved"—from what went wrong along the way. Our human destiny is not to become like Adam and Eve (still less, "spirit-being" versions of Adam and Eve) but our resurrected selves in Christ, in the new heavens and new earth of Rev 21:1.

The creation account does not tell us that learning, growing, developing, and maturing—including learning what's right and wrong—is something that God never intended should happen, any more than human parents would intend that for their own children. The question was only ever going to be the pace at which it happened and who would be "parenting" Adam and Eve in their journey—who was going to teach them. Which brings us to the role of the serpent and the tree of the knowledge of good and evil in all of this.

The Serpent and the Tree

The first thing to notice about God's prohibition of eating the fruit of that tree is that it was *the one little thing* they were asked not to do. This is hardly compelling evidence of a killjoy God who demands meticulous obedience to all manner of petty little rules in a fun-sapping "because I say so" kind of way. It's also often overlooked that (at the outset) there was no prohibition of eating the fruit of the tree of life that was also in the middle of the garden—they were "free to eat from *any* tree in the Garden" *except* that forbidden one (Gen 2:16).

This highlights something else we sometimes come across in a preacher's presentation of the forbidden tree fruit ban: that God did not want Adam and Eve to learn about "the ways of the world." That simply "knowing God" was intended to be enough for them (implying that Adam and Eve forever maintaining childlike naïvety and ignorance, in a purity culture kind of way, was God's original game plan). That for them to learn about right and wrong would be "a bad thing"—awareness that God intended should be kept from them. But to interpret the story that way is to be reading in things that are simply not there. Once again, it's buying into the idea that Genesis is picturing a Neoplatonic pre-fall state of perfection in which God's original plan was for humanity to remain naïve and innocent of such knowledge. But this simply doesn't fit with humanity being born with free will; we cannot make good choices, freely choosing to do right instead of wrong, if what wrong choices look like is concealed from us. It also requires importing a very particular view on what something called the tree of the knowledge of good and evil must be all about.

So if that wasn't what was happening, what was? A better reading of God's ban on eating the fruit of the tree of the knowledge of good and evil is that it was never intended to be a question of *whether* they acquired such knowledge but of *when*, and from *whom* they would acquire it. To whom they would look to mentor them in the journey of learning about right and wrong—whose voice they would listen to, whose perspective it would be, on what's right and wrong.

The presence of the serpent in the garden is permitted by God precisely for that reason: there had to be an alternative voice for Adam and Eve potentially to listen to, if their human free will was to be authentic rather than token. Otherwise it would be a bit like an election in a dictatorship: the good news is that everyone gets to vote; the bad news is that there's only one name on the ballot paper.

It would be easy to see the story of "the fall" as saying that from that point on, having eaten that fruit, Adam and Eve began to listen to the serpent (the Satan figure) in relation to matters of right and wrong (instead of to God). I think a better reading would be that the serpent simply diverted them to look to themselves for their points of reference. Tactically, that would be just as effective and easier to engineer—after all, no one wants to think they're being dictated to by Satan. If there's an obvious moral in the story it must surely be that Adam and Eve were supposed to learn God's perspective on what's right and wrong, in his timing; instead, they chose to say, "We will decide that for ourselves, thanks very much." If that is a reasonable way of reading what was happening, then Adam and Eve would be no different from us in succumbing to that temptation.

A Creation Story That Begins with Original Sin?

I suspect there are very few people—Christian or otherwise—who are unfamiliar with the term "original sin" and from where it originates, in the story of Adam and Eve and the forbidden fruit. Which by the way was not an apple, despite the popular imagery. Not that it makes a difference either way, theologically. The Bible has no problem with apples per se.[4]

This is not the place for a lengthy discussion of original sin as a Christian doctrine, but stated simply and briefly it is founded on what Paul writes in Rom 5:12: "Sin entered the world through one man, and death through sin, and in this way death came to all people, because all sinned"—a commentary on what happened when they ate the fruit of the tree of the knowledge of good and evil.[5] Through Augustine, in particu-

---

4. Not in the way that it has with cucumbers, melons, leeks, onions, and garlic (Num 11:5—the rebellious Israelites yearning for the "forbidden fruit" of Egypt). To my mind, cucumbers and melons receive a slightly raw deal here, but the condemnation of leeks, onions, and garlic is surely apposite. One of my friendly proofreaders commented, "You do realize that your distaste for garlic is pretty much a minority of one, right? Garlic, ginger and chilli are the holy trinity of cooking. Just saying." I mention this simply as evidence of my willingness to consider other interpretive possibilities before, ahem, dismissing them.

5. Here again, this is offering us a theological truth, not a biological truth. As John Walton points out, "Despite the popular and traditional belief otherwise, it can be easily demonstrated that death was in the system prior to the Fall. I ask the question: did Adam have skin? His statement in Genesis 2:23 shows that he did. We know well today what the epidermis is—a layer of dead skin cells. Since Adam had dead cells, we

lar, this has been interpreted as all subsequent humans sharing in Adam's guilt (perceived to transmit through the male, since the female role in reproduction—the egg—was not known about in Bible times). Although this perspective on sin transmission is a fairly standard Christian idea, interestingly it is not a Jewish one.

Another verse which appears to contribute to that doctrine of original sin is Ps 51:5: "Surely I was sinful at birth, sinful from the time my mother conceived me." This underlies Reformed conservative belief that even before a baby has breathed its first breath, let alone done anything, it is inherently sinful and deserving of condemnation as a sinner: as Wayne Grudem puts it, "Even before birth children have a guilty standing before God and a sinful nature that not only gives them a tendency to sin but also causes God to view them as 'sinners.'"[6] What this leads to is that "as far as God is concerned we are not able to do anything that pleases him,"[7] a state that Calvinists refer to as "total depravity." They begin their gospel from this point—the entry of "original sin" into the world.

The doctrine is problematic on several levels. According to this way of thinking, we are all doomed to God's wrath and judgment even before we've started in life. This flies in the face of both personal accountability for our own actions and decisions and the idea that God is both just and fair (since to condemn all humanity simply for "what Adam did" is not just and fair). Furthermore, on that basis we can have no confidence whatsoever that a deceased baby is not destined for hell (I'm using their concepts here). The reader will need to make up her own mind on the validity of the Calvinist interpretation of these things but suffice to say that in Jewish thinking there is "an age of accountability" (or "an age of reason") corresponding to the ceremony of bar mitzvah/bat mitzvah (around the time of puberty).

All this said, some conservative scholars even of a Calvinist disposition would question Grudem's theology of sin applied in this way. They

---

know that death existed at the cellular level. If plants served as food, then certainly we can conclude that plants likewise died." Hence, what happened at the fall is not that humanity passed from a prior immortality to mortality. To understand what was going on, we need to place more focus on the role of the tree of life, which Walton says was "the means by which mortality could be held at bay"—it was "the antidote," to which only humanity had access. "God provided the tree of life to make death unnecessary. Thus when the human pair was prevented from having access to the tree of life [Gen 3:22–24], death became an unavoidable reality." Walton, *Genesis*, 183–84.

6. Grudem, *Systematic Theology*, 499—cited here as a source, not a recommendation.
7. Grudem, *Systematic Theology*, 497.

would bring these conflicting elements together in a more nuanced fashion that appears to make better sense. Millard Erickson, for example, says that despite children having participated in that first sin (via Adam), they are still accepted and saved (he adds the word "somehow"), even though they have made neither a decision for Christ nor a decision to sin.

> Just as with the imputation of Christ's righteousness, there must be some conscious and voluntary decision on our part. Until this is the case, there is *only a conditional imputation of guilt*. Thus, there is no condemnation until one reaches the age of responsibility. If a child dies before he or she is capable of making genuine moral decisions, there is only innocence, and the child will experience the same type of future existence with the Lord as will those who have reached the age of moral responsibility and had their sins forgiven as a result of accepting the offer of salvation based upon Christ's atoning death.[8]

By "conditional" Erickson means our guilty standing before God lies dormant, as it were, and becomes effective only at a later date. By "imputation" he means "credited" to us (or "debited," as the case may be)—bank account imagery. What, then, is the nature of the conscious and voluntary decision that, as he puts it, "ends our childish innocence and constitutes a ratification of the first sin, the fall"? Erickson suggests two options.

> One position on this question is that there is no final imputation of the first [original] sin until we commit a sin of our own, thus ratifying Adam's sin. . . . This position holds that at the moment of our first sin we become guilty of both our own sin *and the original sin as well*. There is another position, however, one that is preferable in that it more fully preserves the parallelism between our accepting the work of Christ and that of Adam, and at the same time it more clearly points out our responsibility for the first sin. We become responsible and guilty when we accept or approve of our corrupt nature. There is a time in the life of each one of us when we become aware of our own tendency toward sin.[9]

Some would say that these are complex ways of circumventing the core problem with the doctrine of original sin as most people would surely see it: that every single one of us is automatically "screwed" (that's a technical theological term) right from the get-go, purely on account of something

8. Erickson, *Christian Theology*, 639 (italics mine).
9. Erickson, *Christian Theology*, 639 (italics his).

our earliest humanoid ancestors did an eternity ago. Erickson's approach is clearly more nuanced, but it does nonetheless appear that he is starting with the assumption that "original sin" must be right, so we simply must find a way to validate it that sounds at least somewhat plausible.

To be clear, this is *not* to say that Scripture is wrong when it affirms that "all have sinned and fall short of the glory of God" (Rom 3:23). No responsible adult can rightly claim to be without sin from a biblical perspective (1 John 1:10). The question is simply what role Adam's "original" sin plays in that.[10] Original sin is not simply an interesting doctrinal question for theologians to argue about: we should be concerned for the doctrine's potentially damaging impact on parents and families when cited in situations such as infant mortality, not to mention the potential damage to God's reputation (a concern that arises from other Calvinist doctrines as well).

A Creation Story That Begins with Original Goodness

There is no doubting that the creation narrative in Genesis presents us with an explanation of "the way things are" in human life that includes ongoing consequences from "what happened"—specifically, "what went wrong"—in the garden. There was indeed a clear first instance of "sin" entering into the story through Adam and Eve. There is also a clear trajectory through Genesis, as the story continues to unfold, that shows sin broadening out in its effects from that point on—for example, in the story of Cain and Abel, in the very next generation. It would not seem inappropriate to illustrate what happened as human life becoming infected with a highly transmissible virus. Alternatively, perhaps, that human DNA became somehow damaged in its genetic code. Or perhaps that human life was somehow knocked off-kilter—out of equilibrium,

---

10. The reader may care to reflect on why in Scripture (and equally, in the doctrine of original sin) it's "all about Adam" and his sin, with no mention of Eve and her preceding sin: "She took some of the fruit and ate it. *Then* she gave some to her husband, who was with her, and *he* ate it, too" (Gen 3:6 NLT). The answer is not endearing; it reflects cultural assumptions about the subordinate status and value of women in the ancient world that are no longer affirmed today (except by some conservative evangelicals who continue to read Scripture in those ways). This notwithstanding Adam's feeble attempt in the story to blame Eve for what happened and, even, to blame God: "The woman you put here with me—she gave me some fruit from the tree, and I ate it." Not that Eve was averse to trying to shift the blame: "The serpent deceived me, and I ate" (Gen 2:12–13). Disinclination to accept personal responsibility for one's actions is clearly not a new thing.

no longer properly aligned with the Creator's intentions. So there was, in some of those senses, something called original sin that entered into human experience.

All of these seem to be reasonable ways of picturing "what happened," certainly in communicating it pastorally and missionally. However, original sin—in whatever form we present it—is not the point from which the divine-human biblical story begins. Evangelical presentations too frequently begin the story *with* sin and *from* sin—specifically, with and from that "original" sin—when the story actually begins with something called "original goodness."

We see that from the very outset in Gen 1, where on each day of creation God spoke something into being and said it was "good."[11] Then on the sixth day, when he'd completed his initial, foundational creative work,[12] God looked at the whole package together and declared it to be "very good."[13]

This distinction between a story that starts with original goodness rather than original sin is important theologically for several reasons.

One is that this is the reason God's creation is worth saving and we are worth saving, rather than giving up and starting again. Despite what happened, God continues to see his creation from the perspective of original goodness. Sin and the problems sin has caused are not the center of the biblical story any more than they're the center of the gospel. Sin is one of the enemies of the story, that invaded the story, and needed to be defeated through Christ to allow everything that was "very good" in the original creation to reach its intended completion and fulfillment. This "saving" involves a healing and a restoration—a rebooting that allows it to become all that it was intended to be without hindrance. All of these aspects are elements of the gospel.

This is why we should really speak about salvation in terms of the new heavens and the new earth, that we see pictured in Rev 21, rather than just "going to heaven."

---

11. Gen 1:4, 10, 12, 18, 21, and 25.

12. Genesis is describing God's initial creational activity; however, it didn't end there. As a living and active God, who is creational by nature, he continues his involvement with his creation. As J. B. Phillips puts it in Col 1:17, the Son "is both the first principle and the upholding principle of the whole scheme of creation." Cf. Heb 1:3, "sustaining all things by his powerful word." As an aside, this leaves plenty of space for evolution as reflecting continuing divine action within the world.

13. Gen 1:31: "God saw all that he had made, and it was very good."

One of the several problems caused by the flawed "rapture" theology is that it is "us-centered"—it pictures salvation in solely human terms, as if the Christians are to be snatched away to heavenly bliss while the rest of the created order, including planet Earth, is left to crash and burn (along with the non-Christians).

In John 3:16, "God so loved the world," we tend to assume the word "world" means "people." But the Greek word is *kosmos*—from which unsurprisingly we get our word "cosmos"—and although it can be speaking of people (and certainly people are included) its broader reference is to the whole created order.[14] Its primary meaning is actually "a harmonious arrangement." The general sense is of everything being in good order—everything in its rightful place.

Kosmos directly relates to another New Testament Greek word, *kosmeō*—from which we get our word "cosmetics"—meaning to adorn or beautify. It appears in this sense in 1 Pet 3:5. Why do I mention that? Because the same word is used to describe the New Jerusalem in Rev 21:2—the centerpoint of the new heavens and earth—where John says, "I saw . . . the new Jerusalem, coming down out of heaven from God, prepared as a bride beautifully dressed (*kosmeō*) for her husband" and also in v. 19, where he says, "The foundations of the wall of the city were adorned (*kosmeō*) with all kinds of precious stones."

Another problem that rapture theology generates is that it leads to a bad theology of ecology and conservation. Why bother with the environment if Jesus is coming at any moment and it's all going to crash and burn anyway? But it's selfish to presume that we're the last generation—that Jesus is coming back soon, so what does it matter? It's also sobering to realize that Christians in every generation from Jesus' time up until now have thought theirs would be the last, and every single one has been wrong so far. Understanding God's destiny for his creation is vital to having a good theology of creation in the present. Yes, of course there is a sense in which we should live as if Jesus' second coming is imminent; but in terms of our attitude toward creation-care, we should live as if it is very far off.

If we humans rape and pillage the earth's natural resources we've become part of what God intends to save his creation from. We've positioned ourselves on the wrong team. Humanity was not given "dominion" (Gen 1:28) so that we could misuse our power and become abusers. This would be wholly inconsistent with the nature and character of God.

---

14. The word *kosmos* is used in the Septuagint creation account (in Gen 2:1).

We were placed in the garden to steward the created order on God's behalf, to "image" him. We were never owners of creation,[15] but rather conservators and curators.

Reimagining What We Mean by "Heaven"

Another reason that beginning the story with original goodness is important theologically is because if God were to give up on the rest of his creation—to settle for just saving human souls, as if that's what it's all about—then to that extent his enemies would have won. God hasn't then saved the *kosmos*, he's abandoned the *kosmos*. That would be no more than a score-draw[16] in cosmic warfare terms: God gets souls and his enemies get the rest.

Tom Wright—N. T. Wright, when he publishes academically—caused a bit of a stir in December 2019 when he wrote an article in *Time* magazine, where he said this:

> One of the central stories of the Bible, many people believe, is that there is a heaven and an earth and that human souls have been exiled from heaven and are serving out time here on earth until they can return. Indeed, for most modern Christians, the idea of "going to heaven when you die" is not simply one belief among others, but the one that seems to give a point to it all.
>
> But the people who believed in that kind of "heaven" when the New Testament was written were not the early Christians. They were the "Middle Platonists"—people like Plutarch. . . .
>
> The followers of the Jesus-movement . . . saw "heaven" and "earth"—God's space and ours, if you like—as the twin halves of God's good creation. Rather than rescuing people from the latter in order to reach the former, the creator God would finally bring heaven and earth together in a great act of new creation, completing the original creative purpose by healing the entire cosmos of its ancient ills. They believed that God would then raise his people from the dead, to share in—and, indeed, to

---

15. We should never forget Ps 24:1–2: "The earth is the Lord's, and everything in it, the world, and all who live in it; for he founded it on the seas and established it on the waters."

16. A sporting term (normally associated with soccer) to describe a match result in which both teams score the same number of goals.

share his stewardship over—this rescued and renewed creation. And they believed all this because of Jesus.[17]

One of the reasons that Western Christians so easily slip into the assumption that "salvation" and "heaven" is all about saving human souls is a dualism that we have inherited from Greek philosophical thought. We read the Bible in a dualistic way, in which there is a sharp divide between "spiritual things" (which are seen as good and superior) and "physical things" (which are seen as bad and inferior). Dualism says that what really matters is spiritual things. But in Hebrew thinking, creation was never artificially divided into categories like that. All of creation is important, because it's all God's handiwork, it's all one indivisible whole (physical and spiritual), and it was all created as "very good." It's all interconnected and it's all scheduled to be saved through a glorious act of cosmic renewal initiated at the cross.

Dualism also impacts how Christians think about the nature of what we call "heaven." If the physical creation is inherently temporal and of no eternal value, then no wonder it would not be part of God's eternal future—"obviously," many would say. If physical things like human bodies are inherently bad and deeply inferior to spiritual things, then salvation "must" be about the liberation of the real and true spiritual person "trapped" inside that physical human body—leaving physical existence behind for a purely spiritual existence in "heaven" for ghostly, disembodied souls.[18]

And yet, when we see what we call "heaven" described in Rev 21, it rather speaks in terms of a new heaven and earth, a renewal of what Wright calls "God's space and ours" brought together in a like manner to that which we see in the creation account in the beginning. Apocalyptic literature such as Revelation is hard to read at the best of times (we shall say more about this in Part II) but for the present let's simply focus on some of the "big picture" messages that are easy to identify, specifically, the features that are common to the Genesis creation account prior to the "fall" and the new creation account in Revelation:

---

17. Wright, "New Testament," paras. 1–3.

18. Our word "ghost" comes from an Old English word, *gāst*, referring to the disembodied spirit or soul of a dead person. It's now mostly used in relation to an apparition in the physical realm. Its meaning as spirit underlies the term Holy Ghost. The phrase to "give up the ghost" reflects the idea that at physical death the eternal soul/spirit of a person is released to live on in another (spiritual) realm.

- God's original creation and new creation both involve heaven and earth, not just heaven;
- God is personally present in direct, intimate relationship with people—the realms of heaven and earth are together as one;
- There is no death, or mourning, or crying, or pain; and
- There is no temple (i.e., the place where God was perceived to dwell) because the whole created realm is a temple.

In relation to the new heavens and earth, bad things and bad people are excluded; and there is "no longer any sea" (Rev 21:1) because, in the ancient world, the sea was symbolic of chaos and disorder.

How might we visualize this kind of new creation working? With some difficulty! Many questions along the lines of "How will this be?" spring to mind. Perhaps that's the reason that when it comes to these things Scripture so often offers us pictures and parables to explain them. And perhaps that inherent difficulty is another reason that people find it easier to visualize "heaven" as a purely "spiritual" domain.

For me, the best picturing of this is Jesus' parable of the wheat and the weeds (a.k.a., the wheat and the tares) in Matt 13. To summarize, Jesus tells a story of an owner who sowed wheat in his field, but an enemy came under cover of darkness and sowed weeds. The owner's servants asked if they should attempt to remove them, but the owner said, no, not now, wait until the harvest, to avoid harming the wheat at this time. When harvest time came, the weeds were indeed pulled out—and destroyed—so that there was once again only wheat in the field, as the owner had intended. Jesus explained that the owner is God, the field is God's creation, he is the one who planted only good things, and his enemies are the ones who planted bad things. At harvest time—the eschatological "end of the age"—God's angels will take out all of the bad, leaving only the good. It's a great picture of a renewed heaven and earth, saved and restored, with everything that is bad and harmful (such as sin, and Satan, and death, and everything that leads to death) removed and destroyed.

Hence we might sum up "new creation" as "everything that is very good about *this* creation—and life as we know it now—but with all of the bad stuff taken out." God removing all of the things that have gone wrong and all of their consequences. Taking out every enemy that caused them to go wrong and wants to keep them wrong, healing all the damage that the enemies have caused. New creation in Revelation is a healing and cleansing of that damaged creation, and a restoration of original goodness.

Once death (and everything that leads to death, such as sickness and decay) is removed from God's creation and destroyed, what do we have left? Eternal life! Once sin and the damage done by sin is removed from God's creation and destroyed, what do we have left? Righteousness—only good and right things. A direct consequence of this is that the incompatibility of sinful humanity with a righteous God—sin's separating effect on the divine-human relationship—is removed, enabling the dwelling place of God to be permanently among his people, per Rev 21:3.[19]

This way of understanding end-times matters answers a question that bothered me for years: "What will heaven be like?" To be honest, I wasn't really sure whether I would like it. It didn't sound much fun, just floating around on clouds all day, playing harps, wearing white nighties. Or, as preachers would sometimes say—as if they thought how wonderful we would think this sounded (or at least, *how spiritual* we would think it sounded)—"We'll just be worshiping God, day and night, 24/7." Now don't get me wrong, I love a good time of worship as much as anyone. But I would hear that and think, "Surely there must be more to it than that?"

Jesus is describing a world in which all of the best of what it means to be human—everything good that God sowed into his creation in the first place—stays as part of the harvest that God intended. And perhaps this offers us a simple grid for what that new heavens and earth will be like: if something concerning this present life is inherently good—once any damage done by the enemies of human life and human thriving is healed, cleansed, and restored—then why wouldn't it be part of the future new creation? I sometimes refer to this grid to answer the question whether there will be pets in heaven (a key concern for some congregants, especially the younger ones when a beloved pet hamster dies).[20]

---

19. "God's dwelling place is now among the people, and he will dwell with them. They will be his people, and God himself will be with them and be their God."

20. My wife and I disagree as to whether there will be rugby union in heaven. Obviously, she is wrong. That said, contact sports may have a hard time making the cut (football and hockey also spring to mind), given that per Rev 21:4 there will "no longer be any pain." But perhaps I'm overthinking things.

A Little More on the Problem of Dualism

Dualism imbibes the idea that the spiritual world is "the real" world and "the real me" is a spirit-being, trapped in a sinful and corrupted physical body, in a sinful and corrupted world, from which it is my destiny one day to be freed. Thus seen, salvation entails being delivered from this physical existence to live in a state of disembodied bliss in a spiritual existence that we call "heaven." Dualistic thinking embedded in the modern worldview is the reason that most people visualize heaven in those "spiritualized" terms.

The extent to which such dualistic thinking has become embedded within modern Christianity is especially surprising when the literal bodily resurrection of Jesus is recognized as a core conservative evangelical doctrine (as distinguished from a liberal understanding in which it's seen only as some kind of "spiritual" resurrection). If our destiny is to be only spiritually resurrected as disembodied souls, then why would Jesus need to have been physically resurrected? Especially if physical matter is intrinsically bad, as Neoplatonism suggests. Rather, in multiple places in the New Testament, the resurrected Jesus is pictured as the model—the "firstborn"—of all who will experience resurrection. He is the firstborn both in a preeminence sense and a forerunner sense. Acts 26:23 speaks of Jesus as "the first to rise from the dead." First Corinthians 15:20 says, "Christ has been raised from the dead, the firstfruits of those who have died."[21]

Dualism is a problem that we need to be attuned to, especially as charismatic Christians. The cosmos that God spoke into being is one indivisible whole: it's a spiritual creation and a physical creation all at the same time. It is both together that God said was "very good." The classic Hebrew understanding differs from Greek philosophical thinking in that neither the spiritual (supernatural) nor the material (carnal) is seen as good or bad in and of itself—its "goodness" or "badness" derives solely from the extent to which its features align with the will of God. We should not love the one and hate the other in a "dualistic" way, only that within each which aligns with and advances the kingdom of God (or vice versa).

If anyone was ever "perfect" you would think it would be Jesus. And yet, Heb 5:8 tells us that "even though Jesus was God's Son, he learned obedience from the things he suffered." But he couldn't have

---

21. Cf. Rom 8:29; Col 1:15, 18; and Rev 1:4.

learned anything if he was already perfect in the Neoplatonic sense. Hebrews is not saying that Jesus learned obedience subsequent to prior disobedience, but it is saying that he learned as he grew, and developed, and matured, just as we do; the human Jesus learned in the ways that we learn. Hebrews 2 tells us that in order to have authentically "shared in our humanity" (v. 12), Jesus "had to be" made like us, "fully human in every way" (v. 17). The sole exception to that complete likeness being that he was "without sin" (Heb 4:15).

This means that *to the extent any feature of what it commonly means to be human is not inherently sinful, Jesus shared that characteristic with us.* It is not sinful, for example, to need to learn, and develop, and mature. In fact it's healthy. Unsurprisingly, therefore, Luke 2:52 tells us, in a matter-of-fact way, that "Jesus grew in wisdom and stature" as well as "in favor with God and all the people."

A Few Thoughts on Adam and Eve

To finish this chapter, I just want to take the opportunity to clear up a couple of other important matters in the creation account that might not otherwise get a mention, specifically concerning "Adam and Eve."

It would have been obvious to its original audience that there was a deliberate wordplay going on with these "names." We've become accustomed to thinking that Genesis is talking about someone called Adam, as the name of the first male human. This is unsurprising, given that Adam is a popular boy's name, but the Hebrew word 'āḏām meant humanity or human beings in general. It's not until at least Gen 2:19 onward in the creation account—and most likely not until Gen 4:25 onward—that it's being used as a personal name. Until then, 'āḏām is always talking about humanity: humankind, or the human race.[22] The original hearers would have realized that, of course, when they heard it spoken in community settings. I say "heard" because people didn't have their own personal copies in the ancient world (and still less could most people read or write). This is why Jas 1:22 says, "Don't just be hearers of the word," rather than, as we would more likely say, "Don't just be readers of the word."

What this means is that God did not create a man named "Adam" in his image. God is not biologically male. He created 'āḏām in his image,

---

22. There's another little word play going on, too, that doesn't come across in the English words: the Hebrew for "ground" or "earth" (from which the man was made, per Gen 2:7) is 'āḏāmâ.

not "Adam" in his image—and not "the male sex" in his image (however much men might like to think that and, for some, design a convenient theology around it). Genesis 1:26–27 (NLT) says, "God created human beings in his own image. In the image of God he created them; *male and female* he created them." Wherever the involvement of women is suppressed or diminished, not least in the church, something significant in the image of God is missing. The church is no longer fully reflecting who God is and what God is like. Part of God's perspective on human life and divine-human affairs has been lost.

In Gen 2, God attends to one remaining "not good" that needed attention before his initial creative work was properly completed: human loneliness. In v. 18, "It's not good for *ādām* to be alone." In God's "very good" creation, human beings were made for companionship. We were made for intimacy and for community. So God says, "I will make a suitable helper." Because the English word "helper" implies a subservient relationship, this verse has been read as a biblical mandate for women fitting into and around men's lives, to "help" them—implying that women were created by God to be men's personal assistants. "Suitable," in the sense of "suiting" the man. Cultural assumptions embedded in society have then imposed themselves on the text by limiting that to taking care of children and the home and meeting the needs and wants of the man. Religious interpretations have then further qualified that women need to be "in submission," under the so-called "headship" of men.

From the male perspective, this "traditional interpretation" based on "what the Bible clearly teaches"—and by and large, of course, it does clearly teach that, insofar as it is an ancient world text where its writers and original hearers would have conceived of little else—has been extremely convenient. For a start, it removes half the competition for preaching and teaching roles.

These assumptions concerning women are often perceived (and taught) to be part of something called a "creation mandate"—in other words, that Genesis is "teaching" something intended as timeless divine truth concerning how things are supposed to be between women and men. But although men who wish to maintain women's subservient status vis-à-vis themselves can point to other Scriptures as prooftexts to support them in that endeavor, I'm afraid they really cannot get it from Genesis's reference to the woman as a "helper."

The Hebrew word translated as "helper" in Gen 2:20 is ʿ*ēzer*. John Walton, who is one of the world's foremost Old Testament scholars, says that when the word is used elsewhere it's almost always speaking of God as the one helping his people. God is "the Helper." Walton says, "Nothing suggests a subservient status of the one helping"; in fact, "the opposite is more likely."[23] I very much doubt that even the most conservative complementarian would suggest that there is a biblical creation mandate for God the Helper being in a submissive relationship to his people, under our (male) headship and authority.

The root of the Hebrew word 'ēzer is "rescuer"—or "savior." The way that it's normally used in the Old Testament is in the sense of "riding to the rescue." Genesis 2:20 is talking about a helper in the sense of a stronger person (the woman partner) coming to help a weaker person who needs rescuing or saving (the male partner). Feast on that one, gentlemen, we might say.

---

23. Walton, *Genesis*, 176.

— 2 —

Relationship with God

LET'S BEGIN THIS CHAPTER by reminding ourselves of something we said in the previous chapter: that Genesis is a *theological* account of creation, saying what was most important for the narrative to convey at the time from God's perspective. It is not a *cosmological* account of creation, saying what would have been most important for the narrative to convey from a modern scientific perspective.

Genesis was not written to explain *how* things were made but *why* they were made and *who made* them. It was written not so that modern readers could see the *similarities* between the biblical account and a modern scientific account, but so that its original Jewish readers could see the *differences* between the biblical account and the equivalent accounts of the surrounding nations. Those differences notably featured the nature and character of the one true God of Israel versus the nature and character of their gods.

Modern skeptics will sometimes pooh-pooh the biblical creation account on the grounds that Israel simply "borrowed" the features of other traditional stories of origins for their own; but this is to miss the point. The divine inspiration in Genesis lies not in its significant similarities to these other accounts but in its significant differences. For example, where other nations' accounts saw humanity as created to be slaves of capricious gods, Israel understood humanity as created for friendship with a faithful, loving God. Shared assumptions underlying those stories, such as humans being formed from the mud of the ground, are irrelevant to what God was seeking to have conveyed.

The creation account was written to tell us who God is, who we are, how God relates to us and how we relate to him. It's thus a relational story, not a manufacturing story. Genesis is offering us theological truths, not scientific truths. It was offering, for the people for whom it was written (and before that, in its preservation and repetition as oral tradition), answers to their questions as to who they were as a people-group, why things are as they are in their world, and who their God is: how he features in that. And it was written and conveyed in such a way that it would "make sense" to them in their world.

Without in any sense denigrating the rest of creation, Genesis makes clear that humanity is the high point in God's creative work. As the creational account proceeds, at each step it affirms, "God saw that it was good." But at the end of day six—after making people—"God saw everything he had made, and it was very good." It's only when humanity is created that a "good" creation becomes a "very good" creation.

We see in Genesis that there is a clear and intentional distinction between humans and animals. Apparently, scientists have ascertained that up to 99.9 percent of our DNA is shared with chimpanzees. But, as *Scientific American* said when they reported on it, "That tiny portion of unshared DNA makes a world of difference."[1] As Christians, we might suggest that "world of difference" as *Scientific American* puts it, is the *imago Dei*—the "image of God" in humanity, as Genesis puts it.

Now although Genesis doesn't give us any real detail about what exactly it means by "the image of God"—many a first-year theology student has been caught out by being asked to write an essay on the "trick question" of what the Bible means by the image of God—certain features do seem to be implicit in the story. We might sum these up by three words, each beginning with the letter "R": that we humans were uniquely made with the capacity to *relate* to God, to *reflect* God, and to *represent* God.

The *Imago Dei*: Relationship with God

Our first "R" word is "relating." As male and female bearers of his image (Gen 1:27), we have an *invitation* to be in relationship with him, a *calling*

---

1. Wong, "Tiny Genetic Differences," para. 2.

to be in relationship with others, and a *mandate* to be in relationship with the world around us. Implicit here is that we are to be in "right" relationship—so it's a good question as to what right relationship looks like in each of these spheres.

In terms of relationship with God, it's important that—especially for evangelical Christians—we do not allow our understanding of the gospel to cut in prematurely. We must allow the biblical story prior to Jesus to speak for itself, as it were. In the Old Testament, the notion of relationship with God—and in particular, *right* relationship with God—is presented to us in an evolving way as the biblical story unfolds. We need to listen and learn from the whole story, not go directly from the fall to the cross in one giant leap.

If we look back to the beginning of Genesis, we see pictured how the divine-human relationship was designed to be in the original creation. And if we look forward to the end of Revelation, we see how the relationship is destined to be in the ultimate consummation. In each case, it's relationally centered: picturing a divine-human relationship in which God is personally known and personally present.

In between, we see various forms and expressions of relationship with God in the scriptural account centered (in the first instance) on Israel as God's people. Clearly, from a Christian perspective, Jesus is the centerpoint of the relational story, but again, let's not rush to that too soon. Jesus came into an existing relational story of God and people that had been in existence for millennia. He respected the preceding story of which he was a part and so therefore should we. The story (including its relational ups and downs along the way) shaped and formed his understanding of God.

This threefold invitation, calling, and mandate to humanity comes as a package. Relationship with God does not stand alone. When Jesus was asked, "What is the most important commandment in the law?" he did not answer with one, but with two: love God, and love people. This was not because he misheard the question. Rather, it's because they are effectively indivisible from God's perspective. Indeed, I would argue that, from God's perspective, if we are not doing the second with all of our heart, soul, mind, and strength, then we are not doing the first. I would further argue that—again from God's perspective—loving people is *by definition* loving God; it is how we love him. This is not to deny or decry feelings we have in our heart toward God directly, simply to make sure we do not stop at that, by defining it as that, as a near-exclusive focus on experiential personal piety could potentially mislead us into doing. As to our mandate to be in right relationship with the world around us, this is implicit in the creation story, but all the more important to emphasize as Christians today, since the urgency to protect and restore the planet's ecosystem is now so pressing. A creation-care mandate is evident right from the beginning of the relational story: "The Lord God took *'ādām* and put [him] in the Garden of Eden to cultivate it and take care of it" (Gen 2:15). Though the scriptural writers were unaware of the ecological disasters that would arise in the modern industrialized era thousands of years from their time, we have no excuse.

The story of the Bible is the story of how that relational invitation, calling, and mandate works out, with ups and downs and successes and failures along the way. We see people "getting it" at times and "not getting it" at times.

Back in Genesis, we see God pictured as walking in the garden with Adam and Eve in the cool of the day. We see God conversing with them. We see face-to-face intimacy, with God pictured as personally present. Although the text is describing a personal relationship, with God clearly personified, we do not see him pictured in human form as such (the story is silent on that). It's making a theological point, not an anthropological point.

Even after Adam and Eve's failure that we call "the fall" God does not withdraw from them. In fact, we see him personally making clothes for them, to cover their shame: "The Lord God made garments of skin for Adam and his wife and clothed them" (Gen 3:21; cf. Gen 1:25).

The evangelical notion that "God can't look upon sin" is completely missing from this picture. There is no indication that he had to cover his eyes and look away as soon as there was sin around, which we may well consider encouraging, given that none of us is without sin, and no one except Jesus ever has been. The reality is that God has to look upon sin in this world every day and from the fall onward always has.[2] The commonplace idea that God abandoned Jesus on the cross (Matt 27:46) because the sin of the world was upon him (which derives from the idea that God can't look upon sin) would benefit from revisiting, given that God has never abandoned anyone (certainly no one who did

---

2. Cf. Gen 6:5: "The Lord saw how great the wickedness of the human race had become on the earth"; and 6:12: "God saw how corrupt the earth had become, for all the people on earth had corrupted their ways." I suppose it is possible for God to metaphorically "see" without looking, so to speak.

not wish to be). It is one thing to say, rightly, that unholy people like us are by nature incompatible with a holy God; it is quite another to infer from this that God is by nature distant and given to abandoning people as a consequence. Indeed, the idea directly contradicts scriptural assurances: Heb 13:5 (NASB), "I will never desert you, nor will I ever abandon you," is quoting multiple Old Testament verses (it is not an exclusively post-Jesus idea).

We also see here the first recorded death in creation. One could say, the first death *because* of sin; the first death *for* sin: the animal from whose skin God made their clothing. Was that animal's death to be read as a "sacrifice" (specifically, a sacrifice for sin)? The text does not tell us; though, if it was, its purpose was clearly to cover the shame of sin rather than to absorb any punishment for sin.[3]

Notice that even after Adam and Eve's failure, God is still personally present with them in the same manner; in fact, "they heard the sound of the Lord God walking in the Garden in the cool of the day" (Gen 3:8) is describing something that occurs *after* that failure, and so too does the subsequent conversation about "what happened."

From this point on in the story, however, the relational picture that's been painted so far does appear to begin to change. We still see God speaking to people—for example, in the story of Cain and Abel in Gen 4 (God's conversation with Cain takes place after he has murdered his brother in cold blood; a sin if ever there was one)—and the implication is of God still being personally present, insofar as the story tells us that Cain and Abel brought offerings to him. Keep in mind that this is all now taking place *outside* the garden, the "temple-like" context in which we had previously seen God conversing personally with Adam and Eve. But from the conclusion of this pericope, the face-to-face, direct, personal intimacy that we have previously witnessed seems to be receding. Perhaps a key verse is Gen 4:16: "Then Cain went out *from the presence of the Lord* and settled in the land of Nod, east of Eden." This is not simply a geographical relocation but a relational dislocation.

As Genesis continues, we see God continuing to speak, specifically to Noah and his sons in chapters 6 through 9, but the text does not present that speaking in the context of a visible, personal presence. As the story unfolds, it does feel as if a discernibly widening gap is emerging in the divine-human relationship, as sin continues to take a grip in new

---

3. For more on the place of sacrifice for sin, the shame of sin, and punishment for sin, see Burnhope, *Telling the Old, Old Story*.

and ever more problematic ways. It's as if we are seeing two once-parallel lines—of the story of God and the story of people—increasingly diverging. We see generation after generation named in Gen 5, but there's no mention—and no stories—of God being personally present as he was in the beginning. Genesis 5:9 does say that "Enoch walked with God," but it's a rare exception in a long list of names; what it doesn't say is that God walked with Enoch in the intimate and personal way that things are pictured with Adam and Eve in the garden.

By the time the story gets to Abraham, in Gen 12 onward, we see a few instances of God "appearing" and "speaking," but this includes in a vision and a dream, and through strangers described as angels. So it's not clear how, exactly, God is now appearing and speaking. What we do know is that by the time God introduces himself to Moses he says, "You cannot see my face, for no man can see me and live" (Exod 33:20).

From this point on, we "see" God only indirectly through intermediaries and imagery: fire in a bush that doesn't burn, a pillar of cloud, and a pillar of fire. Figuratively, we "see" a God who is understood to be present with his people, firstly in the tabernacle and then in the temple—in the Holy of Holies—but who is symbolically separated from them by a curtain veil (believed to symbolize the boundary between heaven and earth), beyond which only one person could pass and then only once a year.

We understand this curtain veil to symbolize the separation between God and people; which is why, at the moment of Jesus' death on the cross, we see it being torn in two, from top to bottom, in Matt 27:51, symbolizing that God's personal presence is returning—an "unveiling" if you will—of God once again being personally present, but in a new way. Through Jesus, how things will be in the future in God's relationship with people has begun to invade the present.

If we fast-forward to the new creation in Rev 21 (that we tend to call "heaven" for short) we see a return to a presence of God that we haven't seen in the biblical story since early Genesis. "God's dwelling-place is now among the people, and he will dwell with them. They will be his people, and God himself will be with them and be their God" (Rev 21:3). The face-to-face intimacy has returned: God will personally "wipe every tear from their eyes" (Rev 21:4), as might a parent for a child.

We see pictured in Genesis the way that human relationship with God was supposed to be. And we see pictured in Revelation the way that relationship with God is destined to be. We need to remember that in both cases "picture language" is the medium being used to convey these truths. As with any picture painted with words, we should be cautious of being overliteral in its interpretation. We should look for the big picture themes and ideas rather than overworking the detail. In all picture language, some otherwise hard-to-grasp reality is being likened to something that is easier to grasp, but inherent in that "likening" is a picture's limitations. Pressed too hard for precise conformity, any picture will start to become untrue once its limitations are reached. For example, though we may speak of Jesus as the Lamb of God seated at the Father's right hand, the truth that the phrase is seeking to convey is plainly not that Jesus is a young sheep sitting on a chair in heaven.

The "Now and the Not Yet"

We should see all of Jesus' mission in terms of the coming of the kingdom of God; this is true of relationship with God. The perspective of many scholars—and one that I share—is that kingdom theology is best understood in terms of "the now and the not yet" or "the already but the not yet" of the kingdom. In other words, the coming of the kingdom of God commenced in and through Jesus' ministry but was not at that time completed. It was inaugurated but not fully consummated. Hence, we see some aspects of the coming of the kingdom "now," in part, but "not yet" do we see all aspects in their fullness. Not everything that Rev 21:4 pictures, in terms of what will happen, has yet happened: there still is death, mourning, crying, and pain, for "the old order of things" which is characterized by those things has not yet passed away, as it one day will.

If we apply "now, but also not yet" kingdom theology to relationship with God in these "in-between" times—between Jesus' first coming to inaugurate the kingdom of God breaking into this world and his second coming to consummate or complete that—we *have* a restored relationship with God "already" but we also *don't have* it "yet"—not in its ultimate fullness as Rev 21 pictures it (mirroring early Genesis).

We are living "between the times," as it were, in a period when, through Jesus, personal relationship with God has been restored in a way that echoes the beginning and the future, but in the present it remains to be fully restored. There is much more to come than our current experience. The apostle Paul pictures that when he says in 1 Cor 13:12, "Now we see in a mirror dimly, but then we will see face to face."

The King James says we see "darkly"—the image they were looking at was dim and dark because mirrors in the ancient world were just polished metal. Paul is saying that dim, dark reflections are as good as it gets right now (were he living in our day, of course, a mirror analogy would not work, but it worked well then). The way that we "know God" now—the nature of the relationship we have with God now—is real, but it's only a dim, dark reflection of the way that it once was and one day will be, because the old order of things has not yet passed away. God is not yet fully dwelling with his people in the face-to-face way that he once did and one day intends to again.

This is why Paul says, in 2 Cor 5:7, that in these "in-between" times we have to "live by faith, not by sight." Living by faith does not mean doing mental gymnastics to try to control our thought life. It is not about never having any doubts or any questions. It most certainly is not about "positive confession." Faith is always in God, never in faith. The best synonym for "faith" in our English vocabulary would be "trust"—which is a "doing" word not a "thinking" word. Faith is not "believing" per se, it's living in a way that reflects believing and reflects the kind of God we believe in. Faith is not utter and complete mental certainty, any more than it was for the man who said to Jesus, "I do believe; help me overcome my unbelief!" (Mark 9:24). It's natural for us as human beings to experience a mix of the two, just as it was for him.

The New Testament Greek word that's usually translated as "faith" in our Bibles also meant "faithfulness." In English, we have the two words, which we perceived to have different meanings, but in the Greek there was just the one. Accordingly, in verses where Bible translators have used "faith" we are at liberty to read them as "faithfulness" instead. When we do that, the meanings of those verses often come across quite differently. (So, too, if we substitute "trust.") Living by faithfulness to a God we can't see should characterize our relationship with God in this present "in-between" time. *That* is faith as a "doing" word.

In Jesus' prayer framework that we know as the Lord's Prayer—albeit it's technically the disciples' prayer, of course[4]—what we are asking when we pray "Your Kingdom come" is for God to bring some of the way things will be in the future into our present: a taster of the "not yet" "now." So, for example, when we pray for someone who is suffering, we

---

4. Jesus was responding to the disciples' request for him to teach them to pray his way, just as John taught his own disciples; clearly, the "forgive us our trespasses" part would not apply to Jesus.

are inviting the Holy Spirit to bring a firstfruit of the future kingdom fullness in which there is "no more death or mourning or crying or pain," when God will "wipe every tear" from our eyes, when "the old order of things has passed away"—an old order characterized by the reign of sin and death and everything that causes death, such as sickness.

The *Imago Dei*: Reflecting God

Our second "R" word is "reflecting" God. By "reflecting" him, we don't mean looking like him physically. We mean visibly reflecting who God is and what God is like—being a reflection of his nature and character. We mean loving and giving and caring in ways that reflect God's own loving and giving and caring.

Bearing the image of God means that we have the capacity to be like God in certain ways that other creatures do not possess. For example, the capacity to love as God loves. If you are an animal lover, I am not saying that your dog, or your cat, or your hamster doesn't love you; of course they do. I'm simply saying that it's not the same. We have capacities and characteristics by virtue of being made in the image of God that they lack. We have special status. And with that special status comes a special responsibility: to be the image of God in this world, not just the image of ourselves. We are called to be "image bearers."

In what *we* are like, people should be able to see something meaningful of what *God* is like. Not because of a physical resemblance, but through the ways in which we reflect God's nature and character. People can't see God, but they can see us—and they should be able to see God in us and through us.

The image of God also means that, unlike other creatures, we have a spiritual as well as a physical dimension to our lives. We are spiritual as well as physical people. We are made with the capacity to engage with the supernatural world and a supernatural God. However, we must not misread that as saying there is a "spiritual" me distinct from the "physical" me—there is not a "spiritual" person who is "the real" me trapped inside a physical body that one day it is destined to be released from. That is not "biblical," that's "gnostic." It's Plato and Greek philosophy speaking.

We are one, integrated, inseparable, indivisible person physically and spiritually. We should therefore be both naturally spiritual and spiritually natural. Our "spirituality" should be natural, not "weird." We should not go from something called "natural" mode into something called "spiritual" mode.

Though "God is spirit" (John 4:24), as people made in his image we have the capacity to engage with him spiritually: to "worship him in spirit and in truth." In prayer, we are invited to commune with a God who dwells in the spiritual realm. As charismatic Christians, we also understand that part of our calling, part of our "imaging," is to reflect the work of the Holy Spirit in exercising spiritual gifts. We ourselves do not have "spiritual powers" in any ownership sense, but we do have the capacity to be empowered by the Holy Spirit—best understood as the Spirit *moving through* us (in which our contribution is characterized in terms of the relationship of a drainpipe to the rain; no more). When it comes to the moving of the Spirit, to say that it's "not all about us" is an understatement—it's *not at all* about us.

The *Imago Dei*: Representing God

Our third and final "R" word is that we're called to "represent" God. The *imago Dei* is the image of God in Latin—that's the term theologians use. But there's another term also, which is the *imitatio Dei*—our calling to imitate God in this world. Not in the sense of impersonating him or pretending to be him, but doing the things that he would do, because we love the things that he loves. The point of being the *imago Dei* is that we should also become the *imitatio Dei*.

God did not create us as in his image just so we would *feel* good (though in one sense we may, because it's a very special privilege). Rather, we were created in his image to *do* good. Evangelical alarms may be sounding at this point, as they always do when "works" are mentioned! But fear not; good works are not to "get us" saved, they're a heartfelt, natural response to "being" saved. This is not a new idea—it's not a new way of conceiving of the place of good works. It's precisely how Israel understood how Torah worked, as well. It was a "thank you," not a "please."

However "Reformed" an evangelical one might be, we would surely recognize that good works should play no less important a part in our lives as they did in Jesus' life; otherwise, neither the *imago Dei* nor the *imitatio Dei* would mean very much. We ought not to be afraid of the term "good works." In Acts 10, when the apostle Peter—who must surely have known Jesus as well as anyone, and specifically, what Jesus thought about "works"—is speaking to the gentile Cornelius, he says that God "accepts from every nation the one who fears him *and does what is right*." Peter continues, "You know what has happened throughout the province of Judea, beginning in Galilee . . . how God anointed Jesus of Nazareth with the Holy Spirit and power, and how *he went around doing good*."

I like Holly Carey's definition of "a disciple" in the Gospels: a person who is "doing what Jesus wants done." As Scot McKnight notes in his Substack book review,[5] this is especially insightful in turning our attention away from questions such as who is and isn't a disciple in an "in, or out?" membership club sense. Carey is responding to the question as it is typically posed, "Did Jesus have female disciples?"—to which the typical response is "no"—which is then deployed as a male way of delegitimizing women in ministry (supposedly honoring a timeless biblical model). Carey's alternative proposal is to focus our attention on a rather different and better way of posing the question: "Did the women in the Gospels do the things that Jesus wanted done?" Rather than focusing on status, this looks to actions. Here, of course, the answer is a resounding "yes"—often in favorable contrast to the men.[6]

In Eph 2:10 (ESV), we see the *imago Dei* and the *imitatio Dei* coming together: "We are *his workmanship*, created in Christ Jesus *for good works*, which God prepared beforehand that we should walk in them." Faithful Jews in the biblical era never believed that "good works get you to heaven" and nor do they now; unfortunately, that's a caricature which still has traction within some quarters of evangelicalism. It's a gross misunderstanding of "the law" (which biblically is speaking of the God-given Torah that mediated the covenantal relationship between Israel and God, not of "legalism" in some generic sense). The Jewish relationship with the God of Israel was always defined by faith, never by works: "The righteous shall live by faith"—said *three times* in the New Testament—is directly quoting Hab 2:4.[7]

---

5. McKnight, "Women Who Do."
6. Carey, *Women Who Do*.

7. Interestingly, the most frequently quoted verse—eight times—is "Love your neighbor as yourself" (Lev 19:18). I don't think the New Testament writers had "warm and fuzzy feelings in our hearts" in mind here, rather, it was doing good toward them. Cf. Jas 2. To the extent that such repetition can be viewed as indicating significance—I believe it generally does, and not least when in this case it forms part of the Great Commandment (Matt 22:36–40)—Christians who fail to see the central importance in God's eyes of "what I do" alongside (or even over above) "what I believe" may have cause for reflection.

In the parable of the sheep and the goats,[8] it is often not noticed that the basis for the destiny of eternal life for the "sheep" is their doing good toward the people Jesus loves (which he deems to be doing good toward him). The "eternal punishment" destined for the "goats" is predicated on their failure to do so.[9]

> "Lord, when was it that we saw you hungry and gave you food, or thirsty and gave you something to drink? And when was it that we saw you a stranger and welcomed you, or naked and gave you clothing? And when was it that we saw you sick or in prison and visited you?" And the king will answer them, "Truly I tell you, just as you did it to one of the least of these who are members of my family, you did it to me."

Once we set aside a "works-righteousness" fixation—that because "good works don't get you to heaven," we must do all in our power not to do things that might suggest we think that—we notice afresh an abundance of Scriptures that speak of the importance of what we do, and specifically, of doing good. This includes a role in our eternal destiny; *not* as the *basis* of our acceptance by God, but as the *fruit* of our acceptance by God—a heartfelt response, in the ways that he himself would have us respond. The parable of the talents is but one example (Matt 25:14–30), which immediately precedes the parable of the sheep and the goats and forms part of an end-times eternal destiny discourse by Jesus.

So humanity was made with the capacity to relate to God, the capacity to reflect God, and the capacity to represent God. We are not physical *representations* of God, but we are physical *representatives* of God.

In the ancient world, an image or an idol was believed to carry the "essence" of that which it represented. The other nations therefore made images of their gods, believing them to carry that essence with them. In contrast, Genesis is saying don't make images of your God (Exod

---

8. Matt 25:31–46.

9. This is one of the key substantiating passages for those who conceive hell in terms of eternal conscious torment (reflecting, as it does, the phrase "eternal punishment"). Undermining such a reading, however, is (a) absence of other similar references in Scripture, (b) the fact that this is said in the context of a parable, and (c) its incompatibility with the nature and character of God that we see in Jesus. More likely than Jesus having in mind a literal meaning for that phrase, which would be inconsistent with how parables were to be interpreted, is that "eternal punishment" was an example of the genre of hyperbole—deliberate exaggeration to shock the audience and grab their attention: "What I'm saying here is really important; you need to really reflect on it." On genre, see Part II, and specifically chapters 3 and 4.

20:4; Exod 34:17; etc.) because God has created *you* to be his image and likeness, and to carry his essence in this world. Radically different! It's interesting that the New Testament Greek word for "image" is *eikón*—from which we get "icon."

The Biblical Story as a Relational Journey

One of the potentially puzzling things about the nature of the Bible as the word of God is that based on that customary title one might expect it to be front-loaded with propositions; indeed, to mostly comprise propositions. In theology, a "proposition" (or a "propositional truth") is a commandment by God, or a truth statement about God or from God. In practice, however, the vast majority of biblical content is not that. It's narrative—in other words, stories that form part of a "big story" of God and people. The best way to characterize this big story is that it's a relational journey. It narrates people's encounters with God, right and wrong perceptions of God, successes and failings as people of God, and what being in relationship with God does and does not look like. If as Bible readers we are focused only on mining the text for propositions, we are, to say the least, missing a trick.

Central to being in relationship with God is understanding who God is as a person, grasping his nature and character. How we understand what God is like, what things are most important to him (and equally, what things are least important or of no importance in the scheme of things) is critical to that relationship.

For example, if we primarily understand God to be defined by wrath, anger, and hatred of sin (all of which can be found in Scripture if we read things that way, or we've been taught to read things that way), our relationship with God will be strongly colored by that. If, on the other hand, we primarily understand God to be defined by love, mercy, grace, compassion, and kindness (all of which can also be found in Scripture if we read things that way), then our relationship with God will be strongly colored by that! Suffice to say that in Scripture God is very clearly identified as love: "God is love" (1 John 4:8, 16). He is never identified as wrath or anger.

The relational journey that we see in Scripture does not reflect a linear progression. It isn't mapping a continuous upward progress in people getting to understand God better and better. It isn't reflecting better and better people of God, living in better and better ways. These are the things we might expect to see. But if it's characterized by anything, it's lots of ups and downs. It's more like a game of Snakes and Ladders, or a seemingly never-ending game of Monopoly where the characters go round and round the same circuit, experiencing the same issues time and again ("Go directly to jail; do not pass Go, do not collect $200") as well as some of the same blessings time and again ("You have won second prize in a beauty contest; collect $10"—though the manufacturers, perhaps unsurprisingly, discontinued this particular reward back in 2021).

If we read Scripture searching only or mainly for the propositions or proposition-like statements, we will get a lopsided view of things. It can also cause us to think that we're finding propositions in places they don't exist, places they were never intended. If we are primarily looking for statements of timeless divine truth, we will miss the narrative (storied) character of most of the content. We will see it as mere "filler" surrounding the propositional truths, from which those truths must be dug out. Obviously the propositional truths are important and we should be looking out for them; my point here is to restore our awareness of the value of the storied elements that God has placed centrally within Scripture—overwhelmingly within it, in terms of its majority content.

Engaging well with the narrative parts of Scripture means having our antennae tuned to picking up the signals in the relational stories that are being told. It means paying attention to the characters not just in their strengths and successes as idealized role models, but also in their weaknesses and mistakes. This means having a conversation with the text—at times, indeed, arguing with the text—as the rabbis would do. Preferably, doing so in community. It means being attuned to the humanity, and the human weaknesses, and the oh-so-common flawed human perceptions in the text. The times that people were getting God right and the times they were getting him wrong. The ups and downs in their relationships with God, with kin, and with others. Scripture is a relational story composed of relational stories, some to do with God and people, and some to do with people and people.

A critical point to stress is that it is no mistake that so much of the biblical content is narrative in this way. It is similarly no mistake that the word of God has nothing authored by Jesus, which could quite easily have happened, had God so intended—just as the apostle Paul dictated to a scribe in writing his letters to churches, so also could Jesus. Instead, we cannot help but notice that everything in the Bible comes to us through the recollections and experiences of people. Even the ascended Jesus' firsthand communications to early churches in Rev 2–3 are via John of Patmos through a prophetic vision.

Throughout Scripture we see divine-human coauthorship, in which the humanity appears alongside the divinity—the human element alongside the divine element—with far more of a nuanced "light touch" for the divine role than we might have anticipated. For example, in the introduction to the book of Revelation, John characterizes his writing as "from me and Jesus" (I'm paraphrasing Rev 1:4–5).

In no sense do any of these features and characteristics undermine the Bible's inspired status (per 2 Tim 3:16) but they do help to frame what that looks like in practice. That said, "inspiration"—which literally means "God-breathed"—remains an elusive and mysterious concept. Perhaps from God's point of view that is quite deliberately so. Had he so intended, he could quite easily have described its nature in other ways; for example, he could have used words like "inerrant" or "infallible." But as Fee and Stuart remind us, "That it is the inspired Word of God is primary; the precise nature of inspiration is secondary."[10]

Inspiration may be an enigmatic concept, but I think we can at least say that it means the Bible we have in our hands is the Bible that God wants us to have, with all of those features and characteristics incorporated, for us to work with and grapple with.[11] Evangelical Christians, in particular, do well to keep these features and characteristics of the text in mind when affirming the "authority" of Scripture. The propositions are one thing—even then, of course, we still have to determine which were speaking timelessly and which were speaking in time-bound contexts—but to ask how narrative, poetry, story, and song function authoritatively is an important question. What *is* clear, however, is that those parts function both relationally and conversationally; moreover, they are no less inspired or significant than the propositions.

---

10. Fee and Stuart, *How to Read the Bible*, 97.

11. The fact that different traditions in Protestant, Catholic, and Orthodox circles have slightly different Bibles (with or without an Apocrypha) is a challenge when it comes to what is and is not "the word of God." Perhaps God has permitted this for good reason from his perspective; it certainly makes it a little harder to idolize Scripture. The reality is that all traditions have their "canons within the canon" in terms of the priority they grant to certain verses, passages, doctrines, and stories, so perhaps we could characterize the whole thing in terms of a pebble thrown into a pond: the strongest ripples in "inspiration" terms are situated closest to the pebble's point of entry (the books we all agree on) while the weakest are toward the boundaries (the books we don't).

So, the story of the Bible is a story of relationship; it's recounting the journey of the divine-human relationship, with inescapable implications for all relationships. It's the story of what it means to know God personally, and the implications that flow from knowing God personally, as experienced by many generations of our forebears in faith.

The Central Place of Jesus in the Relational Journey

Whatever our preferred way of explaining the gospel—specifically the doctrine of the atonement, the literal meaning of which is how through Jesus God enabled us to be made "at one" with him—at its heart the gospel is God's relational initiative toward us. If we are minded to prefer a legal metaphor centered in the divine law courts with God as judge, we must keep in mind that before it's ever a legal concept it's a relational concept. The central concern of the gospel, when stated well, is not broken law that requires punishment but broken relationship that requires restoration. The wounds suffered by the suffering servant messiah figure in Isa 53 are healing wounds inflicted by sinful humanity, not punishing wounds inflicted by God (as a close reading of that text makes clear, especially in the Septuagint). We shall say more on this "how?" question—how God's relational initiatives toward humanity are presented in Scripture, including in and through Jesus—when we look at other big themes in this Part I.[12]

When Jesus was asked, "Which is the most important commandment in the Torah?" he had 613 to choose from. He could easily have said, "obey" the Lord your God, or "serve" the Lord your God, or even "fear" the Lord your God, since all of these ideas are found. But he didn't. He chose "love the Lord your God." With all your heart and soul and mind and strength. And although he was only asked for one, he couldn't resist adding another one: "Love your neighbor as yourself." That's because loving people is an inescapable implication of loving God—at least in the way God understands it. Relationship—and specifically, right relationship—is at the heart of Jesus' choice of commandments.

Whatever you may have heard about so-called "imputed" righteousness and "imparted" righteousness and the like, the concepts underlying righteousness are really very simple. They start with all of our

---

12. For a short and simple treatment of how the doctrine of atonement has been understood and explained from New Testament times till now, see Burnhope, *Telling the Old, Old Story.*

relationships being right: right with God, right with one another, right with ourselves, and right with our planet.[13] We understand being "made right" in our relationship with God thorough what God in Christ has done for us; "staying right" and "doing what's right" are what we "in Christ" are called to be and to do for him, continuously enabled by his abundant grace, love, mercy, and forgiveness.

What we can say, in closing this chapter, is that throughout the biblical story, throughout that relational journey, God is the one who takes the initiative. God is the one who reaches out. God is the one who "comes to us." This will become all the more apparent as we move into our next big theme of "covenant."

---

13. The latter two relationships are inevitably less visible in Scripture, since the biblical writers had less awareness of them; but, in any event, they derive directly from an "all our relationships being right and staying right" reading of Scripture.

3

Covenant

IN THIS CHAPTER WE'RE going to look at one of the biggest "big themes" of the Bible—arguably *the* biggest—and that is "covenant."

Our English word comes from a Latin word, *convenire*, that means to "come together," to "unite," and be "made compatible." Covenant is therefore a framework for understanding the atonement, namely, how we are made "at one," brought together, and made compatible with God. Our term "to convene"—as in "arranging a convention"—comes from the same root.

The word "covenant" appears in the Bible over three hundred times (some thirty-five times in the New Testament); the first is in Genesis and the last is in Revelation. Even when the word itself doesn't appear it's always there as the backdrop. Throughout the Bible it's the basis of the relationship between God and people.

Covenants were in use throughout the ancient world for creating and defining social and political relationships. Unfortunately for those of us seeking to understand and explain the biblical significance of covenant for today, the idea is almost obsolete. At one time, marriage would have been the best example of a covenant relationship, but less so now. Society does not view the commitments that the marriage vows involve with the degree of significance and permanence that it used to. This is not wholly a bad thing (it very much depends on individual circumstances)—for example, external pressures to perpetuate the form of a marriage at almost any cost should never have served to lock one partner in to an unhealthy relationship. Abusive behavior is just as much covenantal unfaithfulness as adulterous behavior; both are violating the marital vows.

In any event, marriage no longer functions so well as an example in today's world. Perhaps the best example today, at least from a technical perspective, would be a treaty between two nations that has the force of international law behind it. You may remember the furor in the lead-up to Brexit when it was suggested that the UK government was planning to break its treaty obligations. Former Prime Minister and now elder statesman Sir John Major said,

> For generations, Britain's word—solemnly given—has been accepted by friend and foe. Our signature on any Treaty or Agreement has been sacrosanct. Over the last century, as our military strength has dwindled, our word has retained its power. If we lose our reputation for honouring the promises we make, we will have lost something beyond price that may never be regained.[1]

That is the sense of the commitment entered into in a covenant.

The Typical Features of Ancient World Covenants

In the ancient world, covenants had a number of standard features. As we run through them, notice how well they describe—and how they make sense of—what God has done for us through Jesus in the "new covenant."

- A covenant created a relationship that didn't previously exist, usually between unequal partners.
- It was founded on or in the light of a historical event.
- It set out commitments—binding promises made under oath—that each of the parties was making to the other, along with the expectations and benefits that would flow from it.
- And finally there was almost always some "ritual act" to "seal" or "ratify" the covenant that was seen as essential to the fulfillment of the promises that were being made. Typically, a sacrifice, and a covenant meal shared together.

---

1. Major, "Statement on Treaties."

Covenants usually involved a great and powerful king called the "suzerain" graciously offering to enter into a relationship with a weaker and lesser king called the "vassal." The vassal would pledge loyalty and obedience to the suzerain and the suzerain would pledge to protect and care for the vassal.

Having entered into a covenant relationship, the enemies of the vassal would now be the enemies of the suzerain; an attack on the vassal would be an attack on the suzerain.

The nature of a covenant meant that the relationship had to be an exclusive one. The vassal king couldn't enter into relationships with other surrounding kings without being guilty of infidelity and betrayal.

Covenant also had a "kinship" dynamic to it. Entering into a covenant was to be extending the family relationship, bringing into the family circle those who were previously—or potentially—enemies. No wonder that throughout the Bible—and especially in the New Testament—we see relationship with God being described in sonship terms, in adoption terms, in "joining the family" terms, and in marriage terms. They are all describing the radical change of status that comes with being included in a covenant relationship.

We can easily see how well these features are describing the features of a relationship with God through Jesus that we are familiar with in the "new covenant."

The similarities continue, especially when we frame it in parallel to Torah—the basis of the covenant that God made with Israel to shape and form its life as a nation once they were delivered from slavery in Egypt.

An ancient world covenant document would begin with the name of the great king, his family tree, and his titles. Then there would be a section describing all the things that the great king had previously done for the lesser king—his historic deeds. That is because what the great king had done in the past was the foundation and the assurance for what he was promising to do in the future. In the Bible, we often see the narration of God's deeds from the past serving in a similar way. Exodus 15:1–18, for example.

After that section came "the stipulations"—the benefits that would flow from faithfulness to the covenant and the adverse consequences from being unfaithful—laid out in a series of "If you do this . . . then I will do that" kind of statements (Exod 19:5, for example).

Since a covenant was seen as a sacred act in which the gods were involved and included, a copy of the covenant would be placed in the temple of the deity. This meant that obedience to the covenant was being placed on the same level as obedience to the gods.

The witnesses were then named—rather as legal contracts today are witnessed by independent third parties. In this case, however, the witnesses were the names of the parties' gods. Often these were very comprehensive lists, such that there would be no divine authorities left for one party to appeal to if they wanted to claim divine justification for violating their covenant obligations.

Engaging the gods in the covenant also served to ratify it in the supernatural realm, with benefits and consequences in the supernatural world as well as the natural world.

There was also provision for the covenant to be read out in public from time to time, the point being that it wasn't just a private and secret agreement between two kings. Its scope and its expectations applied to the people as well. It was part of the "law of the land."

And then last but by no means least would be the ratification ceremony, to bring it into effect. Usually this involved the sacrifice of an animal. The Hebrew word for "covenant" comes from the word for "cutting." What is usually translated as "making" a covenant literally means "cutting" a covenant.

Many Christians—perhaps most Christians—assume that sacrifices in the Bible were always for sin;[2] but one of the main reasons was to ratify or seal a covenant. In that sacrifice, the significance of the promises that were being entered into by each of the parties was being enacted by saying—in effect—"May what is happening to this animal happen to me if I am unfaithful to this covenant." It was certainly a way of getting people's attention to the seriousness of the promises they were making.

One last thing to say about the covenant-sealing sacrifice is that the animal wasn't just being killed for ceremonial reasons. It then became the centerpiece of a covenant meal. And not just in the sense of "Let's have dinner together afterward," as we might say. Sharing in the meal together was part of the making of the covenant. In ancient world culture, to set a meal before someone, to literally "break bread" with them, had covenantal significance.

---

2. They also tend to assume that when the word "sacrifice" is used is it talking about one particular way of understanding the atonement, favored by many evangelicals, known as penal substitution (that, on the cross, Jesus took our punishment for our sin so that we don't have to). But biblical sacrifices never had anything to do with punishment; the animal was never being punished, still less made to suffer grievously. Again, see Burnhope, *Telling the Old, Old Story.*

A Continuous Covenantal Journey

We said at the outset that covenant is the backdrop to the entire Bible—Old Testament and New Testament—because it frames the basis of the relationship between God and his world and it speaks to the nature and character of God. We see in the Bible a continuing series of covenantal commitments running through the whole of the story. Generally these covenantal commitments are made to or through representative individuals at key points in the story (though they always have in their sights a wider people group as well, as we will see in a moment when we briefly run through them).

In every case, it's God who is making the covenantal commitment, taking the initiative. God is the author of the covenant. It is not being "negotiated" between the parties like a trade deal. God is saying, "I am making this covenant with you—I am extending this invitation into a covenant relationship—with blessings and promises." With corresponding obligations on our side—if we want to say "Yes, please" and be part of it—and corresponding consequences if we choose to say "No, thank you" and opt out.

To be outside of a covenant relationship with God when he himself has invited us in is to choose a lonely place.

Now although various covenants are spoken of in the Old Testament, it's best for us to think of them as ongoing expressions of one continuing covenantal commitment by God to his world in various stages. One that required to be reframed, restated, and renewed in the light of different times and different circumstances as the relational journey was unfolding. Perhaps think of it like a relay—passing a covenantal baton.

The journey of Scripture is a relational journey that is defined throughout by covenant. God is, by his very nature and character, a covenant-loving, covenant-making, covenant-keeping, and covenant-fulfilling God. That is why God loves marriage—because it's a covenantal reflection of who he is and what he's like. So, naturally, he wants us to be covenantal in our relationships as well.

Covenant Beginnings in Creation

The covenantal journey begins with Adam and Eve, where we see God's invitation into relationship with him, with blessings flowing from covenantal faithfulness and adverse consequences for covenantal unfaithfulness.

The suzerain's covenantal expectations of the vassals are to be fruitful and multiply (bring about family and community), to enjoy the fruit of the garden (experience life in its fullness), to care for the garden he planted for them (his creation) and, of course, to be relationally faithful to the covenant maker. Adam and Eve's "original sin" was to break the covenant by eating the fruit of the one tree (doing the one little thing) that they had been specifically asked not to do. However, the real sin was not fruit eating per se (it's easy to see that as quite trivial, stand-alone) but rather what it constituted—unfaithfulness to the covenant; listening to the serpent and not trusting in the integrity of the covenant maker. Being open to, believing, and then acting on the serpent's undermining of God's nature and character ("Did God *really* say . . . ?"; "You will *not* surely die . . ."). They bought into the lies of the great king's enemies as to what he was like and broke the covenantal expectation of loyalty and faithfulness.

When it comes to the adverse consequences of breaking the covenant, in one sense the serpent was right (half-truths are always more effective than straight lies). Adam and Eve did not immediately die; though in losing access to the garden they could no longer eat from the tree of life, so death ultimately became a reality of human life. Even then, their banishment from the garden should not be seen as punishment (as an angry God lashing out) but as God's grace at work: his concern was: "What if they reach out, take fruit from the tree of life, and eat it? Then they will live forever!" (Gen 3:22). For humanity to live forever was always the plan, but not in their current state, not under the present circumstances that now characterized human life. As we would see later, the means of bringing eternal life back into human experience would be a (re)new(ed) covenant. Hence, access to the tree of life had to be constrained *pro tem*, pending the time when there would once again be unfettered access in the new creation (Rev 2:7; 22:2, 14).

Though we see consequences from covenant breach in the story, we do not see a lack of forgiveness, grace, or mercy, from the wronged covenant maker. For example, we see God personally fashioning clothes of animal skin to cover their shame (Gen 3:21). It is always within the power of the covenant maker to forgive covenant breach and to withhold or alleviate the adverse consequences provided in the covenant. He is not bound to enact them. Moreover, we see hints of a promised future redemption: a male descendant who would strike down the enemy that has brought this all about (Gen 3:15).

After this covenantally framed opening narrative, the key covenants in the Old Testament are those with Noah, Abraham, and Moses, plus the promise of a new covenant in Jer 31. The covenant with David is also notable because it includes the covenantal promise of a messiah who would be David's son.

The Covenant with Noah

In Gen 9:9, God says to Noah, "I now establish my covenant with you and with your descendants after you and with every living creature." It's "an everlasting covenant"—"a covenant for all generations to come." God says, it's a "covenant between me and the earth," of which the rainbow is a sign and a reminder. And because it's a covenant with all people forever,[3] and it's with the whole of creation, and its terms are unconditional, the overarching covenant promise made to Noah sets the framework for the entire divine-human covenantal relationship from that moment on. The permanent institution of the rainbow seals and signifies the permanence of the covenant; its frequent recurrence throughout all ages across the world serves as a continuing visual reminder for those to whom the covenant commitment was made.

Every subsequent reiteration of the covenantal relationship should be located under the umbrella of that overarching "Noachian" covenant—as subsequent steps along the same covenantal pathway—pointing toward the ultimate covenant, sealed and ratified by the ultimate covenant sacrifice. A new—and almost inconceivable—covenant, through which God in Christ as the suzerain will make the ultimate covenantal intervention to save and rescue his creation from the enemies that have invaded it, damaged it, and enslaved it.

The Covenant with Abraham

As the covenantal journey continues, we see God entering into a covenant with Abraham, in Gen 12 and Gen 15. The immediate covenantal promise was that he would be the father of one people and one nation, but once again we see that already the scope of the promise extends vicariously to all people and all nations. This is important to keep in mind as the story

---

3. Note that at this point there is no Jew-gentile distinction; all of humanity is in sight.

in due course proceeds via Israel. Even at this point, although Abraham is understood as the father of the Jewish nation,[4] the covenant blessing was not just for Abraham or Israel. The intention was that through their blessing the whole earth would be blessed: God would bless them, in order that they would be a blessing (Gen 12:2–3; cf. Acts 3:25).

I suggest this remains God's way: he blesses us in order that we in turn will be a blessing to others (not simply be blessed for our own sake, keeping it for ourselves). If we are not willing to be a blessing—to "pass blessing on"—then we should not be too surprised if God chooses to bless others instead, so that the blessings he wants others to receive can happen.

From this point on, God's covenant commitment to all people and nations that began in creation and continued through Noah is moving toward being channeled into a specific and targeted covenant commitment to one couple—Abraham and Sarah, whose family would grow to become a nation.

The divine-human relational story narrated in Scripture now reaches a fork in the road and becomes two separate, parallel roads, in a manner reminiscent of the Scottish folk song "The Bonnie Banks o' Loch Lomond," the chorus of which is "Ye'll take the high road, and I'll take the low road. And I'll be in Scotland afore ye." One is the road that the nation that will be called Israel will be traveling on and the other is the road that the other nations will be traveling on. Those roads will come together again not in Scotland (it's just a metaphor, folks), but in the person of Jesus later in the story.

The continuing biblical story in the Old Testament will now focus almost entirely on people and events in Israel's covenantal, relational journey.[5] However, the framing of God's plan for the world—initially in

---

4. All four Gospels speak of Abraham in those terms on multiple occasions, though Paul also references him as a gentile. Since the covenant with Abraham precedes the establishment of the Jewish nation and the giving of Torah to frame the Jewish covenantal relationship, Paul uses that to illustrate that gentile believers should take their point of reference for their relationship with God from Abraham and his covenant (rather than Moses and his covenant). See Rom 4, especially v. 16. The active first-century debate about how the two covenants should interface (for Jews and for gentiles) underlies Romans and even more so Galatians. See also Acts 15.

5. Strictly speaking, *Israel and Judah*, the two sibling kingdoms (northern and southern, respectively) into which the Hebrew tribes were divided from around the ninth/tenth century BCE. Each of these nations was within a few centuries conquered and taken into captivity. The writers will variously speak of Israel or Judah, and at times of both. I suggest that the distinctions are not especially material for the average

creation, implicitly, and then later in Noah, more explicitly—makes it clear that in the fullness of time God's covenantal commitment would once again re-embrace all people and nations. Blessing this one family and nation would be a stepping stone to blessing all families and nations.

At this point, the story would have suggested that destiny would be fulfilled through the *nation* of Abraham; it turned out to be fulfilled through a *descendant* of Abraham: Jesus.

The genealogies in the accounts of Matthew (in chapter 1) and Luke (in chapter 3) are easy to skip over because they seem both boring and superfluous, but they are there for a reason. They are situating the coming of Jesus within a family history centered in the covenants and covenant relationships that precede Jesus; what will become the new covenant in Jesus is presented as being in direct continuity. Matthew begins this covenantal history for a Jewish audience by tracing it forward from Abraham to Jesus (situating Jesus' coming within the story of the Jewish nation). Luke, meanwhile, begins the covenantal history for a gentile audience by tracing it backward from Jesus to Adam (situating Jesus' coming within the story of all nations).

From Abraham onward, God's covenantal plan runs through Israel and its journey, but it's one that precedes Israel and ultimately embraces more than Israel.

In due course, we see Abraham's descendants living in Egypt, now so numerous that they constitute a nation—fulfilling God's promise that they would be like "the stars in the sky" and "the sand on the seashore" (Gen 22:17). Originally, the Israelites were refugees from a severe famine, and received as guests, but a new pharaoh feared their numbers and they became oppressed and enslaved (see Exod 1). God's response is that of a suzerain in a covenant relationship acting on behalf of the vassal; indeed, the covenantal relationship which is the basis of God's subsequent actions in the exodus is directly referenced right at the outset:

> The Israelites groaned in their slavery and cried out, and their cry for help because of their slavery went up to God. God heard their groaning, and he remembered his covenant with Abraham, with Isaac and with Jacob. So God looked on the Israelites and was concerned about them. (Exod 2:23–25)

Christian reader of the Old Testament following the broader trajectory of the story (though some may wish to learn more for interest).

God's actions toward pharaoh, rescuing them from their enemies, were fulfilling a suzerain's covenantal commitment in that extended family relationship. In Exod 4:23, God says, "Israel is my firstborn son . . . let my son go."

Moses is, of course, the one through whom God acts in the negotiations with pharaoh to secure the Israelites' release. When God first introduces himself to Moses, at the burning bush, in Exod 3, and Moses famously asks God for his name ("Which god are you . . .?") and God famously responds, enigmatically, "I am who I am" (or equally, "I will be who I will be"), it sometimes goes unnoticed that immediately following this we read:

> God *also* said to Moses, "Say to the Israelites, 'The Lord, the God of your fathers—the God of Abraham, the God of Isaac and the God of Jacob—has sent me to you.' This is my name for ever, the name you shall call me from generation to generation." (Exod 3:15)

Even God's name—the name by which he chooses to be known throughout the generations—is deliberately framed personally, relationally, and hence, covenantally.

So although the covenantal relationship to date—and specifically the covenant with Abraham and his descendants—is clearly the basis for God's actions vis-à-vis Moses and the Israelites in the exodus, we soon encounter a new iteration of the covenantal relationship under new circumstances: Israel's newly constituted nationhood.

The Covenant with Moses

The covenant delivered through Moses, that we call the Mosaic covenant (or the Sinaitic covenant, because it was delivered at Mount Sinai), has a different focus—a far more specific and channeled focus—functioning as a form of constitution for the kind of nation that God wants his people Israel to be. The covenantal document is what we call Torah. Since Christians typically refer to Torah as "the law," it frequently gets bad press, because its role and function is misunderstood, so let's briefly address that.

Firstly, when the New Testament—Paul especially—talks about law, invariably Torah is in mind, rather than "religious legalism" in a more general, universal sense. Law is a technical theological term, to do with genre; it's more than unfortunate that in popular Christian thinking the word has become synonymous with legalistic religion, not least because of the severe damage that has been done to Christian-Jewish relations as a result.[6]

Torah has nothing whatsoever to do with earning salvation by good works—and it never did. It was God himself who gave Torah to Israel and asked them to live by it, just as God had set out his covenantal expectations to Adam and Eve. Obeying Torah was Israel's side of a covenant relationship initiated by God. *Note that the commandments were not given to the world but to God's people*, so we should not read scriptural discussion of the law as if they had been. The commandments were encompassed within God's covenant relationship with Israel.

The core meaning of the word "Torah" is "instruction," "teaching," or "guidance." Like any written constitution, the 613 commandments (as counted by the rabbis) were never expected or intended to embrace all circumstances and situations—to be applied literalistically whether a subsequent context was a good fit or not. To try to shoehorn a commandment into a situation that had something else in mind entirely when first written would, indeed, make it legalistic (when Christians do that, they too are being legalistic, rather than "biblical").[7] This was not the divine author's intention nor was it the covenant participants' understanding. The commandments were a framework within which leaders and elders would be able to discern God's will (God's best) for God's people. It was a guidebook rather than a rule book.[8] Rather than a "textbook," it was a "test-book"—against which to test what might or might not be wise judgment in particular circumstances. It was always inevitable that as circumstances changed, some original commandments would become obsolete, at least in part, rather than remaining timeless (I am not speaking here of any obsolescence due to the coming of Jesus).[9]

6. Along with the (flawed) notion that "the Jews killed Jesus."

7. This is why it is *so very important* for us to understand the original context and meaning of a commandment and, indeed, of anything we read in Scripture that we think may be intended as a timeless propositional truth.

8. Inevitably as Israel's circumstances changed—for example, from being a rural, nomadic people to also being an urban, city-dwelling people, with different forms of lifestyle, commerce, and new and different life challenges—a static, fixed set of commandments was always going to require new interpretations. Very often, different rabbis and rabbinical schools would have different interpretations (we see this in Jesus' experience and the not infrequent times he says, "You have heard it said . . . but I say to you . . .").

9. There is a default evangelical tendency to assume timelessness in biblical propositions and commandments, to what sometimes seems to be the maximum possible

Understanding the covenantal background to Torah enables us to see that obeying the commandments was not to try to earn God's favor; it was the appropriate and grateful covenantal response to already having God's favor.

It's important for modern readers to fully grasp the original context for Torah that is framed by the exodus event: God rescuing his people from slavery in Egypt and bringing them to a promised land where they could be their own nation. As slaves for a considerable period of time (a few hundred years), they had no laws of their own; their laws were whatever their Egyptian slave masters told them they were. Prior to receiving Torah, their only available frameworks for how to live were how the Egyptians lived (the place they had come from) and how the Canaanites lived (the people in the place they had come to). Neither of these ways of living were appropriate to God's people, said the Lord—virtually in those exact words:

> The Lord said to Moses, "Speak to the Israelites and say to them: 'I am the Lord your God. You must not do as they do in Egypt, where you used to live, and you must not do as they do in the land of Canaan, where I am bringing you. Do not follow their practices. You must obey my laws and be careful to follow my decrees. I am the Lord your God. Keep my decrees and laws, for the person who obeys them will live by them. I am the Lord.'"
> (Lev 18:1–5)

Hence, to the extent that we want to understand why certain commandments were given and what they meant in their contexts (especially if we intend to assert some of them for today), it will be necessary for us to know "what they did in Egypt" and "what they did in Canaan." Simply reading the English wording of a commandment in a decontextualized way and making assumptions just from those words on a page will not be enough.

Torah was defining a way of living and of relating to God—and relating to one another—that was radically different from the cultures they'd grown up in and were surrounded by. The Israelites' values and behavior were to be direct opposites to many of the values and behavior of the Egyptians and the Canaanites.

---

extent. Perhaps this is perceived to be taking a high view of Scripture and how it is supposed to function authoritatively. In practice, though, that tends to lead to methodological inconsistency.

Another common misconception among Christians is that it was impossible to fulfill the law. *This completely overlooks the fact that the law itself already anticipated failure to keep it.* An omniscient God always knew that would happen. Nor do we need to be omniscient to realize that—human nature makes it perfectly obvious. Hence, Torah already had provisions for failure built in: sacrifices for sin were *part of* the law. To make sacrifices for sin was part of *fulfilling* the law. We could say that *the only way* to fulfill the whole of Torah was to comply with the commandments that provided for failure to fully keep it!

If it was always going to be impossible to fulfill the law then God would have been playing a "cruel trick" on Israel by giving it to them in the first place. And to compound that by allowing them to be deluded enough to believe that they could (there is nothing in the Old Testament that ever suggests Israel felt unable to fulfill the law God had given them—which is not to say that they believed everyone always perfectly fulfilled it; those are not the same thing).

If God's covenants can be canceled by human failings, then we're all in trouble. Which is why the *new* covenant anticipates our failings as well, as in 1 John 1:8–9 (ESV): "If we confess our sins, he is faithful and just to forgive us our sins and to cleanse us from all unrighteousness." When we participate in the sacrament of communion we are reminded of the new covenant and reminded of its generous provisions for human weakness and failures; what is true for us within our new covenant was true for Israel within its covenants.

One final thought on the covenant in Torah. Christians generally fail to appreciate that prior to the exodus there was no "law" as such for anyone to potentially be legalistic about. The exodus event and the subsequent forming of the new nation was the catalyst for Torah. Before that, there was no equivalent document framing God's expectations of people, just an overarching covenantal commitment and specific things that he asked of individuals. The Old Testament relationship between God and people—both before and after the giving of Torah—*was not and never has been* law centered. The nature of the new covenant versus the preceding covenants is *not* a contrasting of legalism versus freedom, law versus grace, or faith versus works.

The New Covenant Promised in Jeremiah 31

As the covenantal journey continues we see a new covenant promise in Jer 31:31–33:

> "The days are coming," declares the Lord, "when I will make a new covenant with the people of Israel and with the people of Judah. It will not be like the covenant I made with their ancestors when I took them by the hand to lead them out of Egypt, because they broke my covenant, though I was a husband to them," declares the Lord. "This is the covenant I will make with the people of Israel after that time," declares the Lord. "I will put my law in their minds and write it on their hearts. I will be their God, and they will be my people."

Interestingly, this will be a covenant in which Torah still features (v. 33). I doubt that the prophets could have conceived of a time when there would be no Torah, given that it was God's precious covenantal gift to his people—as the psalmist declared, "Oh, how I love your law! I meditate on it all day long" (Ps 119:97). This new covenant would not suddenly be an expectation-free kind of covenant, in which all that mattered was believing the right things (we see no sense of any such ideas in its Old Testament portrayal).[10] Yet in this new iteration, God's covenantal expectations will (somehow) be written on hearts and minds instead of tablets of stone. It will be dynamic, not static. And it will clearly be relational—Jeremiah's reference to hearts and minds cannot but remind us of Jesus' words, "Love the Lord your God with all your heart and mind and soul and strength," as the most important commandment in Torah.

As we read on in Jer 31, we see that this new covenant will be mediated directly, rather than through priests. In v. 34: "No longer will they teach their neighbor, or say to one another, 'Know the Lord,' because they will all know me, from the least of them to the greatest, declares the Lord." This feels like it will be qualitatively different way of knowing God. Perhaps it is foreshadowing the final stage in the covenantal journey—the last and greatest in the series.

And yet even here, in these oft-quoted words, within which Christians locate Jesus' proclamation of a new covenant, we see the promise

---

10. A "law-free" (or "lawless") approach to Christian faith is called "antinomianism" (from the Greek for law, *nómos*). It is one thing to pursue a faith that is not legalistic, but quite another to assume there are no divine expectations for human behavior. "In those days Israel had no king; all the people did whatever seemed right in their own eyes" (Judg 17:6) was a criticism, not a commendation.

clearly framed as "the covenant I will make *with the people of Israel*" (v. 33). As Paul makes clear in Rom 11, it is the gentiles who have been "grafted in" to the Jewish "olive tree"—namely, into a covenantal relationship with the God of Israel—not the other way around.

Salvation—not a word I like to use often, and especially not in missional contexts, since it means as good as nothing to unchurched people—is and always has been framed covenantally. This is true of the new covenant in Christ as much as the preceding covenants with which it sits in continuity.

In what ways might we characterize the new covenant in Christ versus its immediate predecessor in Torah? Absolutely not as a contrast between law and grace! God's covenantal initiatives were always framed by grace and always accessed by faith (it is nothing more than theological anti-Judaism to assert otherwise). Perhaps the simplest way is to see the Mosaic covenant as an invitation to Israel into a covenant "in Torah." Faithfulness to that covenant was defined by faithfulness to *Torah*—by relating faithfully to the written words. The new covenant parallels that as an invitation to the world into a covenant "in Christ." Faithfulness to the new covenant is defined by faithfulness to *Jesus*—relating faithfully to the living Word (John 1:1). The extent to which the commandments in Torah relate to Christians is another topic for another day.[11]

It seems likely that first-century Jewish believers in Jesus would readily have identified with these points of correspondence with the Mosaic covenant, perceiving the nature of the new covenant "in Christ" analogously. To do so would be entirely unsurprising, since the Mosaic covenant was a covenant with which they were intimately familiar, that framed their day-to-day living.

However, that is not the basis on which *gentile* believers in Jesus were being invited to picture the covenantal continuity that is at work here. Paul is at great pains to insist that they take their points of reference from the covenant with Abraham, and before that, with Noah (and, to some extent, with Adam and Eve). Remember that the covenant in Torah was specific to Israel, not to humanity in general. The covenantal journey for gentiles "bypassed" the covenant in Torah from the moment that Israel's and the nations' journeys forked into that "high road" and "low road." Hence, Paul in particular is saying to his gentile audience, "Don't listen to well-meaning Jewish believers in Jesus who think you

---

11. Covered at some length in Burnhope, *How to Read the Bible Well.*

need to 'bolt on' bits of the Mosaic covenant to a covenant invitation from Jesus—authenticated by the moving in power of the Holy Spirit outside of Torah (Gal 3:5)—that is not requiring it. Stay on the covenantal road that God has clearly marked out for you *as gentiles*." The issue being debated in the New Testament period was nothing to do with concerns over something dubbed "Jewish legalism"—still less, that Jesus had come to set everyone free from.

The New Covenant in Christ

How, then, might we best understand the nature of the new covenant in Christ in ways that both make sense to us now and are equally consonant with how first-century believers would have understood it? We should start with what the New Testament writers tell us about the new covenant's features and then marry that to the Jewish understanding of their covenant at the time. We should also take note of what's said about the prophesied new covenant in Jer 31, since this is directly referenced by the writer of the book of Hebrews (Heb 8:8).

At Passover time, in what we call the Last Supper, Jesus was inviting his disciples into a new covenant relationship. They were sharing in a covenantal meal together, "breaking bread" together, invoking the memory of that very first Passover where the lamb was also a covenant sacrifice (*not* a sin offering).

Though roast lamb was no doubt on the menu, the reason that the sacrificial lamb wasn't the theological centerpiece in the Last Supper (as everyone would have expected—as it was in a Passover festival meal) is because Jesus himself would soon be the sacrifice to seal and ratify this new covenant modeled on Passover: "He took the cup after they had eaten, saying, 'This cup which is poured out for you is the new covenant in my blood'" (Luke 22:20; Mark 14:24; cf. Matt 28:20).

It was clearly not by chance that Jesus chose to situate the timing of his sacrificial death to correspond to Passover rather than to, say, the Day of Atonement (which many Christians might assume to be more appropriate, especially if they start their gospel explanation with a focus on sin). This strongly suggests that Jesus saw the covenantal significance of his death more in terms of releasing humanity from captivity and the birthing of a new, expanded people of God than in terms of individual forgiveness of sins (not that that is by any means excluded, of course; Matthew adds precisely that detail to the Last Supper accounts of Mark and Luke).[12]

But there is more: all of the ways in which the atonement is pictured in the New Testament (in other words, how the benefits of what Jesus did for us are pictured and explained) can be seen as actions of the suzerain vis-à-vis the vassal in a covenant relationship. It is frequently debated as to which (if any) of the many biblical metaphors or models of the atonement is the best and most important understanding. Some say it's penal substitution (Jesus took the punishment we deserve for sin upon himself), some say *Christus Victor* (Jesus won a victory over Satan, sin, and death), and some say it's all of the ways that the New Testament speaks about the benefits of what Jesus did for us (the so-called kaleidoscopic view). But to frame the atonement within a covenantal understanding removes any need to choose, or to see them as competing; it is all of the above and more.[13] If there is one overarching idea that frames the new covenantal actions of the divine suzerain on behalf of humanity as the vassals it is perhaps 1 John 3:8 (NIrV): "The Son of God came to destroy the devil's work."

Jesus' covenantal meal with his disciples is the basis for our reenactment of that sacred event in our ceremony of communion, or the Eucharist, or as it's sometimes known, depending on the ecclesial tradition, breaking bread. By regularly participating in the covenantal meal, as Jesus encouraged us to do, we are continuously reminded of God's gracious actions through Christ to invite us into covenant relationship with him; to participate serves as an ongoing reaffirmation of our covenant vows.

A Christian is someone who willingly enters into the commitments of a vassal within the new covenant in Christ—we'll come to what those commitments are in a moment—and who is thereby included in the benefits and promises of the divine suzerain through Christ.

---

12. I find interesting the last part of this statement by a teacher of the law that Jesus affirms in Mark 12:33: "To love him with all your heart, with all your understanding and with all your strength, and to love your neighbor as yourself, *is more important than all burnt offerings and sacrifices*." Considering the profound importance of burnt offerings and sacrifices in Torah (not least, those for sin) this would surely have sounded really quite astonishing to his audience. If we have a low or dismissive view of Torah, then of course we wouldn't spot that.

13. For a short and simple explanation of the various atonement metaphors and models in Scripture, as those have been understood and explained in Christian history, see Burnhope, *Telling the Old, Old Story*.

Proclaiming the gospel is extending God's invitation into a covenant relationship. When Jesus reached out to the outsiders, the outcasts, the poor, the sick, and life's failures in human terms, he was radically covenant extending and covenant embracing. His actions were challenging the religious leaders' definitions of who was inside and who was outside the covenant boundary—what did and did not constitute holiness before the Lord. He was saying, "God does not share your religious view of where and how the boundaries should be drawn." Which perhaps we do well to reflect on today—might there be ways in which our taken-for-granted religious views might put us out of sync with how God sees things?

The New Covenant "Stipulations"

Already we have said that, alongside the benefits, ancient world covenants contained expectations (or, stipulations) on the part of the suzerain vis-à-vis the vassal. What might those be in relation to Jesus' new covenant?

In the format of the Mosaic covenant, those expectations or stipulations were commandments. But this takes us into some potentially confusing territory. On the one hand, the new covenant is not expressly law-centric; rather, it seems to be Jesus-centric. But on the other hand, the New Testament cites many clear expectations for how a Jesus-following disciple is expected to live, many framed precisely as commands—some in specific contexts, some more apparently universal. And in the background, there is also the question of the extent to which Old Testament commandments carry forward, whether some continue to apply to Christians today and if so on what basis—how we are to distinguish the ones that do from the ones that don't.[14]

One theoretical option to resolve this would be to comb the New Testament to compile a list of commandments equivalent to the 613 commandments that the rabbis counted in Torah; but if that was God's intention, then why not just provide everyone with an updated universalized version of Torah—an equivalent to Leviticus in the New Testament? It does seem that something fundamentally different was in view for this new covenant with the nations in Christ compared to the covenant with Israel in Torah.

---

14. A current example of that debate would be the male same-sex sexual behavior prohibited by Lev 18:22 and 20:13—does Paul allude to those verses, and if so does that make them still applicable? This is quite aside from the question of what Leviticus likely had in mind at the time and why.

If an updated Torah was not in view, then what overarching framework might we deduce from Scripture to sum up what God's covenantal expectations "in Christ" and "Christ in us" (to coin Paul's twofold phrasing) might look like? Here is a proposal.

1. Since the new covenant will be a reflection of Jer 31:31–34—namely, "written on hearts and minds"—and there will be no human priestly mediation of its requirements and interpretations, we can anticipate a significant role for conscience and the inner promptings of the Holy Spirit (cf. Rom 14:23; 8:14, 26–27; John 16:13; etc.).

2. We know from Jesus that the most important (twofold) commandment in the law was to love God and love people. Since there is nothing self-evidently time bound about that (no indication of any context-specific limitations) there is every reason to think it continues to reflect God's heart and mind for us. Any behavior on our part should therefore be tested through that bifocal lens (namely, how compatible it would be with those priorities), just as Jesus was saying was the case with all of God's expectations in Torah.

3. Jesus was speaking there in the context of the commandments in Torah; but his new covenant answer then takes it a step further. Loving others is, in Mosaic covenant terms, constrained by loving our neighbor "as ourselves" (in other words, it stops short at the point that an action would *not* be loving ourselves).[15] Jesus, however, took things to a whole new level, modeled on himself: "A new command I give you: Love one another. As I have loved you, so you must love one another" (John 13:34). This modeling of our actions on Jesus' actions reminds us of our calling to be both the *imago Dei* and the *imitatio Dei*.

4. Not only were these words of Jesus self-evidently a command, but he continues in v. 35 that it should be a hallmark: "By this everyone will know that you are my disciples, if you love one another." In other words, this is how people will know that someone is in a new covenant relationship with him. The bar is set high for the quality of that new covenantal love that he's asking us for: how Jesus himself loved.

---

15. For example, Jesus' instruction in Luke 3:11: "If you have two coats, give one away... and do the same with your food." But if you only have one coat, or only enough food for one, then it would not be loving yourself to give that away.

5. Finally, Paul confirms that "love is the fulfillment of the law" in Rom 13:10. He places love at the forefront of divine expectations: "Over all these virtues put on love, which binds them all together in perfect unity" in Col 3:14.

Another way of picturing what it means to be "Jesus-centric" is offered in Rom 13:14, "Clothe yourselves with the Lord Jesus Christ." Or, as the NLT puts it, "Clothe yourself *with the presence* of the Lord Jesus Christ," emphasizing that it's relational. Paul has much to say about what it means to be living "in Christ" and equally, "Christ in you." In this language, we see echoes of how faithful Jews would have conceived living "in Torah" and "Torah in you"—for example, Deut 11:18: "Fix these words of mine in your hearts and minds" (cf. Ps 119:97).

Understanding the place of covenant in the Bible is foundational to understanding relationship with God and the nature and character of God. He is a covenant-making, covenant-keeping, and covenant-faithful God. He is not a fault-finding, covenant-canceling, nitpicking, looking-for-technical-ways-to-get-out-of-it kind of God. Throughout Scripture we see an ever-patient, forgiveness-minded, covenant-renewing God who epitomizes "the Lord is gracious and compassionate, slow to anger and rich in love" (Ps 145:8).[16]

God's lovingkindness and faithfulness in spite of our human failings are reflections of (i) his nature and character, and (ii) the characteristics of ancient world covenants at their finest. Psalm 110:4: "The Lord has taken an oath and will not break his vow."

Each of the New Testament models and metaphors of the atonement is articulating just one of the many benefits of being in the new covenant relationship ratified and sealed by Jesus' sacrifice at the cross (the ultimate covenant sacrifice). We remember this—and reaffirm our new covenant commitments—when we participate in communion/the Eucharist.

The new covenant is one in which God in Christ as the suzerain acts on our behalf in all of the ways that atonement is pictured in the New Testament—to rescue us and deliver us from every enemy that threatens us, harms us, and enslaves us as his extended covenantal family. In the new covenant, reflecting ancient world covenants, our enemies as the vassal become his enemies as the suzerain, including the enemies of Satan, sin, suffering, and death.

---

16. This phrase is repeated with astonishing frequency: see Pss 103:8, 111:4; Joel 2:13; Jonah 4:2.

Some Final Thoughts on the Marriage Covenant

To affirm marriage as a biblical value is entirely correct. However, we do need to be aware (as research would soon show) that marriage in the Bible was by no means conceived in the same terms or practiced in the same forms as society—even Christian society—understands it today. Copying something called "biblical marriage" could lead to some very odd if not illegal results. We ought not to read-in today's understandings of marriage in every instance where we see the word in Scripture.

Nonetheless, it's still true to say that God loves marriage. But *why* does he love marriage? Too rarely do we as Christians ask ourselves "why?" questions (we tend to focus on "what?" questions).[17] The reason is because God loves covenant—covenant commitment, and covenant faithfulness—and marriage is a form of covenant. God doesn't love marriage per se, he loves covenantal relationships, of which marriage is an expression. That's why in human partnering, marriage is the basis he loves to see happen, wherever possible.

Something Christians are inclined to miss is the difference between marriage as a status that two people acquire through participation in some form of ceremony,[18] versus marriage as a quality of relationship that reflects God's covenant heart. From God's perspective it is surely the substance not the form—the content rather than the wrapper—that concerns him and that we should be looking for. The fact that "biblical marriage" (marriage as we see it in the Bible) reflects a number of forms and features that we today would see as being, at best, less than ideal and, at worst, highly inappropriate, should be food for thought.

This basis in covenant is why marital unfaithfulness is not simply to do with having an affair (though that is, of course, unfaithfulness). It equally includes behaving in unfaithful ways toward one's covenant partner, which would embrace any number of unkind, abusive, and harmful practices. There is no reason for a spousal victim to feel pressure to

---

17. Probing with "why?" questions helps us to be thinking theologically, with our minds engaged, to seek to discern the heart and mind of God underlying the things that are said in Scripture (not just what is said, or appears to be being said). When something in Scripture doesn't seem to make much sense, it's all the more important to ask those questions; we *are* allowed!

18. If so, does that mean and include a civil ceremony? Or need it be a religious ceremony? If so, which religions count? For Christians who take their lead on marriage from Adam and Eve, it's unfortunate that the writers of Genesis missed out our earliest parents' wedding ceremony.

perpetuate a marriage covenant that has been broken in that way by an abusive partner, simply for the sake of maintaining a married status. This is to miss the point—to put the cart before the horse; the what before the why—and effectively sanction an abuser's charter. It is not enough for an abuser simply to say "sorry" (especially on multiple occasions) and for that to then shift the burden on to the abused party to forgive (and still less, to forget). Much harm has been done by counsel that seeks to perpetuate a marriage at almost all costs (especially when that cost is falling to the abused party). To cite a trite evangelical catchphrase, it may be "just as if I'd never sinned" in the mind of the wrongdoing party who says sorry,[19] but it is by no means just as if they'd never sinned for the party who has been harmed.

---

19. A crass misrepresentation of biblical justification.

4

The Nature and Character of God

I'VE ALWAYS SAID THAT if there is one thing that is the most important for us to be communicating in all of our preaching and teaching—whatever subject, on the face of it, we may be speaking about—it is who God is and what he is like. Our theology (by which I mean, our understanding, expressed in thoughts and words) of who God is and what he is like as a person will, for better or worse, serve as the lens through which we understand everything else. For example, the things that are and are not important to him; his plans and purposes for us and this world; how he does and doesn't go about things; and how he feels about us.

We could say that who God is and what he's like is the key question that the Bible is asking and answering. It's the starting point for knowing whether—and if so, how—we can be in relationship with him. And perhaps, more importantly, whether we would even want to be in relationship with him in the first place.

Correspondingly, the most important thing on the agenda of the enemies of God is to distort, misrepresent, and get people to believe lies about who God is and what he's like—to try to undermine a relationship, break up a relationship, and dissuade people from a relationship.

For example, if God really is the sort of person that Richard Dawkins says he is then I'm not sure why anyone would want to be in relationship with him. As Dawkins puts it, with barely a hint of hyperbolic rhetoric (ahem):

> The God of the Old Testament is arguably the most unpleasant character in all fiction: jealous and proud of it; a petty, unjust, unforgiving control-freak; a vindictive, bloodthirsty ethnic cleanser; a misogynistic, homophobic, racist, infanticidal, genocidal, filicidal, pestilential, megalomaniacal, sadomasochistic, capriciously malevolent bully.[1]

I suppose there are reasons that someone can believe all that (or at least, suspect it) and still want to be in a relationship with God—fear of hell, perhaps?—but it doesn't feel like they would be particularly good reasons.

It is of course entirely possible to read some passages, in the Old Testament in particular, in a way that corresponds to Dawkins's critique (though I'm sure he knows full well that he is propagating a well-worn caricature to promote his atheistic agenda).

Unfortunately, well-meaning Christians are not immune from unwittingly buying into that caricature in mounting a defense along the lines that, since God is God, he can do as he pleases in this world and it is not for us to judge or second-guess him (that's basically the Calvinist view). I would have to say that if I was God, while I appreciate their efforts, that's not how I would want my character and honor to be defended. The point they are missing is that while by rights God can indeed do as he wishes, it's not what he could do, it's what he doesn't do. It's not about how he could go about things; it's about how he does go about things.

A Developing Understanding

In the stories of Scripture, as the big story unfolds, we see a developing understanding of who God is and what he's like.

Really early on, in Exod 3, we see God appearing to Moses as flames of fire, in what we call the Burning Bush, and Moses having to say to him, in effect, "Excuse me, but which god are you? What's your name? Whom do I say is sending me?" And it's interesting that God doesn't answer him with some impressive title. He describes himself relationally: "I'm the God of your father, the God of Abraham, the God of Isaac, and the God of Jacob." He also takes the opportunity to tell Moses that he doesn't like being boxed in by a name—he will also be "I am who I

1. Dawkins, *God Delusion*, 31.

am" (or, equally, "I will be who I will be," which is the alternative translation). We see in the Old Testament a multiplicity of names by which God is known, all featuring important divine attributes (rather as in the New Testament we see a multiplicity of ways in which the atonement is described, all featuring important elements of Jesus' salvation).

Once we realize that we're seeing a developing understanding of who God is and what he's like that emerges over time, as the story goes on—with some "ups and downs" in people's understanding along the way—we should be looking out for that in the stories that we read. Put another way, we shouldn't make the mistake of assuming that the understanding of God that Abraham had, or Moses had, or Joshua had—the Joshua who's being targeted in Dawkins's savaging of those genocidal texts—was the same understanding that Jesus' disciples had, or Paul had, just because they're all in the same Bible. Remember that the nature of the Bible is that we are eavesdroppers (one could say, voyeurs) on our forebears' stories, watching them trying to figure out who God is and what God is like, in many cases with a lot less information to guide them than we have. Hence, we're allowed to ask the text whether at times in those stories people are getting him right and at times getting him wrong.

God's nature and character is eternally unchanging—but that does not mean that every Bible character's understanding of his nature and character was the same at every point in the story. So, too, in relation to understanding God's plans and purposes. In particular, we must not read our understanding, now, into their understanding, then—and especially not the understandings of those who came before Jesus. We have the benefit of personal copies of the Bible, including a New Testament, plus two thousand years of theological reflection, including not just the early church creeds but also the more recent evangelical statements of faith and confessions of faith.

In Jesus, Everything Changed

With the coming of Jesus comes a sea change in human understanding of who God is and what God is like, even among those who are his historic people. The coming of Jesus—God becoming man—was a game changer. It's as if someone had switched on the lights in a previously darkened room. Suddenly, the shadows are gone and everything in the room becomes crystal clear for the first time. It can now, quite literally, be seen in a new light.

Just to be clear, nothing changed in God or about God; he is and always has been the same in nature and character. What changed was that who God was and what God was like was now revealed in a dramatically new way—not in people's words, or their impressions, or even their encounters, but in a person. It was the moment that the story up until then was waiting for. The coming of Jesus was the ultimate answer to the biggest of the big questions—who is God and what is he like?

The coming of Jesus the Son, fully human like us, gave us the astonishing opportunity to see what God is like in terms that we can understand and relate to. As John 1:18 tells us, prior to that "no one had ever seen God. But the one and only Son, who is himself God, and is in the closest relationship with the Father, has now made him known."

In early Genesis, we do see God pictured as personally present; the accounts of the conversations imply that notwithstanding John 1:18, people did indeed "see God." However, to the extent that Genesis intended to be saying that, it's so far back in the story and recedes so quickly that it has no real impact on the point: God was, indeed, invisible to human eyes. In the later Old Testament narratives, he appears, variously, as fire in a burning bush; in a pillar of fire; and in a cloud. He mostly communicates through the words of prophets. He is understood to be present in the tabernacle and then later in the temple, yet he remains as good as inaccessible to all except a high priest, and then only occasionally. He is near and present, in one sense, and yet also far off and distant.

But now the beginning of Heb 1 sums up the dramatic change that came about through Jesus: "In the past, God spoke to our ancestors through the prophets at many times and in various ways, but in these last days he has spoken to us by his Son. . . . The Son is the radiance of God's glory and the exact representation of his being."

In Jesus, this previously hidden-from-sight, slightly mysterious God is now revealed. Not just someone who is "a bit like God," but as Col 2:9 tells us, one in whom all of the fullness of God dwells in bodily form. Colossians 1:15 in the NLT says that he's "the visible image of the invisible God." Other versions say that he's "exactly like God"; that "Christ is, as God is"; that he's "the exact likeness." And in John 14:9 Jesus says, "Anyone who has seen me has seen the Father." If we want to know who God is and what he is like, we look to Jesus and all our questions are answered.

That last sentence is critically important. Since we know that God's nature and character is eternally unchanging, and we also know that Father, Spirit, and Son are one (sharing in the same undivided nature, character, plans, and purposes) this means that the God of the New Testament whom we see fully and perfectly revealed in Jesus is *exactly the same* as the God of the Old Testament. Jesus is not only what God is like, he is also what God has *always* been like. Every question that anyone ever had in Old Testament times about who God was and what he was like has now been finally and definitively answered in Jesus.

So far so good. But what this means is that in the light of Jesus every previous understanding (and at times, misunderstanding) of who God was and what he was like—how he thought about things, felt about things, and went about things—needed to be subject to review. Everything previously assumed had to be rethought and revisited—in contemporary language, "deconstructed"—in the light of the Jesus who is the "exact likeness" and "visible image" of the God who had never been visible before. Let me say it again: Jesus is what God was truly like *and had always been like.*

So, when we're reading the Old Testament and encountering at times some still-emerging perceptions of God, we need to be reading the text through a "Jesus lens." We need to put our "Jesus spectacles" on and read it through our knowledge of him. Because sometimes what we're seeing is people's assumptions about God, based on what gods were perceived always to be like.

Whenever we see an understanding of who God is and what he's like—whenever we see God being explained or represented in ways that simply don't "fit" with the God we see in Jesus—we know that we're seeing an incomplete and underdeveloped picture. We're seeing people still journeying toward all of the questions of what God is like being fully and finally answered in Jesus.

Prior to that, we're reading a story of people grappling with understanding him. Slowly learning that this God is not like the pagan gods of the ancient Near East—the so-called gods of the other nations. This one true God, the God of Israel, is unlike everything that people at the time thought and assumed that gods were like: the kinds of things that gods always said, and always wanted their followers to do for them, such as annihilating enemies, and taking all the spoils of war as victors always did.

What Jesus is like is the "litmus test" for how well a biblical character's previous perceptions of what God is like—even a "hero" character's perceptions—matched up to the reality. We simply ask: Is this something that Jesus would say or Jesus would do? Is this something that Jesus would want his followers to say or do? We're allowed to question how well people's perceptions at the time were matching up to what we now know through Jesus to be the reality.

For example, in Ps 136: "Give thanks to the Lord, for he is good. His love endures forever." Is that a true perception, in the light of Jesus? Absolutely. But flip over a page, to Ps 137, where the psalmist is raging against the Babylonians because of what they've done, how they've treated them in exile, and he says, "O Babylon, you will be destroyed. Happy is the one who pays you back for what you have done to us. Happy is the one who takes your babies and smashes them against the rocks!" Is that something Jesus would say? No, I don't think so. Not the Jesus who said, "Love your enemies, do good to those who hate you, bless those who curse you, pray for those who ill-treat you" (Luke 6:27–28).

How "Jesus Stories" Teach What God Is Like

When I was writing this chapter, I stopped at this point and Googled, "What does the Bible say about who God is?" The very first result was a website with a list of Bible verses: 101 of them. All were offering factual statements about God that we call "propositions" or "propositional truths." Statements such as "God is love," "God so loved the world, that he gave his only Son," "You, O Lord, are good and forgiving, abounding in steadfast love," and so on. All good, all truths, and all very important. We like propositions and propositional truths. But if we only ever assemble lists of verses with factual statements and think that by definition that's what the Bible has to say about who God is and what he's like then we're going to be missing out.

For example, if we want to do a talk about God's love, grace, mercy, kindness, or forgiveness, and we do a Bible word search for those words, the results won't include the parable of the prodigal son in Luke 15, because none of those words are mentioned. Even though, we'd surely be hard pressed to find a better biblical presentation than that one.

When we're asking what the Bible has to say on something, we're not just searching for propositions. And that's because the narratives (the stories) are there to teach, just as much as the propositions. About a third of Jesus' teaching was in stories called parables. But it's not only the parables. The stories of the things that happened in Jesus' life—the events, and the encounters with people—are teaching us about who God is and what he's like as well. They, too, are truth-conveying.

It's a consequence of living in the modern world that we think of stories and pictures and parables and metaphors as inferior ways of conveying truths. That's because nowadays we see the sciences as more important than the arts and humanities. This is why people (Christians and not) default to reading Genesis as if a scientist had written it, rather than as if an artist or storyteller—or dare I say, a theologian—had written it. No wonder that when we have a science-focused set of expectations we find Genesis comes up short in truth-conveying terms.

If we want to explain to someone what the good news of Jesus is all about in a propositional way, we can quote John 3:16 and John 3:3. But if we want to explain what the good news of Jesus is all about in a storied way and a relational way we can quote the story of the woman caught in adultery in John 8. And the woman at the well in John 4. And the man born blind in John 9. And the man we call the prodigal son and his experience of the father in Luke 15. And the story of Zacchaeus in Luke 19. And the God who cries when he is told his friend Lazarus has died in John 11; one of the shortest verses in the Bible—but perhaps one of the most profound—is John 11:35: "Jesus wept." I would say that all of those stories are teaching important theological truths, wouldn't you? All those stories are of good news being experienced. All of that good news is surely part of the gospel, because the ways in which Jesus was good news for people in those stories are the exact same ways that he wants to be good news for people in our world today. Jesus is consistent! He's the same, yesterday, today, and forever (Heb 13:8).

Now of course, we can and should explain the good news of Jesus by reference to both propositions *and* stories. But let's never forget that it's not a statement of facts and information about Jesus that's the good news, however "theologically sound" it might be. It's not "the Four Spiritual Laws" that are the good news.[2] It's Jesus himself who is the good news. It's knowing Jesus that's the good news. It's understanding who God is through the lens of Jesus that's the good news. It's Jesus

---

2. The Four Spiritual Laws is a "gospel" booklet created by Campus Crusade for Christ founder, Bill Bright. Google it for more information. It is not that it is wrong as such (though its language and approach could be significantly improved to communicate in today's world, not least for an unchurched audience); rather, the problem with this and other similar approaches to "the gospel" is that they are so reductionist. They leave out so much. Including so much that people today care about.

experienced that is the good news. The good news of the gospel includes everything that Jesus said, everything that Jesus did, and everything that Jesus is—then, and now. The gospel includes all of the ways in which Jesus was good news to the people who experienced him.

All of the ways that we see the Jesus of the Gospels receiving someone, welcoming someone, being kind to someone, loving someone, forgiving someone, and explaining what God is like to someone, are part of *the* gospel, because they are all picturing not only what God was like in those situations but also what he will be like in our own parallel situations. The good news isn't just the death of Jesus, it's the life of Jesus as well. This is why it's so important for us to read the Gospels to know the stories. The ways that Jesus understood and explained what God is like then are the ways he wants us to understand and explain what God is like now.

Just in case it sounds like I am being inappropriately overfocused on Jesus in presenting who God is and what he is like, we can also look to what we know of the Holy Spirit. It is not by accident that he is spoken of as "the Spirit of Jesus" in three different places in the New Testament: Acts 16:7, Phil 1:19, and Gal 4:6. This phraseology is not suggesting they are one person (or one person operating in two modes of being); it's speaking of their closeness.

Charismatic Christians might at times convey an understanding of the Holy Spirit that assumes "anything could happen" if he "shows up" (their language, not mine) but this is just folk theology; if we can't see Jesus doing something then we shouldn't expect the Holy Spirit to be doing it. He is not "the weird one" of the Trinity. In nature, character, plans, and purposes—in whatever he does and however he does it—the Spirit is in perfect harmony with Father and Son, because they are one. It is classic, orthodox Trinitarian theology to understand the three persons of the Trinity as one, such that, whenever one is present and active, all three are understood as present and involved.

What this means is that whatever we know about the Holy Spirit will be true of the Father and the Son, and vice versa—it will be a reflection of characteristics that they have in common. Whatever in Scripture speaks of what one member of the Trinity is like will also be describing what the others are like. So, for example, in Gal 5:22–23, when we read, "The fruit of the Spirit is love, joy, peace, patience, kindness, goodness, faithfulness, gentleness and self-control," the reason that the Holy Spirit wants to produce that kind of fruit in our lives is because it reflects what God himself is like—just as we saw that same fruit reflected in Jesus' life.

Isn't that wonderful? I think so. He would hardly want to reproduce characteristics in us that were not fully consonant with what he himself is like. That would hardly be conforming us to the *imago Dei*.

The Holy Spirit also constantly brings us full circle back to Jesus. His mission is characterized by reminding everyone of Jesus and everything he said—John 14:26 (an aspect of the Spirit's inspiration of Scripture). Revealing Jesus to us is an ongoing role: "The Spirit will . . . tell you about me" (John 15:26).

A Bigger Vision of the Good News

John Wimber, the main founder of the Vineyard movement, coined a phrase that's well known in Vineyard church circles: "Doing the stuff." He principally had in mind the supernatural signs and wonders in Jesus' ministry, that as Jesus' followers we, too, are called to do; not of ourselves, of course, but by the presence and power of the Holy Spirit. But there is a wider perspective on "doing the stuff," if we rephrase it more holistically as "making good news happen"—not just in the supernatural realm but in the natural realm as well. In every area of life, Christians are called to *be* good news, to *embody* good news, and to *do* good news. Not *just* to preach good news, as some have mistakenly limited the *missio Dei*.

Even where we see Jesus challenging people, that is part of the "good news" as well. Firstly, it's important to note that the vast majority of occasions in the Gospels where Jesus is seen to be challenging people, it's the religious leaders and religious people that he has in his sights, not the ordinary people. Secondly, his major concern was the ways in which people—again, especially the religious leaders and religious people—were misrepresenting what God was like and what he most cared about. People and their best interests were always at the top of his list. Consequently, he stood against those who were harming the people that God loves, and especially when they were doing it in God's name.

Jesus' particular challenge was addressed to the people in power, especially those with religious power, who should have been doing the most good but in their misguided zeal ended up doing the most harm. In Jesus' time, that manifested as appearing to care more about the law of the Lord than the people of the Lord, which was incompatible with God's perspective. The commandments were given for the good of people, not just to keep God happy (Mark 2:27). Those of us with religious power and influence need to be very careful that our zeal for the doctrines we perceive (or are told) exist in Scripture is in harmony with (and ultimately defers to) our zeal for the nature and character of God that we see in Scripture. The Pharisees were well-meaning, too, but they got the balance wrong and people were the ones who suffered, which made Jesus righteously angry.

The reason that we need to be "good news people" in a holistic way, in all realms of life, is because good news people can't turn a blind eye and stay silent when "bad news" is hurting people and harming people. It's why we can't ignore social justice: poverty, racism, sexism, misogyny, inequality, injustice, and hard-heartedness toward those who are disadvantaged and those who have no power—toward those who are hurting and suffering. This is *not* a "social gospel," it's an intrinsic part of the gospel. Or at least, it is if we ask Jesus what he thinks. A close reading of the Gospels will surely prove that. Yes, there is a sense in which Christians are "a people of the book," guided and led by Scripture, but when it's read well we cannot help but see within it what's known as God's preference for the poor—the powerless, the marginalized, the disadvantaged, and the vulnerable.

The Bible is the story of a God who wants to reveal himself *to* people and be known *by* people. It's presenting the story of our forebears in the faith on their journeys of discovery, of who this God is and what he's like, as they encountered him in their circumstances and situations; in many of which we see ourselves mirrored. The pinnacle of that journey of discovery was Jesus. He is the good news of who God is and what God is like, pending only its fuller, complete revelation in the age to come.

First John 1:1–4 puts it like this:

> We proclaim to you the one who existed from the beginning, whom we have heard and seen. We saw him with our own eyes and touched him with our own hands. He is the Word of life. This one who is life itself was revealed to us, and we have seen him. And now we testify and proclaim to you that he is the one who is eternal life. . . . We are writing these things so that you may fully share our joy.

5

Justice, Righteousness, and Shalom

WE ARE NEARLY AT the mid-point of exploring the big themes of Scripture and perhaps two things are already becoming apparent. The first is that these are not just big themes in the Bible, they are big themes in the heart of God. They are things he cares about; hopefully the chapters to date have articulated why that is so. We could say that the reason they are big themes in the Bible is precisely *because* they are big themes in the heart of God. The second thing becoming apparent is the extent to which the themes overlap. They are intertwined, such that when we talk about one we can scarcely avoid talking about another—if not at times, all of them.

It may not be immediately apparent why the three words in the title of this chapter are grouped together. We shall see in a moment that there is an extremely close biblical connection between justice and righteousness, and the presence of both is key to the concept of *shalom* for human experience—*shalom* meaning not just a slightly nebulous idea of "peace," but holistically "the ways things should be" in life. These values are sourced in God's overwhelming love for his creation, and not least for us, as humanity made in his image. They are concrete expressions of his love, that he wants us to reflect and practice.

> Humans are the special recipients of God's love. God loves each human being, and therefore he demands that we act justly. This forms the context for the repeated biblical intimation that God

takes up the cause of the destitute and oppressed, and therefore he is on the side of the poor. God calls us to be his instruments in bringing about the divine vision of love, justice, and righteousness for all humankind.[1]

Justice and righteousness are biblical themes because in the first instance God himself is just and righteous—it's what he is like. Deuteronomy 32:4 is far from alone in telling us, "All his ways are just; a God of faithfulness and without injustice, righteous and upright is he." Similarly, Jer 9:24: "'I am the Lord who exercises kindness, justice and righteousness on earth; for I delight in these things,' declares the Lord." It's common for these themes to appear together in Scripture when God is in the frame: he *is* just and righteous and he *does* justice and righteousness.

Our English words "justice" and "righteousness" convey somewhat different meanings. People will often campaign for justice, but rarely do they campaign for righteousness, which has particularly religious connotations (justice seems to apply to society, but righteousness only to individuals, as part of an inward piety). Quite often people have a strong view on what justice looks like in particular contexts and situations, while others may disagree. Yet justice still feels more objective than righteousness, which seems to have in mind a set of personal behavioral norms that (to postmodern thinking) should generally not be imposed on others.[2]

It would be easy at this point to digress into a long discussion of the Hebrew roots of these two words, which I think would not be productive. For those who are interested in knowing more at a technical, scholarly level, entries in Bible dictionaries may be consulted.[3] The rest of this chapter will endeavor to explain things more simply, at risk (as always) of some oversimplification!

Righteousness

Words deriving from the Hebrew root for righteousness (the nouns, verbs, etc.) appear well over five hundred times in the Old Testament. Aside from the more obvious righteous and righteousness, we see many other nuances of meaning in different contexts, including integrity,

---

1. Grenz, *Theology*, 76.
2. "What's right for you is not necessarily right for me."
3. For example, Mafico, "Just, Justice"; Scullion, "Righteousness (OT)"; Reumann, "Righteousness (Early Judaism)," and "Righteousness (NT)."

impartiality, justice, deliverance, honest evidence, and saving help. This means we need to think carefully about what an Old Testament word means in its context, and we should certainly avoid "reading in" either the New Testament's use of that same English word—such as in Paul's letter to the Romans—and still less, Reformed notions of righteousness and justification.

If there is one overarching sense of the meaning of righteousness it is "doing the right thing"—doing what is right at all times and in all circumstances. Righteousness is not just some ethereal abstract quality given to someone, or a fictive status granted to someone, it's speaking of what people do or don't do in concrete situations: it's right standing deriving from right behavior. Only God is righteous in the sense of an inherent and permanent characteristic.

In Hebrew thought, righteousness is a relational idea. In other words, it can't be separated from relationships: most obviously, relationship to God (being "right with God") and relationship to others (being "right with people"). Here we see clear echoes of the Great Commandment: love God, love people. In our times, we are conscious of other important relational connections, more so than would have been conceived in Bible times: relationship with self (I'm thinking here of mental health, in particular, and appropriate self-care) and relationship with the planet (concern for the environment: creation care).

A righteous person is someone who loves what is right, pursues what is right, and strives to ensure that all of their relationships are both made right and kept right in every area of life.

It would be easy at this point to leap to some of the instances righteousness is spoken of in Paul's letters in relation to what Jesus has done for us: you may have come across theological ideas called "imputed righteousness" and "imparted righteousness"—righteous status "given" to someone. We will come on to that, but let's firstly see how the understanding that I have just sketched fits with other New Testament verses when it comes to our calling and responsibility. Where you see the word "righteousness" below, try reading "doing the right thing" and/or "all of my relationships being right" instead:

- "Blessed are those who hunger and thirst for righteousness" (Matt 5:6);
- "Practice your righteousness" (Matt 6:1);
- "Seek first his kingdom and his righteousness" (Matt 6:33);

- "Both Zechariah and Elizabeth were righteous before God" (Luke 1:6);

- "Pursue righteousness" (2 Tim 2:22);

- "All Scripture is God-breathed and is useful for . . . training in righteousness" (2 Tim 3:16);

- "Human anger does not produce the righteousness that God desires" (Jas 1:20);

- "Peacemakers who sow in peace reap a harvest of righteousness" (Jas 3:18); and

- "We are looking forward to a new heaven and a new earth, where righteousness dwells" (2 Pet 3:13).

Now of course, these central ideas of "doing the right thing" and "all of our relationships being right" need to be measured against something—some standard, or set of expectations, as to what that looks like. Perhaps this reminds us of chapter 2, talking about covenant. Certainly for faithful Jewish believers at the time of Jesus, that measure or standard was the provisions of Torah, the "covenant charter." Luke 1:6 (cited above) continues, "Both Zechariah and Elizabeth were righteous before God, *walking blamelessly in all the commandments and statutes of the Lord.*" Righteousness meant aligning how you lived your life with the covenant's requirements; it meant to be living "in Torah." A covenantal context reinforces its relational heart and center.

What, then, would be the case in relation to the new covenant in Jesus? Here the equivalent covenantal calling is to be "in Christ" and its reciprocal correspondence of "Christ in us." Rather than a set of static commandments, as was the case "in Torah"—instead of a new list of covenant commandments that would forever need fresh interpretations, as new situations were encountered—we are given an expectation centered on a person and a relationship to that person: Jesus. Righteousness is still characterized by continuity with the Great Commandment that "sums up" Torah (inevitably, we see divine consistency here) but the bar is now raised in what Jesus describes as a new commandment: "Love one another as I have loved you" (John 13:34–35).[4]

---

4. Loving our neighbor as ourself is a lower standard for self-sacrificial love than loving one another as Jesus loved us.

Righteousness remains God's desire for us, as it always has been. It remains modeled on God's own righteousness; it's our calling as the *imago Dei*.

Framing his covenantal expectation in this "Jesus-centric" relational way was "risky," compared to (say) giving us 613 new, updated commandments. But all relationships founded on love are risky, as God knew full well in creating humanity in the first place. A law based on love must also to some degree be a law based on freedom. There is always the risk that someone will play fast and loose with the freedom that it allows; even so, it's still God's preferred approach.[5] Love is risky because there is always the chance—even, the likelihood—that the one loved will not love in return; but love must still allow freedom to choose that, since forced "love" is abusive; it's a counterfeit. If our love is not reciprocated by others, that does not negate God's expectation of us to continue to love, even to the point of loving our enemies (Luke 6:27, 35).

And of course, there is always the risk (we could again say the certainty) that in the new covenant, as with its predecessors, people will fail. In the covenant in Torah, failure was anticipated and provisions were built in. Indeed, *fulfilling* Torah *included* availing oneself of the opportunities for forgiveness and "resetting" the covenant relationship that Torah graciously allowed. So, too, in the new covenant in Christ: "If we confess our sins, he is faithful and just and will forgive us our sins and purify us from all unrighteousness" (1 John 1:9). Participating in communion (a relational word in itself) offers us the regular opportunity to reset our new covenant relationship with God through Jesus: to re-member ourselves (in the sense of a fresh joining) to Jesus.

Finally, a few words on righteousness in the sense it is spoken about by Paul—in Romans, especially. Paul's letters are probably the most studied parts of the Bible, and Romans is probably the most studied of those letters. Especially since the Reformation, "what Paul meant" by righteousness and justification has been debated with some passion. I do not propose to add to that here. For those who would like to know more, the debates between N. T. Wright and John Piper should be informative (easily searched for online). All I would say is that to my mind the Reformed Calvinist perspective articulated by Piper and colleagues

---

5. Jas 1:25, "Whoever looks intently into the perfect law that gives freedom, and continues in it—not forgetting what they have heard, but doing it—they will be blessed in what they do."

is insufficiently relational and excessively transactional in how it is conceived. It smacks of formulae and method.

Despite slightly kicking the can down the road on this, I do not want to avoid engaging entirely. But rather than offering a complete systematic treatment, I will suggest a few brief thoughts.

The first thing to understand is that in the Epistles Paul is mostly (though not exclusively) addressing gentile Jesus-followers. His congregations were mostly (but not entirely) gentile in makeup. Some of those gentiles would have been what were known as "Godfearers" (gentiles who associated with the synagogue because they identified with the God of Israel and Jewish ethics and lifestyle, but who had not gone the whole way—not least in adult male circumcision!—to become Jews). Others, however, would have been former pagans lacking even that Jewish moral framework. In other words, these new Jesus-following believers had no background in the covenant in Torah; as gentiles, they were excluded. Ephesians 2 is addressing such gentiles:

> Remember that formerly you who are gentiles by birth and called "uncircumcised" by those who call themselves "the circumcision" (which is done in the body by human hands)—remember that at that time you were separate from Christ, excluded from citizenship in Israel and foreigners to the covenants of the promise.[6]

Hence, for gentiles, there was no preexisting covenantal relationship with which the new covenant in Jesus could be understood to run in continuity (as Torah did for Jewish believers) in defining God's desire for "righteousness."

Although the new covenant was offered equally to Jew *and* gentile—Jesus' first followers were, after all, Jewish—it was clear that the natural state of the nations was to be "un-right" with the God of Israel: "foreigners to the covenants of the promise," as Eph 2:12 puts it. We need to be aware of this gentile-focused background to a lot of what's being said when we read the New Testament letters. What Paul is saying to previously pagan gentile Jesus-followers in the early churches is not always what he would be saying to Jewish Jesus-followers. The latter would have had a well-established sense of righteousness from an upbringing in Torah; the former would not.

---

6. Eph 2:11–12.

The second thing to say is that however much, in contemporary parlance, God loves us "as we are"—and invites us to "come as we are," to approach him as we are—there is an essential need to be "made right" with him. The gentiles were outside of any covenantal relationship with God. Part of God's love for all humanity was, at the right time, to do something about that. Something that we couldn't do for ourselves.[7] Our most fundamental relationship—before our relationships with others, with ourself, and with the planet—is our relationship with God. That needs to be made right first, as a matter of priority.

Given our powerlessness to do anything to fix that relationship— our only contribution is to desire it and receive it—Paul in Rom 5:17 speaks of the "gift of righteousness." It's a free gift, by the grace, mercy, and kindness of God, through Jesus, that is ours to receive. It brings us into a covenantal relationship with God, starting us off on the right footing, with our past failures in life wiped clean.

Thereafter, our calling as Jesus-followers is to live in covenantal faithfulness—as it always was for Israel, but now defined differently. Life cannot be the same anymore, not least because changing kingdoms means our citizenship changes. Or if you prefer, our direction of travel changes; this is what "repentance" means—turning around and going a different direction in life. Hence, God calls us both to *be* righteous and to *do* righteousness—in each case, as that is defined by him—in a world that we know "isn't right." Which is why, one day, he will make it right. The way that it should be—the way it was destined to be—in a future new creation in which all of the "not right" things, like sin, evil, suffering, and death, are removed and destroyed. As in the parable of the wheat and the weeds in Matt 13.

When death is gone from creation, what does that leave? Eternal life. There is no death to take life away anymore. And when sin is gone, what does that make possible? The permanent presence of God: a righteous God, dwelling in person with his "now made righteous" people. Not simply "as it was in the beginning," but as it was always destined to be.

We *pursue* righteousness and we *do* righteousness because we are in love with God's future—a future that will be characterized by "everything

---

7. In its simplest terms, this is what we mean by "substitutionary atonement." That God in Christ did for us what we could not do for ourselves. There is no need to read punishment (*penal* substitution) into that, however, as if they are synonymous. All of the best ways of explaining the atonement are substitutionary in that sense, but by no means are they all penal (in fact, only in the specifically penal substitutionary model does punishment feature at all—not in sacrifice, ransom, redemption, *Christus Victor*, etc.).

being right." We want to do all we can through both perspiration and inspiration—the Holy Spirit providing the latter—to bring a foretaste of that future "right-ness" for all those suffering wrongs in the present.

Righteousness is far more than some ethereal abstract quality or fictive status granted through a transaction between Father and Son at the cross. Otherwise, Jesus wouldn't have taught his disciples that "God blesses those who are persecuted *for doing right*, for the Kingdom of Heaven is theirs" (Matt 5:10). It's only *doing* righteousness that gets someone persecuted.

Justice

Already we have said that there is a close connection between justice and righteousness, as both attributes of God and characteristics that he wants to see manifested in his people. By definition, we cannot be righteous if we practice injustice or turn a blind eye to others acting unjustly. Once again, we see a relational connection centered in covenant, since justice is framed by laws; in other words, a society's formally stated expectations of those who wish to be part of that society, in "right relationship" to it. For Israel, the covenant charter of Torah was defining not only what righteousness looked like but what justice looked like as well.

Scripture affirms this close connection, this intertwining:

- "The Lord loves righteousness and justice; the earth is full of his unfailing love" (Ps 33:5);
- [The Lord says] "Justice must flow like torrents of water, righteous actions like a stream that never dries up" (Amos 5:24);[8]
- "Blessed are those who act justly, who always do what is right" (Ps 106:3); and
- "The righteous care about justice for the poor, but the wicked have no such concern" (Prov 29:7).

Beyond its specifically crime-and-punishment-focused aspects, perhaps the simplest way that most people would conceive what justice means in societal terms is "ensuring fairness." There are various spheres in which

---

8. For context, the immediately preceding verse says: "Take away from me your noisy songs; I don't want to hear the music of your stringed instruments."

the ethos is manifested, but three in particular: distributive justice, retributive justice, and restorative justice.

Distributive justice is concerned for fairness in the distribution of resources and opportunities. It starts from the standpoint that every person is of equal value and should be granted equal access: *unequal* distribution or access, on any grounds, including due to prejudice, is inherently *unjust*. Another way of describing injustice would be the deprivation of reasonable and basic needs for human well-being when those things are readily available to most. Some would describe distributive justice as everyone receiving their "fair share of the cake," though this can become complicated not simply in what that means in practice but in how it should be brought about. (Communist versus capitalist systems spring to mind.) These equitable principles can be applied not just to individuals within societies, but to nations on the global stage as well.

Retributive justice has to do with the application of the law in criminal justice: in other words, what should be society's right response to crimes? What should be a person's just deserts for committing a crime, ensuring that they "get what's coming to them," fairly and equitably? The answers to these questions have varied very significantly in different cultures and different eras. In England, for example, until penal reform just a few centuries ago, almost all sentencing involved physical punishment, including the imposition of suffering, execution, or deportation. Now, however, we punish wrongdoing primarily through financial penalties and custodial sentences, the deprivation of liberty. Inherent within all criminal justice should be fairness in how the law is crafted at the outset and then how it is applied: without fear or favor—with no unfair influences on the judicial process. It's said that the law should be blind; hence, its regular personification shows Lady Justice blindfolded, holding the scales of justice in one hand and a sword in the other. An area of debate is how to ensure that the punishment fits the crime, and that it is "proportionate." Part of the function of retributive justice is to seek to deter others from following the same path.

Restorative justice goes beyond simply punishing offenders; the concept has to do with "repair"—how victims can receive healing and restoration for the harms they have suffered. It also asks how perpetrators can be helped to understand the harms they have caused and potentially be rehabilitated into the community whose trust they have breached. And it extends to the steps that can be taken to try to prevent reoffending. When a war is ended by an aggressor nation being defeated, attention focuses not only on the appropriate punishment for its aggression but also the appropriate reparations that should be levied on it toward the restoration of the nations harmed. But as with individual offenders, there is also the need for a balance between punishment and restoration—rehabilitation, in due course, into the international community—lest (as happened after the First World War in Germany) an imbalance in punishment versus rehabilitation simply stokes the fires of resentment leading to potential reoffending (in the rise of the Third Reich). There has been much recent discussion of the need for reparations in the context of the historic ill treatment of indigenous people through colonization and the transatlantic slave trade.

Other elements of justice, overlapping with the above, would include "social justice" in terms of people in every segment of society being included and welcomed on fair and equal terms irrespective of race, creed, religion, or gender. This includes being granted equal access to legal representation, having fully transparent access to all of the evidence offered against them, and the legal proceedings being made accessible in the participants' mother tongue (none of which was necessarily the case in years gone by).

It's probably fair to say that almost no one disagrees with the overarching principles involved in all these aspects. Justice is surely a shared value. Opinions may reasonably differ, however, when it comes to what justice looks like in practice. Often, politics comes into play, with public opinion congregating around the ideologies of different political parties of more or less conservative or liberal dispositions (though even those categories themselves come in more than one variety).

Biblical Justice

Throughout the Bible, we see a deep-rooted concern for justice. The framework offered by Torah included multiple provisions to ensure that justice was woven into the fabric of Israelite society. I think it is fair to say that in the Bible we see exhortations to God's people to act justly—to do justice—in all of the elements that we have spoken about above, all of the ways that we see justice understood today. We see these themes running through the text on so many occasions that it is almost invidious to try to select representative examples, but here are just a few that show the broad-ranging value of justice that God required:

- "Learn to do right; seek justice. Defend the oppressed. Take up the cause of the fatherless; plead the case of the widow" (Isa 1:17; cf. Deut 10:18);
- "Speak up for those who cannot speak for themselves, for the rights of all who are destitute. Speak up and judge fairly; defend the rights of the poor and needy" (Prov 31:8–9);
- "When you are harvesting in your field and you overlook a sheaf, do not go back to get it. Leave it for the foreigner, the fatherless and the widow, so that the Lord your God may bless you in all the work of your hands" (Deut 24:19);
- "Do not pervert justice; do not show partiality to the poor or favoritism to the great, but judge your neighbor fairly" (Lev 19:15);
- "To do what is right and just is more acceptable to the Lord than sacrifice" (Prov 21:3);[9]
- "This is what the Lord says: Do what is just and right. Rescue from the hand of the oppressor the one who has been robbed. Do no wrong or violence to the foreigner, the fatherless or the widow, and do not shed innocent blood in this place" (Jer 22:3); and
- "In everything, do to others what you would have them do to you, for this sums up the Law and the Prophets" (Matt 7:12).

In all of these senses and more, justice is deeply biblical. However, "biblical" is not an adjective to be thrown around lightly, without thinking carefully what we mean by it. It's generally overused: what church worth its salt does not claim to offer "biblical" teaching? It would be commercial suicide to advertise church activities as "unbiblical"!

But more to the point is that justice as it was perceived in the biblical period will at times be reflecting the eternal heart of God as to what justice looks like, but at times it will also be reflecting the then-current worldview of the ancient world as to what justice looked like. At times in Scripture, we see the latter more than we see the former; we see what justice looked like then, to them, rather than what it would look like now, to us. We are seeing things that are more properly characterized as "ancient world"—and hence time bound—rather than "biblical" and timeless.

---

9. It's easy to read verses such as this and think, "Well, obviously!" But this fails to recognize how significant sacrifice was for Israel as God's people; it was woven into Torah (sacrifices were a gift to God). We should instead read this as they would—as a shocking attention grabber—and respond, "Wow! So it's *that* important!"

Everything that appears in the Bible is "biblical" in one sense, but not everything in the Bible reflects timeless truths in the way that's normally inferred when Christians deploy the word "biblical" today.[10]

For example:

> If a man happens to meet a virgin who is not pledged to be married and rapes her and they are discovered, he shall pay her father fifty shekels of silver. He must marry the young woman, for he has violated her. He can never divorce her as long as he lives. (Deut 22:28–29)

I think it's reasonable to suggest that this passage is more ancient world thinking on what "justice" looks like than modern world thinking. As Bones might have said in Star Trek (but didn't, to my knowledge), "It's biblical, Jim, but not as we know it." I think we would want to say that these verses are not timeless biblical truth. Note that the "compensation" for the crime is not paid to the rape victim, but to the father, since as a woman she was his property (until she became her husband's property through marriage).[11] Note also that the young woman's feelings and wishes don't appear to come into it.

Similarly,

> If a man who has married a slave wife takes another wife for himself, he must not neglect the rights of the first wife to food, clothing, and sexual intimacy. If he fails in any of these three obligations, she may leave as a free woman without making any payment. (Exod 21:10–12 NLT)

> Anyone who beats their male or female slave with a rod must be punished if the slave dies as a direct result, but they are not to be punished if the slave recovers after a day or two, since the slave is their property. (Exod 21:20–21)

> When the Lord your God hands the town over to you, use your swords to kill every man in the town. But you may keep for yourselves all the women, children, livestock, and other plunder. You may enjoy the plunder from your enemies that the Lord your God has given you. (Deut 20:13–14 NLT)

---

10. All of the Bible's truths are truths. Some are eternal and timeless; some are contextual and time bound. Some statements in Scripture were not being made as truth statements even at the time (as an extreme example, take the serpent's words in Gen 3).

11. The same logic is found in the commandment "You must not covet your neighbor's wife. You must not covet your neighbor's house or land, male or female servant, ox or donkey, *or anything else that belongs to your neighbor*" (Exod 20:17 NLT).

In making these observations, please don't think that I am denigrating Scripture as the word of God. Rather, it's a further illustration that throughout Scripture we see humanity interwoven with divinity—the human element alongside the divine element—with far more of a nuanced "light touch" for the divine role than we might have anticipated.

It is not diminishing Scripture's "word of God" status to observe that we see the human writers' voices coming through in the text, since their worldview reflected what they would have considered "obvious" about life, the universe, and everything: matters of God and the gods included. Of course, we also see the divine voice breaking through as well. For us to distinguish those voices when it comes to application today, wise discernment is needed—ideally practiced in community and with scholarly support.

The interpretive process is firstly to ask ourselves what the biblical writers would have been perceived to be saying, and why it was that they were saying it, in that original context. Then, but only then, do we move on to ask ourselves the quite separate question as to what that might be saying to us in our context, now. Which may be exactly the same; something similar, following the same underlying principle; or (more controversially, perhaps) . . . nothing at all.

The last option is the appropriate reading when we discern that something was time bound in its context. Still equally part of the word of God, of course, and still an inspired text, but not to be copied and pasted directly from "then" to "now" as is.

Reflection on the discussion in this section should enable us to be more circumspect in using "biblical" as an adjective more widely.

The Year of Jubilee

There was a fascinating provision in Torah for what is known as the "Year of Jubilee." Its background lies in the Sabbath—the seventh day of each week during which God's people were to perform no labors and instead enjoy communion with one another and with him; it was "his" day and a religious occasion. Modeled on the Sabbath day came the Sabbatical Year (Lev 25:1–7), once every seven years, when the land is to have a year of Sabbath rest, a Sabbath to the Lord (in other words, allowed to lie fallow).

> The sabbatical year law is just one of a number of laws that protect the landless Israelites (e.g., gleaning laws in Leviticus

19:9–10; Deuteronomy 24:19–21). Lying behind such laws is an appreciation of the land as a gift from God and the obligation on Israel to share its bounty equitably, trusting that God will provide abundantly for all. The recognition that this is just one of a number of laws for the benefit of the poor makes us aware that other laws make provision for the landless during the other six years.[12]

The Hebrew word for Sabbath is *šabāṭ*. The other Hebrew word that is used in reference to the Sabbatical Year is the very similar sounding *šāmaṭ*, which can either mean "letting [the land] rest" (Exod 23:11) or "releasing [fellow Israelites] from debts" (Deut 15:1–2).[13] These were its two key features, alongside a provision for the release of slaves.

Reading on in Exod 25, we see provision for a kind of "super Sabbatical Year" to be celebrated after every "seven Sabbaths of years" (in other words, probably the fiftieth year, following seven sets of seven years including the Sabbatical Years). This super Sabbath is known as "the Year of Jubilee." The fiftieth year differed insofar as its provisions for the release of slaves appear to be broader in scope, debts were canceled, and land ownership reverted to the original families that had owned it.

The reversal of land ownership at a point to come affected the value of land bought and sold during the intervening period, rather as leasehold ownership of a property does today, as the term of a lease runs down. One reason why family land might be sold was in order to pay debts; debt was also a reason for falling into slavery (if you had nothing else to sell, you sold yourself). This provision for reversal was therefore liberating—the Year of Jubilee was characterized by release: freedom and restoration.

We cannot help but see here echoes of Jesus' mission statement in his first sermon in Luke 4:18–19 (NRSV), quoting in part from Isa 61:

> "The Spirit of the Lord is upon me, because he has anointed me to bring good news to the poor. He has sent me to proclaim release to the captives and recovery of sight to the blind, to let the oppressed go free, to proclaim the year of the Lord's favor."

The "theological" significance of the Year of Jubilee, building on the foundations of the Sabbath and the Sabbatical Year, was to remind Israel that

---

12. Barker, "Sabbath," 700. Materials for this section are drawn from this entry.

13. It is not known whether debts were canceled or just suspended for the Sabbatical Year's duration; both are possible readings of the text.

the land belonged to the Lord; they were simply tenants or leaseholders, called to steward it. Hence, the divine owner was exercising his right at the end of that fifty-year lease period to reassume ownership and release the land to its original owners.

There is a concurrent theological significance in the releasing of slaves. It reminded Israel that, notwithstanding the practice of slavery in the ancient world generally, people were not owned by other people, only by God. As his image bearers, people are not to be enslaved and abused. In the Year of Jubilee, therefore, God was also exercising his right to release people to their original owner: himself.

The Year of Jubilee was all about proclaiming freedom—liberty, or release (e.g., Lev 25:10). The Israelites as his image bearers were to behave like the Lord himself, to demonstrate his own nature and character. Multiple times in Deuteronomy God tells them to remember that they themselves were slaves in Egypt but he released them; for example:

> "Remember that you were slaves in Egypt and the Lord your God redeemed you from there. That is why I command you to do this." (Deut 24:18)[14]

Shalom

You may have come across the Hebrew word "Shalom!" (*šālôm*) as a Jewish greeting, along the lines of "good morning" or "farewell." If you've come across it in a biblical context, you'll probably be aware that it's usually translated as "peace." When we think of peace, we generally have in mind one of two things. One is the absence of a state of war or military conflict and the other is a kind of inner tranquility of the soul in the midst of the busyness, bustle, and stress of life. Those understandings are not excluded from the meaning of *šālôm*, but neither is adequate to explain its biblical significance.

Depending on your church tradition, you may be familiar with this benediction drawn from Num 6:22–26:

> The Lord said to Moses, "Tell Aaron and his sons, 'This is how you are to bless the Israelites. Say to them: The Lord bless you

---

14. Redemption (and "paying the price" language) refers to releasing from slavery; we should keep this in mind when the New Testament uses such language in the context of what Jesus has done for us. It has no penal connotations (and arguably no substitutionary connotations, at least not in the sense of Jesus becoming a slave in our place—only in the sense of doing for us what we could not do for ourselves).

and keep you; the Lord make his face shine on you and be gracious to you; the Lord turn his face toward you and give you peace [šālôm]."

In the Old Testament, šālôm is not focused on the negative (the absence of conflict or stress), it's very much focused on the positive. It's referring to a state of wholeness and completeness, where everything in the world, everything in life, is right and healthy—not just on a personal level but in society as well.[15] (The sense of it is captured in the chorus of the Matt and Beth Redman worship song "Blessed Be Your Name" that speaks of when the world is all as it should be.) This state of wholeness and completeness includes cordial relations with others and the absence of need and poverty, sickness, suffering, and untimely death.

There is a clear biblical relationship between šālôm and covenant. In Ezek 34:25, a future covenant centered in David is spoken of as a "covenant of peace." The chapter describes the many aspects of the šālôm promised in God's covenantal commitment: "showers of blessing," fruitfulness, security, and freedom from enslavement. Ezekiel 37 reiterates this covenant of peace, describing it as an "everlasting covenant." An additional feature, with clear end-times significance, is promised in v. 28: "My dwelling place also will be with them; and I will be their God, and they will be my people" (NASB 1995)—which we might compare with Rev 21:3 (NASB 1995): "He will dwell among them, and they shall be his people, and God himself will be among them [and be their God[16]]."

It seems clear that in linking the theme of covenant with šālôm God is indicating the nature of the obligations to which he willingly commits himself in his covenant relationship with Israel and through Israel to the world. In other words, šālôm is the end or goal toward which the creation is journeying under his sovereignty: a time "when the world's all as it should be" in new creation—the new heavens and earth.

In the original creation, God was transforming chaos into order, bringing about an ordered world in which everything was as it should be. The story of Scripture from "the fall" onward is a journey toward the restoration of God's good order through the removal of chaos; the reestablishment of wholeness, completeness, and right-ness, to a state

---

15. The closest single English word might be equilibrium; but no one uses that word, so let's stay with the Hebrew.

16. Per one early manuscript, according to the footnote at this verse in the NASB version.

of šālôm. In Isa 66:12 and 22, in the new heavens and earth, šālôm "will flow like a river."

Reflecting the interlinking and overlapping of so many of these big themes, we see justice and truth joined with šālôm in Zech 8:16–19. In Isa 32:16–17, šālôm appears alongside righteousness and justice: "The Lord's justice will dwell in the desert, his righteousness will live in the fertile field. The fruit of that righteousness will be šālôm." And finally, in Isa 9:6–7, we see the prophetic promise of how this eternal šālôm for God's creation will be brought about through the messianic figure known among other titles as the Prince of šālôm: "Of the greatness of his government and šālôm there will be no end. He will reign on David's throne and over his kingdom, establishing and upholding it with justice and righteousness from that time on and forever."[17]

It would not be unreasonable to see a direct correlation between the concept of the future kingdom of God as it will one day be in all its fullness, as described in the New Testament, and the features of the Old Testament's vision of a future šālôm.

What, then, of the New Testament? Ancient Greek had three words corresponding to elements of peace. One described a state of calmness (similar to how we speak of "inner peace")—used in relation to the Sea of Galilee in Mark 4:39; one described harmony between people (this word doesn't appear in the New Testament); and the one that we see most frequently—used by every writer, except in 1 John—is *eirēnē*, most closely corresponding to the Hebrew idea of šālôm.

It is instructive to read some of the more familiar New Testament verses in which *eirēnē* is used with this deeper and broader šālôm meaning in mind, especially if we've been used to reading them solely in terms of personal, inner peace; for example:

> "Peace I leave with you; my peace I give you." (John 14:27)

> "I have told you these things, so that in me you may have peace." (John 16:33)

> "You know the message God sent to the people of Israel, announcing the good news of peace through Jesus Christ, who is Lord of all." (Acts 10:36)

---

17. See also the famous messianic passage in Isa 11:1–9 (when "the wolf will live with the lamb") that similarly speaks of a time of justice and righteousness when there will be no harm or destruction.

> Therefore, since we have been justified through faith, we have peace with God through our Lord Jesus Christ. (Rom 5:1)
>
> The kingdom of God is not a matter of eating and drinking, but of righteousness, peace and joy in the Holy Spirit. . . . Let us therefore make every effort to do what leads to peace. (Rom 14:17, 19)

In a number of verses, God is described as "the God of peace." The relational centering is reflected in the passages above and in Eph 2:14: "He himself is our *eirēnē*." The God of *eirēnē* brings the *eirēnē* of God that passes all understanding (Phil 4:7) and he does so through his personal presence in lives and communities (Gal 5:22 lists *eirēnē* as one of the features of the fruit of the Spirit).

Finally, echoing Rom 14:19, 2 Tim 2:22 encourages us to "pursue righteousness, faith, love and peace." The same root word, *eirēnē*, is reflected in Jesus' saying, "Blessed are the peacemakers," in Matt 5:9, echoed also in Jas 3:18: "Peacemakers who sow in peace reap a harvest of righteousness."

In sum, justice, righteousness, and shalom are attributes of God himself; they are part of his nature and character, and they characterize his ways and his desire for his creation. They reflect how he made the world to be, how he wants it to be, and how he will one day restore it to be. As his people, he calls us to play our part in loving justice, righteousness, and *šālôm* as he does, since we are to be bearers of his image. Not simply loving those things in a heart attitude sense, but also wanting to bring them about in our world now, as *šālôm*-makers, in partnership with the Holy Spirit. When we pray for people as Jesus taught the disciples to do, "Your kingdom come, your will be done on earth as it is in heaven," we are petitioning the Father for an inbreaking of justice, righteousness, and *šālôm*—a foretaste of the future that he has planned—into lives and situations now.

— 6 —

A People of God

One of the difficulties in explaining to Christians today why the People of God is an important biblical theme is that in both modernity and postmodernity we're used to thinking of relationship with God as an individual thing. The mindset is that we relate to God *primarily as an individual*—that being a Christian is really all about "him and me"—and we see the wider community of the church as primarily there in support of that—to be a resource to serve us in that relationship.

In this way of thinking, the church is just one of a number of service providers to choose from—along with para-church organizations, conferences, devotionals, books, blogs, videos, and self-styled Christian leaders' independent personal ministries. All competing to offer me religious goods and services to pick and choose from, to enhance my walk with God. "Church" is just one more option on the menu for what I feel will benefit me the most in working out my personal faith.

This is illustrated when someone talks about moving churches because "I'm not being fed," it's no longer "meeting my needs," or "I'm not getting anything out of the worship."[1] And most importantly, it's why people say things like, "I don't need to be part of a church to be a Christian." Which in today's individualistic world sounds perfectly reasonable. But through the entire Christian era, until very recently, anyone

---

1. Isn't it supposed to be God who gets something out of the worship?

hearing someone say that would think they were crazy, because it's an individualistic, modern worldview speaking.

When the first coronavirus lockdown happened—and suddenly, far more churches were live-streaming—it was not uncommon for Christians to post on social media that they were watching another church's services on Sundays instead of their own—invariably a bigger church, with more resources (a.k.a., more money to spend on the production) because those services were "so much better" than what their church was offering; they were "getting more out of it." And not only watching personally, but recommending on social media that others do the same. That kind of self-centeredness was a kick in the teeth to small, local churches.

This individualistic way of thinking comes about for three reasons. The first is because it's an integral part of the worldview of the Western world today. Everybody thinks like that, not just Christians. The second is because in a more prosperous world, with wide-ranging choices available in almost every area of goods and services, the customer is king, and we've gotten used to that being the case. In just about every area of life outside of our day job (and even there, it's not wholly absent), we see ourselves primarily as consumers rather than contributors. And the third reason is a continuing reaction against the old idea that a Christian is someone who goes to church (or that people are Christians if they live in a "Christian country").

To counter that last reason, evangelicals were right to say, "No, a Christian is someone who has a relationship with Jesus, not simply someone who attends church at Christmas and Easter or puts 'Christian' on an official form as an alternative to 'British.'"

But it's these three factors—the prevailing worldview of society, a consumer mindset, and a reaction against a births-, marriages-, and deaths-centered "Churchianity"—that have come together in such a way that "personal" has become commingled with—and confused with—"individual." Yes, our relationship with God should always be personal; but no, it should never be individualistic.

A Collective Framework

In the Bible, personal relationship with God is invariably situated within a collective framework. This is not always apparent to modern Bible readers because our worldview colors how we read it; we simply don't "see" the group-centered context in which the stories are taking place (even though, for the biblical characters this would have been obvious; so obvious that there would have been no reason to point it out). We read almost all verses that speak of "you" as "you personally" (i.e., addressed to "me"), rather than to "you collectively."

And yet, so many of God's plans and purposes for his world cannot be understood—and cannot happen—outside of the framework of a collective People of God. In the Old Testament, that collective framework is a People of God called Israel; in the New Testament it's a People of God called the church. The biblical story has never just been about individual people of God in isolation. That's because the fulfillment of God's plans and purposes for his world requires not just transformed individuals but a transformed community fulfilling them together.

Now of course, this is not to say that individuals do not feature prominently in the biblical story—of course they do. Nor is it to say that individuals are not critical to the story—of course they are. But they are not the story; they're not the centerpiece of the story and they're never the end game for the story.

We see that very early on, in Gen 12:1–3, in the story of Abraham, when the "restoration plan" centered on a People of God begins to take shape:

> Now the Lord said to Abraham, "Go from your country, and from your relatives and from your father's house to the land which I will show you; and I will make you a great nation. . . . And I will bless you, and make your name great; and so you shall be a blessing. . . . And in you all the families of the earth will be blessed." (NASB)

God is not promising to bless Abraham just so that he personally will be blessed. He's not being offered personal promises so that he and his family will have a happy life. God will bless Abraham in order that Abraham will *be* a blessing. Abraham will be blessed in order to bring about a family that's blessed, in order to bring about a nation that's blessed, so that through this family and nation all families and nations will be blessed. And God repeats the promise in Gen 22:18 (NLT): "Through your descendants, all the nations of the earth will be blessed." It's an outward-looking, forward-looking blessing; not an inward-looking, self-centered blessing. It has its sights on blessing the whole world, not just Abraham's little world.

God's plan for humanity is (and always has been) for a People of God. A community of people who are different from the world around them, not because they're "strangely religious," (or "religiously strange"), but simply because without imposing themselves on others, they quietly live by a different set of values and ideas of what's right and good. A people whose lives and families and communities are centered in God, not centered in themselves. A people who love and worship the one true God of heaven instead of loving and worshiping the false gods of this world. A people who seek to quietly be the *imago Dei* together—the image of God in this world—and the *imitatio Dei*—imitators of God in this world. People who are really not interested in being different by "making sure everyone knows where we stand" on morality and behavior, who want to "put people right" all the time—after all, it's the Spirit's job to convict, not ours. Rather, to be people in whom God can be seen and through whom he is able to do what he wants to do, which is to show the world what he is like. A community that, by reflecting him so well, will be laying the ground for introducing people into a relationship with him.

Right from the beginning, this plan for a People of God began with a call to come out and be different. Abraham's family at the time were idol worshipers. Jewish tradition tells us that Abraham's father, Terah, was not only an idol worshiper but he made and sold idols. So God says to Abraham in Gen 12, you need to go—you need to leave the place you're living and the people you're living with. You need to come out from under your father's authority—under his lordship, as it were—and come under my lordship instead. Why? Because as the apostle Paul would later say in 1 Cor 15:33, don't kid yourselves: "Bad company corrupts good character." (NIrV: "Bad companions make a good person bad.")

We see this divine plan for a called out and set-apart People of God continuing through Moses and the exodus. Not a brand new plan, but the continuation of the same plan that began with Abraham. When God first introduces himself to Moses in Exod 3, he says, "I'm the God of your father, the God of Abraham, Isaac and Jacob." Same God, same story, same plan.

Soon after they've left Egypt, God says to Moses, say to Israel, "Out of all nations you will be my treasured possession" (Exod 19:6). In the next verse he says, "You will be for me a kingdom of priests." Not just a kingdom *with* priests but a kingdom *of* priests—a group of people in which everyone is a priest. What do priests do? They minister to God and they're intermediaries between God and his world: to bring God to people, and people to God.

Unsurprisingly, given the continuity in the biblical story, these same themes are visible in the New Testament:

> He rescued us from the domain of darkness and transferred us to the kingdom of His beloved Son. (Col 1:13 NASB 1995)

> You are a chosen people, a royal priesthood, a holy nation, God's special possession, that you may declare the praises of him who called you out of darkness into his wonderful light. (1 Pet 2:9)

> He [Jesus] has made us a kingdom of priests for God his Father. (Rev 1:6 NLT)

> You have caused them [God's people, see v. 8] to become a Kingdom of priests for our God. (Rev 5:10 NLT)

Going back to Moses, in Exod 20 God begins the process of giving Israel the law, starting with the Ten Commandments, to set the framework for what it looks like for them to be the People of God.[2]

As you may have noticed, "the law" gets a very bad press in modern Christianity. Partly because people misunderstand it. Partly because of the word "law," which smacks of legalism. And partly because of what evangelicals have inherited from the Reformation: the assumption that the law was about trying to get to heaven through obeying commandments (a.k.a., through "works"). But that was never how faithful Jewish believers understood it.

What Luther and Calvin rightly found to be true of sixteenth-century Catholicism was not something that Jesus or the apostle Paul thought was true of first-century Judaism. Yes, of course, there was some religious hypocrisy around in first-century Judaism. And of course, Jesus and Paul challenged it when they encountered it. But let's be honest: where doesn't that happen, especially among religious people? Christianity is hardly immune from that.

The Hebrew word "Torah" doesn't mean law in the way we think of laws today; it means "teaching," or "instruction." Law as a biblical genre (a type of literature) is a technical theological word. I would always recommend speaking of it as Torah rather than law, to avoid these misleading connotations. Torah was a comprehensive framework that God gave

---

2. *Not what it looks like* for everyone, everywhere, in all times and places to be the People of God, as we will shortly come to.

Israel to lay out for them what it looked like to be the People of God, in their world, in that place, at that time. A people who would be different and distinctive from the other nations in all the right ways.

The most obvious distinctions to the outside observer would have been the dietary laws, keeping the Sabbath, and observing the festivals. But Torah was far more than that. It was a comprehensive set of values and guidelines to provide shape and structure for the whole of life: work, worship, family, extended family, sexuality, justice, righteousness and compassion toward the stranger, the refugee, and those in need. It was describing what being a People of God needed to look like in their world. Some of it may sound strange to us now, but it wasn't designed for us now; it was designed for an ancient world nomadic people living in a Middle Eastern desert three thousand years ago, when we in Britain were in the Bronze Age.

At the start of Lev 18:1–5—in the part of the Old Testament that we call the Holiness Code[3]—God reiterates the point of Torah and why Israel needed to be different:

> The Lord said to Moses, "Speak to the Israelites and say to them: 'I am the Lord your God. You must not do as they do in Egypt, where you used to live, and you must not do as they do in the land of Canaan, where I am bringing you. Do not follow their practices. You must obey my laws and be careful to follow my decrees. I am the Lord your God. Keep my decrees and laws, for the person who obeys them will live by them. I am the Lord.'"

The rest of chapters 18 through 20 then includes prohibitions against the things people did in Egypt and Canaan, like child sacrifice, incest, bestiality, and prostitution; consulting mediums and spirits, and worshiping idols. But these chapters also include positive commands: to use honest weights and measures, to look after the foreigner and not pervert justice, and to take care of the poor.

It's very important for us to understand that practicing Torah was never a way of *qualifying for* the People of God. It was never a way of "getting in." It was the appropriate way of saying thank you for *already being* the People of God—for having already been "included in." It was already-chosen people celebrating having said "yes" to God's gracious and unmerited invitation. It had nothing remotely to do with being saved

---

3. Lev 17–26; so-called because of its frequent repetition of the Hebrew word for "holy." Biblical scholars regard it as a stylistically distinct section within Leviticus.

by works; neither in their minds nor God's mind. It was entirely a heartfelt response to having been saved by grace. The apostle Paul famously said, "The righteous shall live by faith." *But he got it from Hab 2:4*. This was no new idea; it had always been the case.

Being "right with Torah" was how a person knew they were "right with God." It was the yardstick God had given his people so that they would know.

When the rich young ruler approaches Jesus and asks him, "What must I do to inherit eternal life?" in Mark 10 and parallels,[4] he is not saying, "How do I become a Christian? How do I get to heaven? What prayer do I pray? Is it the Four Spiritual Laws?" He's asking (the word "inherit" gives it away) how he can be sure that he's included in the People of God—that he has a share in the inheritance of true, faithful Israel. Surprisingly, perhaps, Jesus does not offer him a modern evangelical answer to his question (that's another clue as to what the man is *not* asking). Rather, he says, "Keep the commandments." Ooh . . . suspiciously like salvation by "works"? Not at all; at least not in the sense that would cause Reformed antennae to start twitching! It's not that Jesus isn't a good evangelical (perish the thought), it's that the question is aiming at something different.

But Jesus doesn't simply leave it at "keep keeping the commandments." As in other encounters with religious leaders,[5] Jesus is at pains to point out whenever people are "missing the point" of Torah: namely, the divine heart behind every law, given in the best interests of people. Not slavish adherence to the letter of the law, to keep God happy. Jesus' clashes with the religious leaders were all to do with them seeing loving God through the lens of loving the law of God, rather than through the lens of loving the people of God. The law was always for the benefit of people, never people for the benefit of the law. Wherever a commandment was being interpreted and applied in a way that meant it was no longer operating for the well-being of people, it was by definition being interpreted and applied wrongly. There's a lesson for us in that: let's never love God's commandments more than God's people or at the expense of God's people.

---

4. The parallels are Matt 20 and Luke 10; the conversations vary slightly in each Gospel (perhaps the same question was asked of Jesus quite often; people often asked different rabbis for their interpretations of Torah on various points). Here I'm synthesizing the accounts to draw out what the conversation was all about.

5. In the Lukan version of this encounter, the man is described as an expert in the law.

This remains a helpful "test" for us to apply today: If we insist on imposing a commandment, will the fruit of it—the outcome—be *for* people or *against* people? Per John 10:10, will it be life *enhancing*, or life *harming*? If it's the latter, then perhaps we need to go back to what Jesus said concerning the Sabbath, which was front and center in the Jewish understanding of what was most important to God—as central a feature of "what God wants" as any commandment—and rethink our insistence.[6]

A Personal Faith Within a Community of Faith

Now of course, it's one thing to emphasize the importance of being the People of God collectively,[7] as a much-needed corrective to rampant modern and postmodern individualism, but how does that interact with the need for our faith to be personal as well? And the answer is—as so often in the Christian life—that it's a combination of "both/and." The gospel is not just what good news looks like in the life of an individual, it's also what good news looks like in the life of a community. It's not just good news between me and God. As was the case with God's commandments in Torah, so many of the things that the New Testament calls us to be and to do as the People of God can only happen in a community and group setting.

So yes, of course our faith should be *personal*. It should begin from the starting point of a personal encounter with Jesus. And we should never leave that behind; it should continue to be centered on an intimate, personal relationship with Jesus. But it should never be *individualistic*. It should never be detached from an intimate personal relationship with the People of God that we call the church.

And I don't just mean being technically part of some airy-fairy thing called "the church universal." That is just an individualistic cop-out. I mean the nitty-gritty, messy, disappointing—and at times embarrassing and inadequate—thing that is the church in our localities and communities. By all means vote with your feet and have nothing to do with truly bad churches and especially toxic churches and toxic leaders. Sadly, they do exist. But that aside, if we can't find a local church that's good enough for us, then we're probably thinking way too highly of ourselves. Join one and help to make it better.

---

6. Perhaps that's why Jesus chose it as his example.
7. Another word for that would be "corporately."

I rarely have any problem with people "deconstructing" what church is. That can be perfectly healthy. *Provided that* at the same time they're building a vision for constructing what church *should* be. And, that they're actually intending to do something about it.

Jesus said, "I am the Light of the world" in John 8; but he also said, "You are the light of the world" in Matt 5. And he gave us not just one but two pictures of what that looks like. We are called *individually* to be like a lamp in a home—giving light to those immediately around us. But we're also called *collectively* to be like a city set on a hill—one that can be seen from miles away—because of the light that's generated by all of our lights together. We need to be lighting up the world in both these ways; not just in an individual, personal way.

Our witness to those who don't know Jesus is not just conveying information to which individuals can give mental assent and be personally saved. Arguably that was so in modernity (certainly the approach taken toward apologetics suggests that it was assumed to be effective), but today, especially, people want (and need) to see and experience the gospel in a community of God's people. They want to see what the good news of God actually looks like in concrete life experience, how our stories of our encounters with God might change their story—how what we have found to be true could become true for them, too.

What will be the characteristics of that kind of Christian community? Basically, it will be being like Jesus. Loving one another; loving the unlovely; being kind, gracious, forgiving; preferring one another over ourselves; being sacrificial; and basically just being great human beings—all because of our love for Jesus and the way that the Holy Spirit taking up residence in our lives has transformed us. Notice that we can only do those things in relation to others; none of them happens within our "inner self."

The need for an authentic, visible experience of the gospel lived out in Jesus' church is one reason why the appallingly ungodly behavior of numerous celebrity Christians in recent times has been so damaging to the gospel: the very people who deigned to preach and teach morality on behalf of Jesus being shown to be not just flawed—everyone knows we're all flawed—but blatantly hypocritical. No wonder that postmoderns are skeptical toward institutions and the authority claims of those who represent them, churches included. The sooner that evangelicalism ends its love affair with big-name celebrity preachers that draw the crowds the better. Authenticity and humility (over entertainment and performance) is at a premium.

Called Out and Set Apart

In the New Testament, we see this theme of being a called-out and set-apart people reflected in the life of the early church. In 2 Cor 6:14–17 Paul says,

> Do not be yoked together with unbelievers. For what do righteousness and wickedness have in common? Or what fellowship can light have with darkness? What harmony is there between Christ and Belial?[8] Or what does a believer have in common with an unbeliever? What agreement is there between the temple of God and idols? For we are the temple of the living God. As God has said: "I will live with them and walk among them, and I will be their God, and they will be my people." Therefore, "Come out from them and be separate, says the Lord. Touch no unclean thing, and I will receive you."[9]

Since Paul's audience would have been mostly gentiles—relatively recent converts from paganism, with no background in traditional Jewish morality and ethics, surrounded by a very pagan urban environment—he is needing to speak to them in ways that would have been largely unnecessary for faithful Jewish believers.

New Christians who come from a largely unchurched background today face many of the same challenges as Paul's audience. But it's really important that we "get" what the Bible is and isn't saying on this—what it means to be "called out" and "set apart." "Do not be yoked together with unbelievers" is fraught with potential for misunderstanding if deployed inappropriately.

I remember a preacher saying many years ago, "God wants us to be 'in the world' but not 'of the world.' The problem is that too many Christians are 'of the world' but not 'in the world.'" And that is the challenge: to be in it—where the people are—but not of it. The gospel should not be taking us out of the world, but it should be taking the world out of us.

What do we mean by "the world"? First John 2:15 tells us not to love the world or anything in the world: "If anyone loves the world, love for

---

8. Another name for the devil.
9. Paul is citing Isa 52 and Lev 26.

the Father is not in them." And yet in John 17:15, we see Jesus saying, "My prayer is not that you take them out of the world" but that you "protect them from the evil one" while they are in the world.

Clearly Jesus is not talking about the physical creation here. God has always loved his creation, from the beginning of time. In this context, "the world" has in its sights those attitudes, behaviors, and priorities that we encounter in society which are patently antithetical (even hostile) to the kingdom of God, incompatible with the nature and character of God that we see in Jesus, and with living a life that glorifies him.

Sometimes these attitudes, behaviors, and priorities are spoken of as the "spirit of the age"—not in the "evil spirits" sense (though at times it's not to be ruled out), but rather in the Zeitgeist sense, which the dictionaries tell us is the unique spirit, nature, or climate that sets an era apart from all other eras. You could say the cultural waters that society is swimming in, but is generally unaware of, because it knows nothing else. A Zeitgeist is everything that a particular society takes to be "obvious" about life—and finds it hard to see why anyone would ever have thought differently. Another word for this would be "worldview."

It's very important for us to be aware of worldviews as Bible readers and interpreters, because the most common mistake Christians make is to read the Bible as if it was written today: reading it through a modern lens and interpreting its words accordingly.

Another thing that's very important to realize is that, despite pulpit rhetoric to the contrary that we may hear about our current era— "demonizing" it in one form or another—it is by no means worse than the preceding eras from a Christian perspective. All eras and their associated worldviews have pluses and minuses. It's beyond naïve to blame the current "ungodly, worldly culture" for the challenges the church is experiencing in its mission or its message. Rather, our task is to maximize our opportunities to engage with the many pluses in the postmodern worldview; recognizing that a modern gospel based on modern points of reference will largely not compute for postmodern people.

As citizens of the kingdom of God, we're called to be "an alternative society"—but that's an alternative society *within* society, not one that has *opted out* of society. We're called to love the world in the sense of the people of the world, which is the sense in which God loves the world, per John 3:16. And we're called to love the world in the sense of everything that God said was "very good" about the world on day six of creation.[10] What we shouldn't be loving is anything that's part of the weeds sown by the farmer's enemy in the parable of the wheat and the weeds in Matt 13. It's those that we need to beware of entangling ourselves in without realizing.

Sometimes you'll hear people say, "Love the sinner, hate the sin," as a way of trying to frame these challenges. But we need to be careful with that kind of language. In fact, I recommend against thinking or speaking in those terms, because postmodern people won't get the distinction you have in mind. What they will hear is you hating them, because in their worldview who they are and what they do is not so easily separated, as it used to be in modernity. The ways of thinking have shifted away from *guilt* for things we've *done*—which in modernity could easily be forgiven and taken away, because they weren't part of us—to *shame* for who we *are*, which in postmodernity isn't so easily taken away, because who we are is seen as a part of us. We will be more effective by explaining the healing and restorative effects of the cross than its exoneration from the effects of legal guilt. "Love the sinner, hate the sin" also reinforces the impression that the church is more focused on what it's against than what it's for (which is surely a great shame). If we spent more time focusing on what we're for, maybe what we're against would scarcely need to be said.

---

10. We should never read John 3:16 as talking only about people. The whole of creation is in sight. The Greek word for "world" is *kosmos* and it means the entire created order, of which we are a part (but it's not "all about us").

7

The Enemies of God

When we talk about "enemies" in a spiritual context, we usually think about what's called "the Unholy Trinity"—the world, the flesh, and the devil. But I want to start this chapter with something you might not immediately think of as an enemy, which is "sin."

The Enemy Called Sin

When the apostle Paul talks about sin, it's interesting that it's almost always in the singular: sin, rather than "sins." He's focused on sin as a hostile power. He talks about it in terms of a personified enemy that wants to deceive us, control us, and enslave us, and to rule and reign in our world. This may remind us of way back in Gen 4 where God says to Cain, "Sin is crouching at your door; its desire is to have you."

We live in a world that's been broken and damaged by sin. We are people—and we live among people—who've been broken and damaged by sin. Sometimes we suffer *from* sin and sometimes we conspire *with* sin. All of us experience sin as both victims and perpetrators. Sometimes it's more one than the other; some people experience it more as one than the other. We "do" sin and we suffer from sin—from specific sinful acts and from the consequences of living in a sin-infected world. But Jesus died *for* sin and to save us *from* sin—to win the victory over sin—in all of the ways that it affects us, so our gospel good news must be broad enough to reflect that.

Sin is one of a number of religious words that don't communicate well outside of a religious context, but perhaps the best way to explain it in nonreligious language is in terms of selfishness. The very worst kinds of sin can be characterized as hyper-selfishness: selfishness that's "out of control," that doesn't care whether it hurts people or how much they get hurt, pursuing the things that someone wants. Old Testament scholar Chris Wright helpfully builds on this:

> The narratives of Genesis 4–11 describe inter-human disorder at every level: envy, violence, murder, corruption, vengeance, arrogance. The rest of the Old Testament adds to this list all the other social sins of greed, injustice, socio-economic oppression, abuse of the poor, abuse of women and so on. In relation to these, one could add the ecological dimension, since our relationship with the earth is spoiled and the *shalom* that we should enjoy in our created environment is disturbed. The earth itself suffers because of human sin.[1]

Sin is an enemy that infiltrates our values, our behaviors, our relationships, and our ways of thinking. It embeds itself in our institutions, our politics and our social structures, in our justice systems and our injustice systems. Sin is like a virus that's highly infectious and none of us are asymptomatic—we're all infected and we all infect others. Sin is the original global pandemic.

These ways of thinking about sin are in contrast to how it's often explained in preaching the gospel, where the problem of "sin" becomes the problem of "sins," defined as the list of things that I personally have done wrong, for which I need to be forgiven so that I can go to heaven when I die. This reductionist version of the gospel says that all I need to do is pray a prayer and say sorry. And then all the things that I've done wrong—however bad they may have been, and whoever got hurt in the process—will instantly be forgiven and forgotten. It will be "Just-as-if-I'd-never-sinned." Which, in case you've come across that expression, is *not* a biblical definition of "justification," it's a caricature of justification. It's not the gospel, it's a parody of the gospel.[2]

---

1. Wright, "Atonement," 70.
2. This is not to say that none of those components feature in the gospel; the problem comes when they become the virtual be-all and end-all of the way we explain it. When for the sake of supposed simplicity we leave out so much that's vitally important.

When Zacchaeus encountered Jesus in Luke 19, we don't see him saying, "Now I've 'said sorry' it's all forgiven and forgotten. Praise God, it's now 'just as if I'd never sinned'!"—with Zacchaeus feeling forgiven and assured of heaven (once saved, always saved). Rather, he said, "Here and now I'm giving half my possessions to the poor—and if I've cheated anybody out of anything, I will pay back four times the amount." In response to which Jesus said, "Today salvation has come to this house." That is not a "cheap gospel," that's an expensive gospel, from someone who "gets it."

We shouldn't confuse the fact that all have sinned, which biblically we have, with all sins being equal, which biblically they're not. They're certainly not equal in terms of their consequences for the people who are harmed by them. In our passion to share the grace of God with the abusers, we must not be insensitive to the suffering of those they've abused, for whom it will not instantly be "just as if they'd never sinned." The expectation that we sometimes hear said that a victim of adultery, or domestic violence, or systematic abuse, now has to "forgive and forget" because the perpetrator has "said sorry" needs to be radically revisited, both theologically and pastorally, starting with grace and sensitivity, rather than dogma and prooftexts. The way we explain the gospel must be good news to the victims at least as much as it is to the perpetrators.

Biblical Hebrew had over fifty words for sin. Chris Wright says the problem of sin is much bigger than individuals getting personal forgiveness for the things they've done:

> In its broad Old Testament perspective, sin has a devastatingly wide range of effects. It breaks our relationship with God, one another and the earth; it disturbs our peace; it makes us rebels against God's authority; it makes us guilty in God's court; it makes us dirty in God's presence; it brings shame on ourselves and others; it blights us from the past and already poisons the future; it ultimately leads us to destruction and death.[3]

The New Testament Greek words for "saved," "salvation," and "savior" come from the *sōtēria* word-group, from which we get soteriology, the theology of salvation. It has a broad range of meaning, including rescuing, healing, restoring, and liberating. Salvation is far from just being

---

That said, I do believe that "Just as if I'd never sinned" is profoundly unhelpful on several levels.

3. Wright, "Atonement," 71.

forgiven for our sins and going to heaven when we die. We need saving from what sin's done to us and to our families, and to our relationships and our communities. As well as forgiving, people need rescuing, healing, restoring, and liberating. We need to be proclaiming a gospel of the kingdom in which Jesus is experienced as good news in all of these ways, both "now" as well as "not yet."

The World, the Flesh, and the Devil

When the Bible talks about "the world," sometimes it's talking about the creation (or planet Earth) and sometimes it's talking about people. But when it talks about the world as an enemy, it means in the sense of 1 John 2:15: "Do not love the world or the things in the world. The love of the Father is not in those who love the world." As The Message helpfully paraphrases it, "Don't love the world's ways. Don't love the world's goods. Love of the world squeezes out love for the Father" (MSG). We spoke about this in the previous chapter: that as Christians we are called to be "in the world, but not of the world."

James 4:4 picks up on that: "Anyone who chooses to be a friend of the world becomes an enemy of God." In other words, an inappropriate relationship with the world means "joining the other side."

Over the centuries Christians have really struggled to understand the difference in practice between this "in" versus "of." In what ways are we supposed to be different? To what extent are we to engage with the culture and to what extent are we to distance ourselves from the culture? How do we love people and be with people without doing what they're doing some of the time? How can we be "normal" (in the right sense) without doing the things that most people "normally do" (in the wrong sense)? "What would Jesus do?" is not at all a bad start, but it doesn't always give us the answer. He lived in first-century Israel, not the twenty-first-century West.

There's no slam-dunk easy answer to this because it's as bad to disengage from the world as it is to over-engage with the world. But let me suggest four simple things:

1. Make sure we're really listening to the Holy Spirit speaking to our conscience. What is that "still small voice" saying (NIV: that "gentle whisper")?[4] What is our "inner peace" saying?[5]

2. Ask ourselves: Would God love what I'm doing, or would he be saddened by what I'm doing? Could I "look him in the eye" right now?

3. Is my doing this, being part of this, as a Christian, something that will enhance God's reputation or damage his reputation, in the eyes of people who don't know him? and

4. Is it compatible or incompatible with the godly values that we see in Scripture? These will be our points of reference for sensing the voice of the Spirit in relation to 1 through 3 above.

OK, so let's move on to our next enemy: "the flesh," where we're thinking primarily about how Paul uses that term, and especially in Romans. The Greek word that gets translated as "flesh" has more than one meaning. Sometimes Paul is talking about his physical body; sometimes bodies generally; sometimes he's talking about the human race; and sometimes—most often—he's talking about human nature: what we as people are naturally like, and especially what we're like without God.

One reason the flesh is an enemy is because it's weak, and it's lazy, so it's a soft target. It's inclined toward wanting the wrong things and doing the wrong things—like a car that gradually veers toward the curb when you take your hands off the steering wheel. So for us as Christians who have the Holy Spirit living inside this body of flesh there's often a conversation going on. At times it's a battle going on, between what the flesh is saying and wanting and what the Holy Spirit is saying and wanting.

The principal biblical concern over "the flesh" in Paul is allowing it to be "lord" of our lives: when our natural feelings, wants, and desires are allowed to rule over us—whatever suits me and whatever would please me. It's seeing something, finding it attractive, and wanting it—like Eve in the garden: "When the woman saw that the fruit of the tree was good for food and pleasing to the eye, and also desirable for gaining wisdom, she took some and ate it." The flesh tells us to listen to our natural desires and give in to them, even that it's wrong to suppress them (which sometimes it is, sometimes it isn't—context is everything).

4. 1 Kgs 19:12.
5. Col 3:15.

The world and the flesh work together. When we're tempted, it's our flesh that's being targeted. The world is tempting us to want the wrong things that we see "out there" and the flesh is wanting us to give in to those temptations "in here." First John 2:16 names them together: "Everything in the world—the lust of the flesh, the lust of the eyes, and the pride of life—comes not from the Father but from the world."

Lust is not simply wanting the wrong things; it's wanting too much of things, even when those things are OK in themselves. Lust is a desire to have things and to own things that is out of control. It's craving for more and ignoring boundaries of what's right and wrong in order to get it, and then to justify it. It's seeing things and wanting things and deciding that—come what may—we're going to have those things.

We can easily see how lust and consumerism are best friends. And how capitalism can be their running mate. Lust is not just about sex, it's also about possessions and money and power and pride.

And then, finally, our enemy the devil. Christians generally make one of two mistakes when it comes to the devil: they either see him in everything, or they see him in nothing. They give him credit for way too much, or they give him credit for way too little. As C. S. Lewis famously said, "There are two equal and opposite errors into which our race can fall about the devils. One is to disbelieve in their existence. The other is to believe, and to feel an excessive and unhealthy interest in them." How do we avoid an imbalance in either direction?

The possible activity of evil spirits is one of the things to which we need to be sensitive in pastoral ministry if we believe in the supernatural and in supernatural enemies (as charismatic evangelicals generally do). But we also need to remember that in Bible times they had no category for mental illnesses. So, we see Scripture describing *the visible effects* of what's wrong with someone in *ancient world categories*. It is not diagnosing the *medical causes* of what's wrong with them in *modern world* categories. We need to be wise here and listen to the medical profession, just as we would with physical illnesses; the problem could be either, or both, or neither. Don't leap to conclusions either way. Remember, too, that when it comes to praying for healing for someone, it's the Holy Spirit who heals, not our diagnosis or our vocabulary. Let's hold back from evil spirits language, which can spook people and ultimately contributes nothing.

A biblical theology of Satan tells us that the problem of evil is not just a human thing (though, sadly, we humans don't do too bad a job even on our own). There's also a personified evil being in the spiritual realm with a will, and a purpose, and a strategy to contend with. It's unhelpful to mentally picture him as a little red devil with horns and a forked tail, not least because it trivializes him and leads people not to take him seriously. Second Corinthians 2:11 says that we shouldn't be ignorant of his schemes, but we probably will be if we think of him like that.

It's also important that we don't use Satan as a scapegoat for things that are down to us—a version of "the devil made me do it." The devil has no power to "make us" do anything unless we choose to. As Jas 4:7 says, "Resist the devil and he will flee from you."

Satan is mentioned in seven books in the Old Testament, but we don't see a developed understanding there—but note that most commentators identify him with the serpent right back in Gen 3. However, when we get to the New Testament he's mentioned in three-quarters of the books—135 direct references and nearly 150 if we include indirect references. The word "Satan" comes from the Hebrew and "the devil" from the Greek. There's a variety of other names and titles used as well, many of which are ways of describing what he's like. And it's these names and descriptions that give us the best insight into who he is and what he does. The root meaning of "Satan" is an adversary, an accuser, and a slanderer. Keep in mind that "accuser" and "slanderer" are not the same thing. To slander someone is to accuse them falsely, to spread lies about them, whereas accusations may be true. So *when they are* true, it's Satan's motivation for the accusations that is under the spotlight, which is to condemn people, and make them feel bad, and to keep them like that. Rather than, as Jesus would, coming alongside them and lovingly drawing them into repentance and forgiveness.

Satan is also a slanderer and false accuser of God, and he tries to get us to buy into that: to doubt God and doubt his love, by cynical, undermining questioning. The very first words that Satan (in the person of the serpent) speaks in the Bible are in Gen 3:1: "Did God *really* say . . .?"

The root of Eve's problem was getting into conversation with Satan in the first place. Once we give what he says credibility, by starting to debate with him, we're making ourselves vulnerable, allowing his subtle and cynical undermining to take root in how we think of God. In John 8:44, Jesus calls him not just "a liar" but the "father of lies."

So expect him to lie to you, convincingly. Expect him to lie to you about yourself, about other people, and about God. And expect him to exaggerate things that may have truth in them, but are being deployed with bad intentions—weaponized to suit an unclean agenda, seeking to disable spiritually and emotionally. It's that element of truth that enables him to disguise himself and pretend to be an "angel of light" (2 Cor 11:14).

Satan is also called "the prince of this world" by John (John 12:31, 14:30, and 16:11) and "the god of this age" by Paul (2 Cor 4:4). Those are his domain—at the moment. As he did with Jesus in the wilderness, his strategy is to get us to buy into what the world is offering—to play the game of life by the world's rules. He has his own parallel kingdom, where he rules and reigns, governed by a totally different set of values. It's there as an alternative to the kingdom of God, where Jesus rules and reigns, governing by his set of values. The word "antichrist" doesn't only mean "against"—it also means "instead of."

Biblically, there are only two options: the kingdom of this world or the kingdom of God. Either the one rules and reigns over us, or the other rules and reigns over us. The kingdom of this world is the default option. Colossians 1:13 says that God has rescued us from the kingdom of darkness and transferred us into the kingdom of his Son. That "choice of kingdoms" is the challenge of the gospel—it is so much more than praying a prayer and receiving assurance of heaven for when we die.

The devil is the one "conducting the orchestra" of all of the forces that are God's enemies. They conspire together to oppose God's will and God's plans and God's best for our lives. They have no positive agenda, only whatever steals fullness of life and seeks to damage and destroy lives. That is the bad news of their kind of kingdom. But Jesus offers us the good news of his kind of kingdom. We see the stark contrast in John 10:10: "The thief comes only to steal and kill and destroy. I have come that they may have life and have it to the full."

So as Paul says, let's not be "unaware of his schemes" (2 Cor 2:11). Always remembering that "the reason the Son of God appeared was to destroy the devil's work" (1 John 3:8). We need to be sufficiently familiar with all of his works, infiltrating all aspects of human life, that we are attuned to how we can join Jesus in that mission.

An Axis of Evil

The phrase "Axis of Evil" was first coined by US President George W. Bush back in 2002, in the aftermath of the 9/11 attacks and prior to the invasion of Iraq. He was referring to a group of nations with common goals in state-sponsored terrorism targeted at the free world. The roots of the phrase are in the Axis powers of World War II—Germany, Italy, and Japan—and it's been used to speak of other states since that time. More recently, Senate Minority Leader Mitch McConnell referenced "US Faces New 'Axis of Evil' (in Iran, China and Russia)" in an October 22, 2023, *Newsweek* article.[6]

Whether we use Axis of Evil language to think of the world, the flesh, and the devil, or stick to the traditional "Unholy Trinity," these three influences work together and feed off each other. All are, in their own ways, opposed to the kingdom of God (which is the rule and reign of God in our lives).

"The world" is everything "out there" (the society and culture around us) that wants to shape our attitudes, our behavior, and our sense of right and wrong "in here" (inside us). The world specializes in telling us that "it's OK" to live and behave like other people do, telling us that it's what "normal" people do. Offering us every reason under the sun why, just because we're Christians, we shouldn't be different and we needn't be different. The world is feeding us the idea that the lifestyles, values, and behaviors that we see in the world—in advertisements, social media, movies, and soaps—are "normal" and OK; that it would be the worst thing in the world for us as Christians to come across as weird, or old fashioned, or religious fanatics. Even convincing us how bad that would be for our witness, if we did.[7]

"The flesh" is our natural human nature released to behave in ways that are unconstrained by God's perspective. The word "unconstrained" here is important: there is nothing intrinsically wrong with who we are as human beings. As the psalmist said, "You created my inmost being; you knit me together in my mother's womb. I praise you because I am fearfully and wonderfully made; your works are wonderful, I know that full well" (Ps 139:13–14). But this does not mean that everything to do with human nature is always healthy in how it is expressed.

For example, while selfishness comes naturally to most of us and is an unhealthy thing, sexual appetite and attraction (which also comes naturally) can be either healthy or unhealthy, depending on how it's

---

6. Kika, "US Faces."

7. I am not advocating being weird or old fashioned or coming across as a religious fanatic. There is no merit in that. Though I am sometimes challenged by a definition I once heard, that a fanatic is "someone who expresses their love for Jesus more enthusiastically than you do."

outworked. It can bring blessing or trouble. The fact that it can "go either way" is why in a moment of pragmatism the apostle Paul said,

> To the unmarried and the widows I say: It is good for them to stay unmarried, as I do. But if they cannot control themselves, they should marry, for it is better to marry than to burn with passion. (1 Cor 7:8–9)

This is a curious statement in several ways. Let's leave aside that it doesn't immediately offer a very romantic view of marriage centered on being lifelong soulmates and best friends (sexual expression being uncomfortably to the fore in Paul's words). His candor does, however, point to the fact that sexual desire is a powerful force in human nature and not to be taken lightly. (Rather as James speaks of concerning the tongue—"a tiny spark can set a great forest on fire" [Jas 3:5 NLT]—we fail to recognize its power at our peril.)[8] Paul is pointing to God having provided a covenantal setting called marriage as a means of helping to facilitate something that has the potential for many problems to be channeled in a way that brings the potential for much good and much pleasure.

Inevitably, given the worldview of his day, Paul has in mind opposite-sex relationships. In our day, however, we may be minded to wonder whether that same principle—based in pragmatism and starkly honest reflection on one aspect of what it means to be human—is valid for the same reasons in same-sex relationships. We will only ever consider such a question, of course, if we believe four things to be the case at the outset: (i) that sexual desire is an equally powerful force in homosexual people as it is in heterosexual people, and hence something which the church should be willing to recognize; (ii) that same-sex attraction is homosexual people's *natural* orientation—in other words, it is as natural for them as opposite-sex attraction is natural for the heterosexual majority—something of which the ancient world of the biblical writers was unaware; (iii) that conservative focus on the sexual element of a relationship is significantly overstated relative to the many other important qualities and characteristics of Christlike discipleship; and, most importantly, (iv) that God recognizes all of these points and empathizes with those affected. It is primarily different views on these four points that lead Christians to arrive at different conclusions for or against same-sex relationships today.

---

8. Notwithstanding the need to navigate James's hyperbole in chapter 3, it's quite interesting to read vv. 2–12 with sexual attraction (rather than the tongue) in mind; both are powerful forces in human experience that have the power for good and bad outcomes.

Pastoral accommodation need not, of course, be synonymous with unqualified affirmation (what was Paul himself advocating in 1 Cor 7:8–9, if not pastoral accommodation?). There's no question that Paul, personally, felt that singleness with celibacy was the preferred choice—said in what we now call a heterosexual context, of course[9]—but he did not believe it to be worthy of a doctrine to be imposed on everyone, or even on one segment of society. This was not so in relation to other opinions he held strongly. Take, for example, short hair for men and long hair for women: "If anyone wants to be contentious about this, we have no other practice—nor do the churches of God" (1 Cor 11:15–16).

A relevant comparison point for conservative evangelicals might be pastoral accommodation toward divorced and remarried couples coming to church, whose relationships surely only the most fundamentalist-minded Christians would want to see break up for the sake of promoting doctrinal purity. Is divorce and remarriage God's best? Clearly, no. But we live in an imperfect world where many things are not as they ideally should be or would be. Rather than applying Jesus' clear denial of divorce and remarriage in Mark 10 and Luke 16 legalistically—*note that the passages offer no exceptions*—churches that are pastorally sympathetic toward divorcés prioritize the good in a faithful, monogamous, lifelong, formal commitment of two people to each other (even second time around), over the not-good of being alone, with no church-affirmed outlet for their God-given human desire to love and be loved in life through to death. Conservative evangelical churches should surely be expected to be consistent in relation to both, since applying a consistent hermeneutical approach would inevitably lead to the same conclusion: no acceptance of same-sex marriage *and no acceptance of divorce and remarriage*.[10]

---

9. There was no word in any ancient language for "homosexual" or "heterosexual." Everyone was believed to be by nature what we would now call "heterosexual." This is why same-sex behaviors were condemned as "unnatural."

10. As conservative scholar Darrin W. Snyder Belousek (opposed to same-sex marriage) explains, "Congregations reluctant to extend accommodation to same-sex couples must ask themselves why they should accommodate some situations that deviate from the creational ideal, such as divorced-remarried couples and never-married parents, but not accommodate other situations that also deviate from the creational ideal, such as same-sex couples. . . . Expecting sexual discipline of gay believers while accommodating the sexual sins of straight and married believers is simply hypocrisy." *Marriage*, 252.

8

Messiah

I ALWAYS FIND IT surprising when preachers talk about "the Messiah" with what seems to be a taken-for-granted assumption that their listeners will know what they're talking about, that it should somehow be "obvious." Messiah is a specifically Jewish notion, embedded in the God of Israel's relationship with Israel. The messiah was "their" messiah, not the whole world's messiah. That we as Christians are able to recognize Jesus as the fulfillment of the messianic promise to Israel and be the beneficiaries of a messiahship that was graciously extended to the gentile world are secondary consequences for which we can be grateful. But to be clear, the gentile world was not waiting expectantly for a messiah; the Jewish world was.

Moreover, "messiah" is not synonymous with "Son of God." Though we, now, may speak of Jesus in both respects, we should not read that into either the word itself or first-century Jewish messianic expectations; indeed, the opposite would have been the case in terms of divine identity.

So, note to preachers: don't be sloppy in using messiah language—even at Christmas!

Perhaps some of this conflation arises from the fact that although the term "messiah" comes from a Hebrew word meaning (and often translated as) "anointed," or "anointed person"—for example, in 2 Sam 22:51—its Greek equivalent is *christos*, from which we get our English word "Christ." Greek was the lingua franca of the Mediterranean world in the first century, so it's not surprising that the New Testament writers would use *christos*, though on two occasions in John (presumably for the benefit of a Greek-speaking audience that was at least in part Jewish) we see it appear in tandem with a different Greek word deriving from the Hebrew, *messias*. For example, in John 1:41, "The first thing Andrew did was to find his brother Simon and tell him, 'We have found the Messiah' (that is, the Christ)." For the most part, though, the New Testament simply uses *christos*, such as in the famous declaration of Peter in Matt 16:16 (ESV), "You are the Christ, the Son of the living God!"[1]

Although *christos* speaks of a title, or role, many Christians assume it's like Jesus' surname. Hence, to speak of "Christ" or "Jesus Christ" can sound rather formal to an English-language listener; far less personal than "Jesus," which implies we're on first-name terms. In fact, it's simply saying "Messiah," or "Messiah Jesus." But if we substitute the word "Messiah" for "Christ" when reading aloud, or in conversation, it can come across as if we're trying to sound pseudo-Jewish, or trying to sound clever, or both!

Christians tend to assume there was a self-evident preexisting Jewish expectation that the messiah would be someone like Jesus, so the only question was whether Jesus was, indeed, that person. That is not quite the case; or at least, the expectations of who the messiah would be and what he would be like were diverse and far from clear.

> Because a central tenet of Christianity has always been the conviction that Jesus was the Christ (the Messiah expected by Israel), much attention has been paid to the study of Jewish expectations of the Messiah. The Christian focus upon the person of Jesus has led to an undue concentration on the *person* of the Messiah in Jewish thought, even in the works of recent scholars. One should realize that in the Old Testament the term "anointed" is never used of a future savior/redeemer, and that in later Jewish writings of the period between 200 B.C. and A.D. 100 the term is used only infrequently in connection with agents of divine deliverance expected in the future.[2]

As a result, when we're looking at how messiah is a "big theme" throughout the scriptural story, we need to approach it differently than doing a biblical word-search for "messiah." We need to look from the perspective

---

1. The "Simon" in John 1:41 is the "Peter" in Matt 16:16 (unsurprisingly also known as Simon Peter).

2. De Jonge, "Messiah," 777.

of the New Testament writers as to how they understood the relationship between the Old Testament and Jesus as the Messiah. We need to look at the prophetic trajectory in the Old Testament more broadly, to perceive the features of God's future redemptive plans and purposes and how (through whom) they would come about—not necessarily pictured in and through a specific person who is named as messiah. And we will have to consider how "anointed" features. In all cases, that means reading the Hebrew Scriptures through a more specifically Christian grid (in other words, looking back, with hindsight, from a Christian perspective, based on what we now know) than we are perhaps used to doing.

In both Testaments, we are looking to identify the messianic expectations: the manner in which God's promises to deliver his people and establish a new age of peace, prosperity, and healing would be brought about—sometimes, but not necessarily, described as through a messianic person. It is these expectations that we can then see as fulfilled in Jesus, even though the specific designation of "Messiah" (or even of an anointed one) may be absent.[3]

Already we have said that one of the qualifications for being a "big theme" is that it "bookends" the canonical story. In Gen 3:15, we see the first hints of a redemptive one who is a descendant of Adam and Eve (a male "offspring") who will strike back and, by implication, fatally wound the serpent that has caused things to go wrong for humanity. God says to the serpent, "He will crush your head, and you will strike his heel." With the opportunity to be Monday-morning quarterbacks, we can see this as a first prophetic hint toward Jesus, with the second part saying to the serpent, in effect, you will *merely* be striking his heel at the cross, but he will be fatally crushing your head at the resurrection. This may remind us of what Joseph said to his brothers, in Gen 50:20: "You intended to harm me, but God intended it for good to accomplish what is now being done, the saving of many lives," which we could imagine as a declaration to Satan by the resurrected Jesus. And in the last three chapters of Revelation, we see the redemptive story of Scripture reaching its prophesied conclusion with the fatal wounding that began at the cross being completed in the removal from creation and destruction of "that ancient serpent, who is the devil, or Satan" (Rev 20:2). A characteristic of the new heavens and

---

3. This is not necessarily unusual in Scripture. For example, we see the concept and characteristics of "kingdom" present in the background to texts even when the word itself does not feature. So, too, with "covenant."

earth is that "nothing impure will ever enter it, nor will anyone who does what is shameful or deceitful" (Rev 21:27).

An Anointed One

The verb form of that Hebrew word for messiah (*messias*) means to apply oil. When it's used in relation to people, it's invariably to do with anointing someone as part of appointing them to a specific role or status. Given the intertwining of the God of Israel with Israel's governance and leadership throughout the biblical story, it is entirely unsurprising that this anointing is presented as God's initiative. Hence, we often see the phrase "the Lord's anointed." The one who is anointed is serving as God's servant and representative. There is at least the implication of an anointing of the Spirit (a gifting) to accompany that calling, and in places it is expressly stated. For example, in 1 Sam 16, in the anointing of David, we see that "from that day on the Spirit of the Lord came powerfully upon David" (v. 13). In Isa 61:1, the prophet says, "The Spirit of the Sovereign Lord is on me, because the Lord has anointed me" with empowerment for the mission. We see Jesus citing these words of Isaiah in Luke 4, in his first recorded sermon; clearly Jesus saw his own mission and empowerment in the same terms. When Peter spoke in the house of the gentile Cornelius in Acts 6, part of his explanation is that "God anointed Jesus of Nazareth with the Holy Spirit and power." It is from these biblical connections, seen in the Old Testament in particular, that charismatic Christians derive the basis of the "anointing of the Spirit" in spiritual gifts today, with some claiming to be anointed by God in a role, such as that of prophet.

In the Old Testament, anointing mostly occurs in relation to kings, (high) priests, and on occasion, prophets.[4] Normally, these would be distinct roles, but in the New Testament we see Jesus fulfilling all three in his person. A central feature of anointing in the Old Testament is its application to kings, and specifically to King David, especially in a prophetic sense—looking toward a future king who would be from David's family. It was this desire for a coming "Davidic" king, anointed by the Spirit, whom God would one day send to rescue and redeem his people, that principally shaped the expectations of Jewish people at the time of Jesus.

---

4. Examples of each would be King David, Aaron and his sons, and Elisha.

The Perspective of the New Testament Writers

In the writings of the New Testament, we see all of the above coming together in relation to Jesus as Messiah. For example, in Acts 9, when Paul begins his ministry, speaking in the synagogues in Damascus, his key concerns are asserting that Jesus is both Israel's Messiah and Son of God (Acts 9:20–22). Similarly in Corinth, in Acts 18:5, where he was "testifying to the Jews that Jesus was the Messiah." So, too, his colleague Apollos in Acts 18:28: "proving from the Scriptures"—which would, of course, have been the Old Testament—"that Jesus was the Messiah."

Jesus' messiahship and messianic mission features throughout the New Testament. Once we know what we're looking for, we are able to see it as a central theme for many, many encounters in the Gospels: people asking themselves whether this expected messianic figure, in whom so many Jewish hopes rested, could possibly be this man, Jesus.

In Mark 15, Pilate's questioning of the arrested Jesus is focused on: "Are you the king of the Jews?"—no doubt because of the implied political threat that such a claim would involve, but also because the messiah's kingly inheritance as a male descendant in the line of David was a well-known popular expectation.

Shortly before that, in Mark 12, Jesus questions the understanding of the Jewish theologians as to the messiah's identity: "Why do the teachers of the law say that the Messiah is the son of David?" (v. 35). Jesus is saying the relationship of the prophesied messiah to King David is more figurative than biological:

> "David himself, speaking by the Holy Spirit, declared: 'The Lord said to my Lord: "Sit at my right hand until I put your enemies under your feet."' David himself calls him 'Lord.' How then can he be his son?" (Mark 12:36–37)

When Jesus rides into Jerusalem on a donkey shortly before his execution, the crowds hail him with "Hosanna to the Son of David!" "Blessed is he who comes in the name of the Lord!" (Matt 21:9 and parallels). Jesus is often addressed as "Son of David" in the Gospels. The apostle Paul clearly saw this Davidic association as important in the preamble of his letter to the Romans, speaking of "the gospel [God] promised beforehand through his prophets in the Holy Scriptures regarding his Son, who as to his earthly life was a descendant of David" (Rom 1:2–3).

Moving away from this predominant idea of the messiah as a king, the Samaritan woman whom Jesus encounters at the well in John 4 was expecting a coming messiah (v. 25),[5] but as a result of Jesus' words of knowledge concerning her life story she wonders whether this man—who is clearly a prophet (v. 19)—could be that messiah (v. 29). This is significant for the messiah's identity, since signs and wonders are generally associated with the office of a prophet, such as Moses or Elijah, rather than a king. In John 6:14, after the feeding of the five thousand, once the people saw the sign that Jesus performed, they began to say, "Surely this is the Prophet who is to come into the world." Similarly in John 9:13–41, when the Pharisees question the man born blind whom Jesus healed, they ask, "What have you to say about him?" and the man replies, "He is a prophet!" In Peter's speech to the crowd at Solomon's Colonnade in Acts 3, he cites Moses in Deut 18:15 as speaking prophetically of Jesus: "For Moses said, 'The Lord your God will raise up for you a prophet like me from among your own people; you must listen to everything he tells you'" (Acts 3:22).

Perhaps surprisingly, we see only a handful of instances of Jesus being spoken of in terms of anointing, or as the anointed one. One is in Luke 4:1, where Jesus cites Isa 61 in relation to himself, and three are in Acts 4:26–27 and 10:38.

A further title with which Jesus identifies himself is the well-known "Son of Man." This is not simply a way of identifying with humanity (though no doubt it reflects that, too) and nor is it just being modest (choosing Son of Man over Son of God). No doubt Son of Man language would assist Jesus avoiding being tagged with the potentially more incendiary term of messiah (to the extent he wanted to conceal his messianic identity)[6] and far more so, Son of God (not that this would have had Trinitarian—or even, binitarian—implications at the time). But the primary reason is that Jesus clearly saw himself in terms of the Son of Man character in Daniel,[7] a text with which his contemporaries would have

---

5. No doubt this was reflecting the expectations of her community (she would not simply have been sharing her personal beliefs as an individual).

6. We see a desire to conceal his identity in the Synoptic Gospels, but not in John.

7. Daniel 7, 11:35, and 12:2–3 give an indication that the death of martyrs can atone, within a "Son of Man" context. Scot McKnight suggests that Jesus "thought of his death in terms of a divinely destined martyr for his prophetic calling"; as a prophet, "he would have pondered over Scriptures that might shed light on his destiny—and at least one place he might look to see his life inscripturated would be Daniel 7." McKnight, *Jesus and His Death*, 155. Note that other Old Testament references to Son of Man should not

been very familiar, not least in inspiring them to continue to trust the God of Israel despite their suffering under Roman occupation (so too, the narratives of the suffering servant in Isa 53 and the Maccabean Martyrs in 2 Macc 7:37–38). For example, Jesus' conversation with the man born blind whom Jesus healed in John 9:

> Jesus heard that they [some Pharisees] had thrown him [the healed man] out, and when he found him, he said, "Do you believe in the Son of Man?" "Who is he, sir?" the man asked. "Tell me so that I may believe in him." Jesus said, "You have now seen him; in fact, he is the one speaking with you." (John 9:35–37)

Little in the Old Testament speaks of either the messiah or a messianic mission in Son of God terms, but that is not in the least surprising, given that God's primary concern at the time was to ensure that Israel thought of him monotheistically—as the one, true God of the whole earth—rather than as a territorial god in Israel, just one among many.

A Broader Vision of "Messiah"

There is one final point to be made on the biblical concept of the messiah. Once we recognize that Scripture speaks as much or more about the messianic mission than a messianic person named as such, a whole raft of language describing an anointed one sent by God to fulfill the prophetic passages concerning God "putting right" everything that is presently wrong in his creation, as part of the ushering in of a new age, can be seen as embraced. Titles, roles, and characteristics such as savior, redeemer, victor, and healer, whether the word "messiah" appears or not.[8] For example, the prophetic passage in Isa 9:6–7 that the early church saw to be fulfilled in Jesus as Messiah:

> For to us a child is born, to us a son is given, and the government will be on his shoulders. And he will be called Wonderful Counselor, Mighty God, Everlasting Father, Prince of Peace. Of the greatness of his government and peace there will be no end. He will reign on David's throne and over his kingdom, establishing and upholding it with justice and righteousness

---

be read as speaking of Jesus or the Messiah (for example, throughout Ezekiel)—rather, of a male human being.

8. For example, the testimonies of Simeon and Anna in Luke 2:25–38.

from that time on and forever. The zeal of the Lord Almighty will accomplish this.

While it is feasible to see this passage as speaking of a human person who would be called Wonderful Counselor and Prince of Peace, that clearly cannot extend to being called Mighty God and Everlasting Father. We see these divine associations echoed in the angel's words to Mary in Luke 1:32–33:

> "You will conceive and give birth to a son, and you are to call him Jesus. He will be great and will be called the Son of the Most High. The Lord God will give him the throne of his father David, and he will reign over Jacob's descendants forever; his kingdom will never end."

The only kind of king who can reign forever is one who lives forever; the divine Father-Son relationship being spoken of is not, therefore, simply metaphorical in the way that Israel is called God's son (Exod 4:22).

However, this Son is *not only* a divine figure but also a human figure, descended from David, and thus fulfilling Israel's Davidic messianic expectations. Hence, divinity and humanity—Son of God and Son of Man—come together as "both/and" in the identity of this one person.

In both passages we see the "king" characterization prominent, foreshadowing the message of the inbreaking kingdom that was at the heart of Jesus' ministry. Indeed, in Matthew in particular, the gospel itself is "the Gospel of the Kingdom" (Matt 4:23, 9:35, 24:14; cf. Luke 16:16). And yet, this king is distinctly unlike any earthly king: "See, your king comes to you, gentle and riding on a donkey" (Matt 21:5, fulfilling Zech 9:9). This king exemplifies the meek inheriting the earth (Matt 5:5). This king endures violence done to him (Isa 53), rather than exacting violence on others.

— 9 —

The Kingdom of God

THE BIG THEME OF the kingdom of God is a key emphasis in the theology and praxis of church movements such as the Vineyard (where I served as a pastor) and others that have been significantly influenced by the ministry of the late John Wimber, such as churches related to Holy Trinity Brompton (HTB) and New Wine, in the UK.

Compared to the other big themes we've been looking at, where we've often started with Genesis and tracked them through to Revelation, the kingdom of God is a bit trickier. Surprising though it may seem, although the phrase is found ninety-nine times in the New Testament, it never appears once in the Old Testament. However, that doesn't mean it was a brand-new idea that came out of nowhere.

When John the Baptist began his ministry, Matt 3:2 tells us that his message was: "Repent—for the kingdom of heaven is at hand." ("Kingdom of heaven" is Matthew's way of saying "kingdom of God," in deference to a Jewish audience, because it avoids using the divine name.) And when Jesus began his ministry, Matt 4:17 tells us that his message was the same: "Repent—for the kingdom of heaven is at hand." Notwithstanding the absence of express Old Testament language, it seems that both were taking it for granted that their audiences would know what they were talking about.

Kingdom in the Old Testament

The theme of the kingdom of God is present in the Old Testament in three main ways.

Firstly, the idea that God is king over everything. "The Lord is King for ever and ever" (Ps 10:16); "Say among the nations: the Lord reigns" (Ps 96:10); and "The Lord has established his throne in the heavens and his kingdom rules over all" (Ps 103:19 ESV).

Secondly, the idea that God is specifically king over Israel. For the first few hundred years in the promised land, Israel had no king, because they saw God as their king, which was very unusual in that world. But in the time of Samuel they started asking for a king—"Give us a king to lead us" (1 Sam 8:6)—because they wanted to be like the other nations (vv. 5 and 20). They wanted a king who would "go out before us and fight our battles" (v. 20), even though that was God's role: "The Lord your God who is going before you will fight for you" (Deut 1:30); "God is the one who goes with you to fight for you against your enemies to give you victory" (Deut 20:4). God always expected that one day Israel *would* have an earthly king. It was anticipated way back in Deut 17:15: "Be sure to appoint over you a king the Lord your God chooses." But it had to be the right kind of king, at the right time. Not like the kings of the other nations, which is what the people were demanding in 1 Sam 8.

And thirdly, there was a prophetic expectation of a king from heaven who was to come, a messianic king who would establish God's kingdom on earth and his rule over the nations. A key passage is Dan 7:13–14 (ESV):

> I saw in the night visions, and behold, with the clouds of heaven there came one like a son of man, and he came to the Ancient of Days and was presented before him. And to him was given dominion and glory and a kingdom, that all peoples, nations, and languages should serve him; his dominion is an everlasting dominion, which shall not pass away, and his kingdom one that shall not be destroyed.[1]

---

1. Daniel 2:4—7:28 is written in Aramaic. The NIV footnote for Dan 7:13 says, "The Aramaic phrase *bar enash* means *human being*. The phrase *son of man* is retained here because of its use in the New Testament as a title of Jesus, probably based largely on this verse." Presumably for the same reason, the NASB 1995 capitalizes "Son of Man," while the 2020 edition leaves it lowercase per the NIV.

When Christians read this today, it's easy to "already know" that it's talking about Jesus the Son of God, but this would by no means have been obvious at the time (the description simply envisages a heavenly ambassador "like a son of man"—meaning, like a male human being).

Another element of the prophetic expectation is that this coming king would be a descendant of King David:

> "When your days are complete and you lie down with your fathers, I will raise up your descendant after you, who will come forth from you, and I will establish his kingdom. He shall build a house for my name, and I will establish the throne of his kingdom forever." (1 Sam 7:12–13 NASB 1995)

Then in v. 14 comes an intriguing little postscript—intriguing in hindsight, that is: "I will be a father to him and he will be a son to me." Once again, we must be careful not to read too much of what we know now into what it would have been perceived to be saying at the time,[2] which would have been metaphorical (as Israel was spoken of as God's son in Exod 4:22 and indeed, Adam in Luke 3:38). In any event, "Son of David" became a messianic title.

These prophetic threads principally framed expectations of the messiah in first-century Israel. There was another thread as well: a suffering servant messiah, in Isa 42, 49, 50, 52, and 53, but that received less attention. Which is no great surprise, given that Israel was suffering under oppressive Roman occupation. They much preferred to think about a "conquering hero" kind of messiah than a "suffering servant" kind. It wasn't until the early church reflected at length on Jesus and the things he said that they were able to join the dots.

Kingdom in the New Testament

This sets the scene for what we find in the New Testament: Jesus' self-understanding and, more broadly, the New Testament writers' understanding.

The king and kingdom theme emerges very early in the story, when the magi ask Herod: "Where is the one who has been born king of the Jews?" (Matt 2:2). We also see why Herod was so troubled when

---

2. Not least in the light of what follows it: "When he commits iniquity, I will correct him with the rod of men and the strokes of the sons of men, but my lovingkindness shall not depart from him."

he heard that. After all, *he* was the king of the Jews! As an unpopular puppet king propped up by the Roman legions, the risk of insurrection would always have been in his mind and the thought of having to contend with a popular pretender to the throne, who might have the backing of the people, would have been deeply concerning. The circumstances were such that a potential king of the Jews would likely be popularly presumed to have been sent by God. No wonder Herod lashed out so violently (Matt 2:13, 16–18).

This popular expectation of a messianic descendant of King David who would bring liberation and a new golden age for Israel is reflected in those needing healing crying out to Jesus, "Have mercy on us, Son of David." And the children shouting in the temple, "Hosannah to the Son of David." It explains why on Palm Sunday, the crowd were shouting, "Blessed is the King who comes in the name of the Lord," from Ps 118. And why Matthew says, "Behold, your king is coming to you, humble, and riding on a donkey," from Isa 62.

As we read through the Gospels we can't miss references to the kingdom. The Greek word for kingdom appears well over one hundred times. It was also the subject that Jesus told most parables about—around one-in-three. So what is "the kingdom"?

Let's start with what it isn't: the kingdom is not "going to heaven" when you die. When Jesus said to one of the religious leaders, "You're not far from the kingdom" (Mark 12:34), he didn't mean, "You're going to die soon." And kingdom is not another word for "church." The church should be an expression of the kingdom, reflecting the characteristics of the kingdom, but by definition it isn't the kingdom.

The kingdom of God is anywhere that the rule and reign of God is happening. Anywhere that God's "ruling" and "reigning" is being experienced. The kingdom is present in any place—in any life and in any situation—where God is visibly ruling and reigning as king. Wherever the power and authority of God is active and present. Wherever Jesus' Lordship is visible and tangible. The kingdom is present wherever God's enemies that are hostile to human life and human well-being are being defeated. Wherever there is healing, and deliverance, and answers to prayer—wherever the Spirit of God is putting right things that are wrong—the kingdom is happening and the kingdom is present. All of this is summed up in "Your Kingdom come, your will be done, on earth as it is in heaven," understood in both a present sense of firstfruits and a future sense of fullness.

Christians often assume that the miracles in Jesus' ministry were "to prove that he was God." But that wasn't their primary function. They were signposts—pointing to the fact that the rule and reign of God was breaking-in to this world. We should really call them "signs" and "wonders" instead. When we talk about "the coming" of the kingdom, we're talking about the restoring of the authority of God in the earth. We're talking about God becoming king. We're talking about the defeat of every enemy that's invaded his creation and challenges his reign.

OK—so far, so good. But one of the things that can be confusing when we read the Gospels is that sometimes Jesus says the kingdom has come, now—that it's arrived, in and through him and his ministry—but other times he says that it's still to come, in the future. In Matt 12:28, Jesus says, "If it is by the Spirit of God that I drive out demons, then the kingdom of God has come upon you." But in Matt 26:29 he says, " I will not drink from this fruit of the vine from now on until that day when I drink it new with you in my Father's kingdom." In the Sermon on the Mount, Jesus said we should seek the kingdom as a first priority, suggesting that it's something we can expect to experience now (Matt 6:33). But he also said we should pray for the kingdom to come (Matt 6:10), suggesting that it isn't here yet.

How do we reconcile this apparent conundrum? Various ideas have been posited over the years, but the most obvious way of approaching it is to synthesize these apparent contradictions by recognizing that both are true. It's a case of "both/and," not "either/or." The kingdom is here already, because the coming of the kingdom began in Jesus' life and ministry. But the kingdom is also still to come in all of its fullness at a time in the future when Jesus returns and ushers in the end of the age. So it's "here already," but also "not here yet." This is what is meant when people talk about "the now, and the not yet"—or the "already" and the "not yet"—of the kingdom.

Implications of a "Now" but "Not Yet" Kingdom

Again, so far, so good. But what about the in-between times in which we are living? Between the inauguration of the kingdom in Jesus' life and ministry, and his return to "finish the job," as it were? Here opinions will differ, depending on one's view of spiritual gifts in this present age. Charismatic Christians will say that those are just as much for today as they were in Jesus' ministry and in the early church. Noncharismatics will say that they ceased sometime thereafter—that God in effect phased them out. So which is it? I have to start from the standpoint that, however much I may not regularly see signs and wonders today (for example, the extent of supernatural healing that was so prevalent in Jesus' ministry), and however much it's necessary to recognize that the claims of modern-day prophecies and prophetic words can be problematic, I cannot see any rational basis to say that spiritual gifts should not be part of Christian experience.

It may now be that I will fail to do justice to the alternative views, which I think congregate around one of two perspectives. The first is based in experience: we just don't see enough of the supernatural moving of the Holy Spirit in anything other than occasional answers to prayer and relatively minor healings, *so* occasional and minor that those gifts appear to have ceased as a practical matter. I understand that. The other view is harder to acknowledge: that spiritual gifts ceased once we had the Bible. This strikes me as problematic for a number of reasons. The first is that it smacks of rewriting the Trinity as God the Father, God the Son, and God the Holy Scriptures. If I was the Holy Spirit I would not be too pleased about being pensioned off—"Thanks for some great work, we really appreciate everything you've done." There seems no obvious reason why he would be withdrawn from moving in this world, not least if the kingdom was advancing. The second is that we are scarcely comparing like for like here: the supernatural moving of the Holy Spirit in kingdom-bringing activity versus a book (even if it is an inspired book). By implication, it's replacing an experientially centered faith with an intellectually centered faith, in which information replaces transformation (I do wonder the extent to which this is unwittingly driven by Enlightenment rationality and the worldview of modernity).[3] Thirdly, the very idea of God supposedly replacing the role of the Spirit with a role for the Scriptures undermines what Scripture itself says. There is no place in the Bible where spiritual gifts ceasing is remotely hinted at. I cannot think of anything credited to the work of the Holy Spirit that could be replaced like-for-like by the work of the Bible. Hence, to take such a view is surely undermining the integrity of inspired Scripture rather than affirming it. We would need to take a blue pencil to everything that is said about spiritual gifts, or at least to rewrite it all in the past tense. And finally, I can't see any basis on which

---

3. Hiebert, "Flaw of the Excluded Middle."

we can pray to ask God to supernaturally transform lives and situations at the same time as believing that God intervening in the natural world through the Holy Spirit does not happen anymore. Otherwise, prayer becomes a token gesture, limited to generalized niceties like world peace and "Dear God, please be with so-and-so." Whatever the limitations may be in our present-day experiences of supernatural spiritual gifts, none of the above seem good reasons to deny their continuance.

To be clear, noncharismatic conservative evangelicalism does not deny the working of the Holy Spirit in this world today, but it limits that to certain (primarily cognitive) functions, like conviction of sin or persuasion of the truth of the gospel. The artificiality of that divide (which, again, is likely due to the mindset of modernity) is probably obvious.

So let's look at the charismatic view or at least, given that there is more than one version, the one that reflects the Vineyard and movements influenced by John Wimber (which arguably have the most developed articulation of the kingdom in the popular domain). The remainder of this chapter will broadly follow that view.

Jesus has commissioned us and empowered us through the Holy Spirit to continue to do the works of the kingdom. As Wimber used to say, to "do the stuff" that Jesus did. He was thinking of John 14:12, where Jesus says: "Whoever believes in me will do the works I have been doing." The Holy Spirit anoints and empowers us in the same manner that he anointed and empowered Jesus, so that we too can do the same kinds of things in Jesus' name and authority.

We presently live in the "in-between" times between Jesus' first coming and his second coming, when he will "complete the job" and the kingdom will come in all its fullness. Until then, we have *some* of the kingdom but not yet *all* of the kingdom. We experience firstfruits of the kingdom but not the complete harvest. Firstfruits are the same as the harvest in quality, just not yet in quantity. They reflect that the harvest has begun, but not all of the harvest has yet arrived. Second Corinthians 5:5 says that God has given us the Holy Spirit as a "first installment," or a "down-payment." Ephesians 1:14 says the Holy Spirit is a deposit, guaranteeing our future inheritance. These are ways of describing how the Holy Spirit is active in the world today in a "now, but also not yet" sense.

Anyone who is familiar with house buying in England will know that there is a two-stage process: "exchange" (of contracts) and "completion" (of the sale/purchase). Both events mark contractual commitments voluntarily entered into that then become binding on the parties.

Between exchange and completion, the buyers and sellers are living "between the times." The typically 10 percent deposit on exchange guarantees that completion is certain to happen at a future point in time. Nothing can stop it, no one can "gazump" you. Exchange of contracts is the critical moment for the buyers, when the property will definitely now be theirs. From that moment on, the buyer "owns" the house in one sense but also "doesn't" own it. They own it "already" but "not yet." There is certainty as to the outcome, but neither buyer nor seller receives everything that is pledged to them until completion.

Another way to picture this is the period between D-day and V. E. day in the Second World War. D-day was the decisive moment when the allied forces successfully invaded mainland Europe and the enemy forces were on the run. Victory was assured from that moment on. But it still took nearly a year—from June 1944 to May 1945—before the victory was completed. During that "in-between" time there were still battles to be fought, enemy resistance to be overcome, and battles that would be lost along the way.

The "already, but not yet" of the kingdom helps to explain why not everyone we pray for is healed now. This is liberating for anyone who's blamed themselves for "not having enough faith" when a loved one was not healed despite prayer. The "already, but not yet" of the kingdom releases us to ask God to intervene in situations—to look to him, expectantly and enthusiastically—and to invite the future to break in to the present, but without blaming ourselves if it doesn't happen. Or even worse, blaming the person being prayed for because *they* obviously didn't have enough faith, or because they must have had unconfessed sin in their life, or other such nonsensical folk theology—all of which is so damaging and condemning, when healing doesn't come (and could never be God's intended outcome).

So we should never tell people to "claim" their healing, and we should never tell people they "already have" their healing—that they "just need to believe it and not doubt it"—when self-evidently they *don't*. That has nothing to do with faith—it's just false. These are ideas that originate in heretical Word of Faith Pentecostalism (the so-called "name it and claim it," health-and-wealth prosperity gospel).[4]

The Bible encourages us to have faith, but—and this is *very* important—faith is not a formula. Faith is not straining to get mental certainty

---

4. On which, see Pentecostal theologian Fee, *Disease*.

about an outcome. We don't qualify for answers to prayer based on how much faith we've got. Otherwise, our faith is in faith, not in God. Faith is being faith-ful—in regularly and expectantly asking God to move: inviting the kingdom to come into this situation, for the Holy Spirit to bring a foretaste of how things will be in the future into how things are in the present. And faith is still believing in God, still loving God, and still faithfully praying for people, whatever the outcome was last time we prayed.

Biblical "promises" are much misunderstood in popular Christianity and worship songs. All of God's promises are true, but not everything he promises is for now. Healing is not guaranteed in this life—however many Bible verses we memorize, or claim, or remind him about (all of which verses I suspect he knows already). The final defeat of death is a prime example: everybody still dies. Even those who receive healings in this life still die, and they likely later suffer from other sicknesses as well. All of God's promises *are* true now, but not all of them will *come* true now, so not all of them can be *claimed* for now.

The theologian George Eldon Ladd was very influential for the early Vineyard. He said this: "Jesus' proclamation of the presence of the kingdom means that God has become redemptively active in history on behalf of his people." That is what we look to, with encouragement, and excitement. The quote comes from one of his books, the title of which says it nicely: *The Presence of the Future*.[5] Some of what that future will be like is here with us now, through the presence and power of the Holy Spirit; post-Pentecost, the future has *already* invaded the present. But not all of that future is here yet.

We pray for healing; sometimes people are healed and sometimes they're not. It's our understanding of the kingdom that helps make sense of that. It provides the basis for our expectations of God's interventions in this world—for when they do and don't happen. Just to be clear: it's not a perfect answer. It's part of an answer.

So, does "now, but also not yet" mean that it's kind of *que sera sera*—"Whatever will be will be"? Not at all, for three reasons.

Number one is that when we pray for someone we know that we're doing something that Jesus encouraged us to do. In Matt 6:8–10, in the Lord's Prayer, he said: "This is how you should pray: your Kingdom come, your will be done, on earth as it is in heaven." When we pray along those lines, what we're doing is praying for some of the future to

---

5. Ladd, *Presence of the Future*, 172, and *Gospel of the Kingdom*, 79–80.

break in and "come now" in that situation. To bring some firstfruits of the way things *will* be, into the way things *are*.

Number two, God has given us the gifts of the Holy Spirit for now: 1 Cor 12–14.[6] He has not given these passages for framing on the wall or posting as pithy little truisms on Facebook. They're for living, and experiencing, and doing: words of wisdom, words of knowledge, gifts of healing, prophecy, and so on.

Always remember that a "gift of healing" is not God's gift to the person praying; it's God's gift to the person being prayed for. The person praying is, quite frankly, irrelevant. We're just called to be faithful in praying. As someone once said, we're not the rain, we're only the drainpipe. There are no "special anointed ones"—"Men of God" or "Women of God," with special powers—that we need to stand in line to try to get them to pray for us (or chase round the country to attend their meetings). We should place a very high value on the role of the Holy Spirit, and a very low value on our role.

This is why, in a pithy John Wimber-ism to do with "doing the stuff," "everyone gets to play";[7] not just a few special, anointed ones. In saying that, we're not just being nice—it's expressing a theological truth: anyone can pray and get the same results, it doesn't matter who.

And number three, we trust in God's nature and character. We don't put our faith in "faith," we put our faith in who God is and what God is like. That he's a good, good Father, who loves to give good gifts to his children (Matt 7:9–11). It's relational, not transactional. Formulae and prooftexts don't heal people or supernaturally transform situations, God does.

For all these reasons we should pray confidently and expectantly with an excitement that we're doing what Jesus wants us to. But we always leave the outcome with him.

I don't often have reason to quote John Calvin, but I do like this thing he said: "We must make the invisible kingdom visible in our midst." That's a great mandate for kingdom theology. Not just in physical healing, which we shouldn't put on a pedestal on its own (however enthusiastic we may be to see it happening more often) but in every aspect of what life looks like when the rule and reign of God visibly and tangibly breaks into someone's life situation: whenever the enemies of God—those enemies of

---

6. Yes, you read that right. Read chapter 13 as if it's part of Paul's teaching on the gifts of the Spirit in 1 Cor 12 and 14, rather than just extracting it for weddings.

7. Which is an easy-to-remember way of speaking of "the priesthood of all believers."

human life and human well-being, the activities of an enemy who comes only to steal, kill, and destroy per John 10:10—are visibly in retreat.

So our prayer is always, "Come, Holy Spirit," and bring the rule and reign of God. Bring more of God's future into our present.

PART II

How They Said It: The Genres

Introduction

ALTHOUGH WE SPEAK ABOUT the Bible as a book, in reality it is a collection of books, written in different places, with many different contributors, in many different contexts, for many different purposes, over a long period of time, and all taking place within what we now call the ancient world. In many cases, the written-down accounts were preceded by orality: in other words, passed on across long periods of time via the spoken word rather than the written word. The idea of an oral tradition underlying our written Bibles probably seems an alien concept, not least because it would mean that the Bible's "inspiration" spanned a long period of time as well; it didn't just occur at one particular moment of "writing down." The Old Testament texts were put into writing during a period from the end of the eighth century to the second century BCE, by various authors from different backgrounds. Although only one name may be associated with some of the biblical books (Isaiah, Jeremiah, and so on), this should not lead us to assume anything like a single author at a single point in time. We must be aware of the roles of multiple contributors, redactors, and collators in bringing them to us in the final form we have them today.

This background illustrates how problematic is the notion of "original manuscripts" or "autographs" (meaning, a first, original version of a biblical book, prior to any copy being made) that is presumed in many evangelical statements of faith as the basis of the Bible's "inerrancy" (and hence its authority). Not only do we have no such original version of any book, but it simply ignores the way in which those books for the most part came about. It is a dogmatic claim (sincerely intended) that is at odds with what scholars know about the Bible's developmental history.[1]

Within both Old and New Testament Scripture, we find many different styles of writing, called "genres." We're familiar with this word today in a number of artistic fields, such as music and drama, as well as in literature. When I teach classes on biblical interpretation, I will often set a group exercise to identify as many genres as possible in one of those fields in two minutes; whatever the field, the winning group usually comes up with well in excess of twenty.

In the literary world, we encounter genre when we visit a library or a bookstore. Everything is organized by genre. The simplest categorization of genre is fiction versus nonfiction; but we all know there are multiple subcategories for each. The same is true of the Bible. Hence, the genre of a piece of writing is crucial in terms of what it is saying and how it has chosen to say it. If we are to correctly grasp what any piece of writing is saying, we must take full and proper account of its genre.

A simple example from a biblical genre that we're likely familiar with may suffice: a parable is a work of fiction. A parable is not a true story.[2] When Jesus said, "A man had two sons . . ." (Luke 15:11), there was no such man. Jesus didn't say, "I'm about to tell you a story I made up about a man who had two sons, please don't take it literally," because he didn't need to. Everyone knew that he was about to tell them a made-up story. Nowadays we might make that clear by starting with "Once upon a time," but in Jesus' context it wasn't necessary. Parables were a genre of the day, and they had their own interpretive "rules" that went with them. So, in order to read them as the original audience would have read them—or rather, as they would have heard them—we need to follow their rules.

To ignore a biblical writer's choice of genre is to disrespect not only the writer but also the divine author, since he clearly acquiesced in that.

---

1. In no sense does this literary background undermine Scripture's authority (except insofar as we try to argue for its authority based in something that does not exist and for the most part never did exist). Nor does it undermine the Bible's "inerrancy," provided that, by that, we simply mean its entire trustworthiness and reliability as the inspired word of God that he intended us to have in the form that we have it (which is therefore "mistake-free" from his perspective).

2. Parables *are* true, but in a different way (which we will come to).

It's hardly holding Scripture itself in the highest regard, either, since the genre is a built-in feature of the inspired text. To assume that what the biblical writers wrote should be interpreted in accordance with our literary expectations is de facto saying that our genres are superior to their genres (or that ours are what theirs ought to have been). Perhaps most importantly, ignoring or misreading the genre is likely to distort the meaning and miss the point.

Things do get a tad more complicated, insofar as one book can quite easily—and frequently does—include more than one genre within it. In the Gospels, for example, at a minimum we encounter narrative (a story), history (events that actually occurred), parables (made-up stories used for teaching purposes), overstatement and hyperbole (exaggerations, as attention grabbers), idioms (jargon, sayings, and euphemisms), instructions (commands), and prophecy (forward-looking statements concerning future events). There's even song lyrics (but sadly, no tune) in Mary's song, in Luke 1.

Even within a genre, there are significant differences in the writing styles and vocabularies used by different authors—as indeed is the case today. Even when the subject matters are ostensibly the same, a children's book is written differently from an adult book and an academic book is written differently from a popular book. When Nicholas Thomas Wright writes academic Christian books, he is N. T. Wright; when it's a popular book, he's the more folksy Tom Wright. His vocabulary and content is fashioned accordingly.

Writing styles and vocabulary can also tell us about origins. Tradition associated the authorship of the book of Hebrews with the apostle Paul, but in due course, as knowledge of the ancient Greek language and writing styles of that era increased, by comparing the language and style of Hebrews with the known Pauline Epistles, biblical scholars were able to establish that Paul was not its author (he remains anonymous).

Perhaps the easiest way to think about why (and how) genre affects understanding is to compare different sports. If we go to a sports event for the first time, we are highly unlikely to know what's going on if we have no idea of the rules of the game. Some of what we see may—rightly or wrongly—seem quite intuitive (dare I say, obvious) at least on the surface, but a good deal of what's going on may remain a mystery, even if we have watched that same sport many times. What we can't do—especially if we're wanting to tell others what's happening—is to just guess, or assume that it corresponds with what we know from elsewhere about something else. If we suppose that the rules of football apply to the game of rugby, or try to play cricket the way that baseball is played, we will cross numerous foul lines. We will at best be laughed at and at worst be asked to stand down. So, too, biblical genres have interpretive "rules of the game" that come with them, with which we need to "fit in" and conform to, if we are to pronounce on what's happening on the field of play with any measure of assurance.

The Meaning of "the Meaning"

Before we go into the various genres, we need to take a moment to revisit the meaning of a text or passage. At its simplest level, this is simply to ask the author the question, "What do you mean?" So far so, good; except that in the case of the Bible we do not have the authors available to answer that for us (at least not this side of eternity).[3] All we can do is to aim for the next best thing: to reconstruct what they likely had in mind, as best we can determine that from the various hermeneutical tools available to us, just one of which is, of course, genre.

When a preacher uses a phrase such as "So what the apostle Paul is saying here is . . ." we need to realize that this may simply mean, "Well, that's what I assumed it meant when I prepped the sermon. It reads like that to me. And it fits very well with what I want to talk about this morning." The problem is that this is fraught with the potential to be "reading into" a passage a meaning that *isn't* there (which is called eisegesis) rather than "drawing out" from a passage a meaning that is there (which is called exegesis).

But is that preacher *really* that wrong? After all, many of us will have been part of a midweek home group "Bible study" where, having read a passage, everyone shares in turn "what this passage means to me" or is "saying to me." The group's contributions may or may not bear any resemblance to what the apostle Paul had in mind. They are not wrong, as such, *but they're talking about something different*. None of the group is talking about "the" meaning of the passage—in terms that the author would relate to—but rather something "meaningful" that they, personally, have drawn

---

3. If I can get an appointment in heaven to meet with him, I have a whole host of questions for the apostle Paul. He will probably be very busy putting straight a number of scholars and theologians on a host of interpretive points (I can give him a list to work from), but I guess with all eternity available I can be content to wait in line.

from it; something that they find significant for their life. *Which may or may not bear any relationship to the author's intended meaning.*

To the extent that "what this means to me" is the Holy Spirit "breathing out" of the passage (inspiring *us*) then it's entirely valid from a personal devotional perspective. Indeed, within reason that need bear no resemblance to that original meaning.[4] But it is *not* "the" meaning. This is what people are really getting at when they say, "What this means to you is not necessarily what it means to me." Please don't confuse that with unbridled postmodern relativism. It's rather like what draws someone to become a Christian: it may be any one of a number of aspects of the good news of Jesus that causes them to decide to commit their life to him. "What drew me, may not be what drew you," is the reality we see in listening to new believers' testimonies.

One way of illustrating this might be to think of a piece of art—a painting, or a poem, perhaps. The artist will have meaning in mind, but he or she also invites the audience to find meaning *for themselves* in it and through it: "I love that painting because . . ." In that context, meaning can indeed mean almost anything. But that does *not* apply when it comes to a biblical text, where what a person *finds* meaningful is to be distinguished from its meaning.

The process to arrive at a text's meaning is to determine (as best we can) what it would have meant—what it would have been "saying"—to the original author and their audience. This requires us to leave our world behind and immerse ourselves in the biblical writers' world—their place and time, their concerns, their reasons for writing, how what they wrote would have been "heard" in their context, and why they wrote what they did, using the words, ideas, and idioms that they did. This includes taking full account of the original authors' worldview. In most cases, this will have been a contemporaneous Jewish worldview, but in all cases it will have been an ancient world worldview. (A worldview is all of the things about life—"the way things are"—that are taken to be "obvious" by people in a place and time, so much so, that they rarely if ever need to be articulated.) In inspiring Scripture, God did not bypass the writers' worldview, he worked with it and within it—he accommodated it in order to be able to communicate meaningfully into that time and place

---

4. By "within reason" what I mean is that this "meaning for me"—or "what it's saying to me"—that we are finding in a passage must correspond to the nature and character of God that we see in Jesus; for example, in terms of morality, behavior, ethics, and so on. It's only from the Holy Spirit if it does.

(God may be timeless, but the people he was working with were not, so divine pragmatism was unavoidable).

Beware talking about something called "the biblical worldview"—which you may often hear preachers doing—because although there is a sense in which it can be valid, that which is timeless in Scripture (and hence could be considered to be part of a "biblical worldview") first needs to be disentangled from that which was time bound within the writers' worldview. In other words, based on what we now know (but they didn't) would they still have said what they said? Would we (or would we not) say something different about that now? We should never only be interested in *what* the Bible says, but also *why* the Bible said it.

Once we have determined (as best we can) what something would have meant—what it would have been "saying" to the original author and audience, and why—then we can move on to the quite separate question of what it means (what it's saying) to us. Which might be exactly the same, or something similar, based on the same principles or values, or . . . nothing. That last possibility is not as radical as it may sound; it's simply to say that while everything in the Bible is *for* us, not everything was *written to* us. Not all truth in the Bible is timeless; some is time bound. We are not supposed to "copy and paste" anything or everything from then to now with minds in neutral; that is not biblical faithfulness, it's just foolishness.

One final thought relates to the meaning we find in Scripture more generally. All readers bring their own perspectives and concerns with them when they approach a text; none of us comes to it entirely neutrally in what we expect to find. So, for example, readers for whom "kingdom theology" operates disproportionately as a primary hermeneutical lens will tend to see "kingdom" in everything (even, at times, when it isn't there), because it fits well with their community's expectations. So, too, Calvinist readers, Arminian readers, conservative readers (theologically and culturally), feminist readers, liberationist readers, Pentecostal readers, LGBT-affirming readers, and many others, will all find themes, meanings, and interpretive conclusions that are consonant with the perspective of their particular community. It is as good as impossible to detach ourselves from our presuppositions, even if we might wish to.

Moreover, to be included within a community typically requires that a reader be constrained by the perspective and interpretive expectations of that community. Rarely in the popular Christian world is interpretive diversity genuinely welcomed, even when that diversity is within the boundaries of Christian orthodoxy. Which is a great shame, since to engage with the insights of scholars and theologians who do not "think like us" is both enriching and challenging. It's how we learn, and how we grow.

In this Part II, we will address the most prominent genres found in Scripture and which are the most interesting from a Bible reader's point of view. There are of course other rhetorical devices that we should be on the lookout for, such as irony, assonance (similar sounding words placed together—in the original languages, not the English!), puns (wordplay), tropes (such as metaphor, synecdoche, and metonymy), and euphemisms (for example, in relation to matters of death, sex, and bodily functions, a tendency we see in languages to this day).

1

Narrative/History

THIS CATEGORY OF WRITING that we might call "stories" comprises the majority of Scripture. The word "narrative" is preferable, however, because we tend to think of stories as works of fiction, like "bedtime stories," and hence not "true" stories. Self-evidently, the Bible is historical writing; we shall come on to its relationship to "history," as we use that term today.

In order to be interpreting narrative well, we need to be aware of how it was understood in the authors' world—what mattered to them in that category; how they defined it. Our interest is in the literary conventions of their day, to which the biblical writers necessarily conformed in what they wrote, and which the presence of a divine author "behind the scenes," as it were, did not overturn. The Holy Spirit's contribution to the inspired text did not include superimposing twenty-first-century literary conventions for our benefit, to meet our expectations as contemporary readers. What the biblical writers wrote must be received, from a genre perspective, on their terms, without demanding that it conforms to our ways of thinking nowadays.

Narrative in the Bible is invariably the setting for its teachings; stories are the contexts in which truths and commands are conveyed (for example, Torah is given in the setting of the Israelites' rescue from slavery in Egypt and deliverance to a promised land). It is not a series of sermons. All of its individual stories form part of one big story, compiled with one aim throughout: to explain who God is and his relationship with people, especially *his* people. It's a historical account, set in history, but its historical aims are subsidiary to its theological aims, so its material is organized accordingly. This means it is selective in both content and chronology, happily allowing "gaps" in time (in, for example, family trees). It is not a transcript of 24/7 CCTV recordings of all of the persons and events in those places and times, any more than was the case for Winston Churchill's four-volume *History of the English Speaking Peoples*. In addition, the writers serve as expert commentators interpreting for the reader or hearer the significance of the people and events whose stories they recount. Though the Bible is framed around the stories of people, and includes the tales of many biblical heroes, it always ultimately revolves around God. He is the central character; he is the ultimate hero of every story.

> Old Testament narratives are not just stories about people who lived in Old Testament times. They are first and foremost stories about what God did to and through these people. In contrast to human narratives, the Bible is composed especially of divine narratives.[1]

So far, so good; and so far, uncontroversial, one would think. But when it comes to the Old Testament, in particular, we encounter our first big shock. Though presented to us in historical accounts, the narrative genre seamlessly blends "history" as we nowadays would define it—namely, real people and real events that actually happened exactly as presented—with elements of folklore and legend. This is most obviously true of matters that are clearly not eyewitness accounts, such as the days of creation in Gen 1.

Mention of some of the Bible reflecting folklore and legend (or, "myth," which is a technical literary term but tends to be thought of today as fiction pretending to be fact)[2] tends to sound alarm bells for us as modern readers, since we are very focused on something being "true" as opposed to "false." The implication of something being "untrue," of course, is that it is intended to deceive. The controversy over what we now know as "fake news" illustrates that.

---

1. Fee and Stuart, *How to Read the Bible*, 75.

2. There are technical distinctions between these three terms that scholars ague about but need not concern us here.

And yet, such concerns really begin with misreading the genre that we're talking about—applying a modern lens to what we are reading.

In parables, for example, everyone knows that they are "made-up" teaching stories. They convey truth, but not because of the actuality of the persons and events. They teach truths that are true, but they don't use statements of fact as their vehicle.

So what is the difference between a parable (an obviously "made-up" story that is nonetheless teaching truths) and some of the Old Testament stories? Only that the parabolical features are blended with the historical features, genre-wise. The stories are not so "obviously" made-up, in how they are presented.

The key thing to keep in the forefront of our thinking about this genre is that it is equally as divinely inspired as any strictly "historical" narrative. The elements of traditional folklore, legend, and myth in Old Testament accounts that originated in the oral history of Israel and were ultimately committed to writing as inspired Scripture were deeply significant for who they were as a people and who their God was. And not just significant but, thanks to the storied manner in which they were conveyed, easily memorable—in the same way that parables such as the good Samaritan, the lost sheep, and the prodigal son are memorable. As a modern audience, we may struggle to cope with this genre if we are fixed on the necessity of everything that is presented to us as "history" having necessarily to conform precisely to "real" people and events in the way we define things today.[3]

To suggest examples from history of stories that have been memorialized as similarly significant for who a people group are—and see themselves as aspiring to be—is a potentially risky venture, but in the case of English history we might think of the story of Robin Hood. Here we see folklore and legend so deeply intertwined with elements of history, through many centuries of transmission, that it is impossible to now separate them. However, the key thing is that the significance of the story of Robin Hood is not dependent on its precise correspondence to an identifiable "real" person or events.

In relation to Scripture, the reality is that until the last few hundred years or so there was no reason for most people to think very much about these things. No one knew any better about where human life came from, so the biblical account was as good as any other; why would a good

---

3. The problem comes not from the text itself but from the expectations that modern readers (usually unconsciously) impose on the text.

Christian not simply "believe" in Adam and Eve as historical fact? But the discoveries of modern science and historical study meant that the previously taken-for-granted definition of "history" as presented in the Old Testament had to be rethought (for example, the age of the earth and the origins of the universe). For sure, some of this perceived need to rethink things was influenced by an Enlightenment skepticism concerning the divine role, but by no means all. Fundamentalists, of course, found the whole thing deeply unsettling and reacted by asserting the necessity of the continuing historical accuracy of everything in the Bible, in strident terms. The "literal" truth of Scripture concerning "scientific" statements became a hill to die on, or at least a line in the sand not to be crossed for fear of the slippery-slope consequences.

To identify the genre of biblical narrative as a blending of history and legend does not mean it's a newfangled modern idea that should be opposed as part of a culture wars battle for biblical truth (as fundamentalists tend to see things). The simple fact is that it's only in modern times that we have found the need to think about it; the question didn't previously arise. In reality, there is no need for us to relate to the stories any differently—we are still concerned for the theological truths we find there—we just have to loosen our grip on a previously assumed complete factuality in the conveying vehicle.

When it comes to the New Testament, things are rather different. The events recorded are more recent in time. Their basis in history as we define it today is more tangible. Nonetheless, some factors that we have observed in relation to Old Testament narratives do still pertain, not least concerning matters where the ancient world worldview is self-evidently being reflected. So, too, in the writers' selective choice of material (for example, as John tells us in John 21:25, "Jesus also did many other things. If they were all written down, I suppose the whole world could not contain the books that would be written") and the details and perspectives that they chose to include.

In *A Basic Guide to Interpreting the Bible*, Robert H. Stein comments helpfully as follows:

> The interpretation of biblical narrative presents some unique problems. This is especially true for those who deny the historicity of the events recorded in them. If, however, the meaning of a biblical narrative is determined by the communicative intent of the author, then the historicity or lack of historicity of the events recorded in it does not in any way change the meaning of the

account. The account means what the author willed to say by the account, whether the event described in it is true or untrue. Thus both critical and evangelical scholars can work together in seeking to understand the meaning of biblical narratives.[4]

We should finish with a few words on the book of Acts. Though it serves as a continuation of the Gospels—especially Luke's Gospel, since he is the author of both—we tend to read Acts rather differently; or perhaps I should say, we tend to apply it differently.

> We seldom think of the Old Testament histories as setting biblical precedents for our own lives. On the other hand, this is the normal way for Christians to read Acts. It not only tells us the history of the early church, but it also serves as the normative model for the church of all times. And this is precisely our hermeneutical difficulty.
>
> By and large, most sectors of evangelical Protestantism have a "restoration movement" mentality. We regularly look back to the church and Christian experience in the first century either as the norm to be restored or the ideal to be approximated. Thus we often say things like, "Acts plainly teaches us that. . . ." However, it seems obvious that not all of the "plain teaching" is equally plain to all.[5]

The question of "application," in a nutshell, is whether what we see in Acts is being presented to us as a pattern to which all churches everywhere should seek to correspond and indeed, to which all Christians' individual experiences should expect to correspond. Is Luke simply *describing* what *did* happen in certain places and times, or *prescribing* what should happen in every place and time? And even if Luke has in mind that he's presenting a *norm*, are we to take that as *normative*?

Fee and Stuart propose that our assumption should be that "unless Scripture explicitly tells us we must do something, what is merely narrated or described can never function in a normative way."[6] I think they are essentially correct in this, though I would propose an exception. In early Acts, I think it not unreasonable to infer that Luke is presenting the Jerusalem church as a model of what "being" the church (as opposed to the modern idea of "going to" church) looked like in the period

---

4. Stein, *Basic Guide*, 97.
5. Fee and Stuart, *How to Read the Bible*, 75.
6. Fee and Stuart, *How to Read the Bible*, 97.

immediately after Jesus. Acts is offering us a window on what "church" was like for the people who knew him personally, led by the people who were his close friends—who knew his teaching, who knew what mattered to him, and who wanted to be a community that reflected him. The two paradigmatic passages I have in mind are Acts 2:42–47 and 4:32–35 (both NLT), which together read:

> All the believers devoted themselves to the apostles' teaching, and to fellowship, and to sharing in meals (including the Lord's Supper), and to prayer. A deep sense of awe came over them all, and the apostles performed many miraculous signs and wonders. And all the believers met together in one place and shared everything they had. They sold their property and possessions and shared the money with those in need. They worshiped together at the Temple each day, met in homes for the Lord's Supper, and shared their meals with great joy and generosity—all the while praising God and enjoying the goodwill of all the people. And each day the Lord added to their fellowship those who were being saved.
>
> All the believers were united in heart and mind. And they felt that what they owned was not their own, so they shared everything they had. The apostles testified powerfully to the resurrection of the Lord Jesus, and God's great blessing was upon them all. There were no needy people among them because those who owned land or houses would sell them and bring the money to the apostles to give to those in need.

I don't think it's necessary to draw up church membership rules based on what we read here, but I do think we need to firstly recognize and then secondly aspire to the values that underlie the picture that Luke paints of being and doing church together, not least because it wholly undermines the individualistic modern assumption that being a Christian is all about (and really only about) "me and Jesus," which confuses a personal relationship with an individual relationship. In the collective, group-centered worldview of the Bible, today's rampant individualism would have been unthinkable. The church as described in early Acts is the necessary antidote.

I stress that I am looking at these passages as offering us exemplars of values to be lived out in community, not instructions to be institutionalized as membership rules. But it would mean a church with the following characteristics:

- "Devoting themselves." The Greek word is in a present continuous tense: they were "continually devoting themselves"—they "kept on devoting themselves."

- As Jewish believers, they didn't need teaching about the God of Israel and his ways. The "apostles' teaching" was therefore *teaching about Jesus* from those who knew him personally—who he was; what he was like; what was important to him; how he understood the nature and character of God; and how to be like him (cf. Matt 28:20).

- Sharing Jesus-centered meals together, in one another's homes—extending generous hospitality and friendship.

- Not just open homes but open pocketbooks, too—sacrificial generosity, reflecting a profound love toward others.

- Prioritizing worshiping together, including communion/the Eucharist.

- A focus on "one-ness" in heart and mind, united in Spirit (cf. Eph 4:3–4).[7]

- The almost inevitable popularity of this kind of church in its surrounding community, its almost inevitable resultant growth, and the blessing of God that surely comes when a church reflects his heart in these kinds of ways.

I have not highlighted miraculous signs and wonders in this list, not because we ought not to have a heart to see them but because we are not their architects in the same way. We can and should be expectant and desirous, but *we* cannot "make" them a characteristic of church, as we can the above.

Although the full title of the book is the Acts of the Apostles, we might well wonder as we read through it whether it shouldn't be the Acts of the Holy Spirit, since he is the main character. The moving of the Holy Spirit is the first key theme we see (one that continues throughout). The second key theme is a progression of the extension of the messianic kingdom from Jerusalem into Judea and Samaria. And the third is the inclusion of the gentiles in the people of God through Jesus (bypassing the need to become Jewish through Torah).

---

7. Rather than evangelicalism's tendency to focus on one-ness in matters of doctrine (agreement on certain secondary beliefs) as its basis of acceptance and unity.

The picture that Luke paints reflects the fulfillment of the resurrected Jesus' words in Acts 1:8: "You will receive power when the Holy Spirit comes on you; and you will be my witnesses in Jerusalem, and in all Judea and Samaria, and to the ends of the earth." In each case, that this extension and inclusion is God's plan and purpose is evidenced and confirmed by the outpouring of the Holy Spirit.

Contrary to the assumptions of the early Pentecostals, Acts is not offering a timeless chronology for Spirit-reception by individuals becoming Christians (first for regeneration, second for empowerment) and nor for that matter was the day of Pentecost an example of the gift of speaking in tongues per 1 Cor 12 and 14.[8]

---

8. Acts 2:5–11 could not be clearer: "Now there were staying in Jerusalem God-fearing Jews from every nation under heaven. When they heard this sound, a crowd came together in bewilderment, because each one *heard their own language being spoken*. Utterly amazed, they asked: 'Aren't all these who are speaking Galileans? Then how is it that each of us *hears them in our native language*? . . . We hear them declaring the wonders of God *in our own tongues!*'"

— 2 —

Commandments

COMMANDMENTS ARE PART OF a biblical genre known as law. This can be rather confusing for several reasons. Firstly, at times the whole of what we know as the Old Testament is spoken of as the Law (for example, by Jesus, in John 10:34, where the phrase he cites from "in the Law" is actually from Ps 82:6). Secondly, the Law is used to speak of Genesis through Deuteronomy, otherwise called the Pentateuch (though none of the commandments are in Genesis). And thirdly, for most Christians the idea of "law" is very negative. Since the Reformation, it has been associated with legalism; the Reformers read Paul in Galatians and Romans as calling out both Jewish legalism and human legalistic tendencies, trying to please God (get to heaven) by our own efforts rather than by the grace of God and Christ's work alone. However, the circumstances of sixteenth-century Catholicism that the Reformers rightly challenged were not those of first-century Judaism to which they were wrong to draw close comparison. The law never worked like that. Practicing the law was, for faithful Jews, their heartfelt response to God's gracious initiative in inviting Israel to be his people.

Giving the law to Israel was God's initiative; it was his law, not Moses' law. It was given as a comprehensive framework for "how to live right" as a nation under God, to a gaggle of former slaves who had grown up in slavery and had no land or laws of their own. It was a fast track answer to living as the people of God.¹ All nations have laws, and Israel needed them too; they embraced both individual behavior, religious behavior, and civil behavior. Before the modern era, all societal governance commingled what we would now call the secular with the religious. This had nothing to do with legalism, Jewish or otherwise.

It is unfortunate that the word Torah (the Old Testament commandments to Israel) is usually translated as "law," since although that's correct as a technical term for the genre, in the popular Christian imagination it's all too easily associated, negatively, with legalism. Torah actually means teaching, instruction, or guidance.

If there is a $64,000 question that springs to mind for any Christian when it comes to the commandments in Scripture, it has to be, "Which ones apply to me?" If God has seen fit to include instructions—"Do these things; don't do those things"—addressed to humanity (or at least, to believers; those who want to be included in the people of God and be on good terms with him) then we surely need to take those instructions seriously. So which ones . . . ?

We know that the Christian Bible has always included both Old and New Testaments. Evangelical statements of faith invariably include language such as the following (taken from the UK Evangelical Alliance's "Basis of Faith"): "We believe in the divine inspiration and supreme authority of the Old and New Testament Scriptures, which are the written Word of God—fully trustworthy for faith and conduct."² No distinction is made here between the Old and the New. So it would be logical to start from the assumption that all biblical commandments apply to us, cover to cover. But very soon we run into problems, especially if we are somewhat squeamish: the Old Testament commandments concerning animal sacrifices! Even with a priest on hand to do it for us, it's a very unpleasant thought. Fortunately, we are rescued by the fact that the prescribed place to make those sacrifices was the temple in Jerusalem (before that, the tabernacle, a mobile temple-tent which preceded it), but neither exists any more.

Of course I am being slightly facetious here, since most Christians know that the sacrificial system was "old covenant" (as it's routinely called)—to do with the biblical nation of Israel—and doesn't apply to "new covenant" believers in the light of Jesus' sacrificial life, death, and

---

1. In particular—and many of the commandments directly reflected this—*not* to be living like the Egyptians (the land they'd come from) or the Canaanites (the land they were going to). See Lev 18:1–5.

2. Evangelical Alliance, "Basis of Faith."

resurrection. Which suggests that *none* of the Old Testament commands apply to us, since they were *all* given by God within the context of the covenant relationship with Israel. And basically, that's the right way to think about Old Testament commandments: that none of them apply to us per se. The very worst way of thinking about Old Testament commandments is to try to separate the ones we think we should be obeying from those we think we shouldn't (and still less to be selecting on the basis of how appealing or unappealing they are).

The reason for the *per se* above is that there is an "exception" of sorts—when a commandment found in the Old Testament is explicitly restated in the New Testament. But rather than its purpose being to muddy the waters in terms of whether Old Testament commandments do maybe still apply,[3] that "restatement" is really a fresh statement of a specific New Testament expectation. The new covenant has covenantal expectations just like the covenants that preceded it chronologically. So bottom line, our focus as Christians today can and should be on what is said in the New Testament, without trying to also dust down and repurpose a selection from the Old Testament (however worthy we think some of them might be).

It's a category error to think that the new covenant is a "do what you like, anything goes, because you are 'not under law'" kind of arrangement. All ancient covenants had expectations of the parties to them, and so too does the new covenant. Of course we are not saved by what we do, but being already saved by grace *into a covenant relationship* means we gladly take on board God's covenant expectations—assuming, of course, that we have understood what it means to be saved in the first place. Getting our hands on a Get out of Hell Free card to keep in our back pocket in case we might need it one day does not count.

However . . . the New Testament is somewhat inconvenient in failing to group those expectations in one place. It's something to be aware of if ever you are tempted to describe the Bible as "God's Instruction Manual" for human life. To avoid embarrassment, be prepared for someone asking

---

3. We are not expected to search the Greek text for "echoes," "hints," and "allusions" to Old Testament commandments that are "as good as" restatements. The New Testament writers guided by the Holy Spirit were perfectly able to be explicit in relation to an Old Testament commandment if and where they wanted to be. The danger in searching for "echoes," "hints," and "allusions" would be that we find the ones we want to find and miss the ones we don't. As Fee and Stuart put it, "Only that which is *explicitly renewed* from the Old Testament law can be considered part of the New Testament 'law of Christ' (cf. Galatians 6:2)." *How to Read the Bible*, 139 (emphasis added).

you to show them where the instructions are. The rabbis counted in the Old Testament and came up with a list of 613 commandments; are we supposed to do the same in the New Testament?

I took a time-out to Google the question: "How many commandments are there in the New Testament?" The first result came from an organization based in Australia. They identified a list of... wait for it... 1,050![4] So much for the idea that only Old Testament faith was legalistic![5] Since this was clearly an unsatisfactory answer, I concluded it had to be wrong and scrolled down; the next search result was a more reasonable sounding 684, though still rather a lot to have to remember.

To have any chance whatsoever of fulfilling so many expectations, it would seem necessary to try to establish some kind of hierarchy, to identify the main New Testament commandments, under which other (less important) ones could be grouped. I think there is a process that we are invited to follow, beginning with some things that Jesus said in the Gospels; not because the rest of the New Testament is any less Scripture, but because the Jesus of the Gospels was and is the mediator of the new covenant (Heb 9:15). He is the Word of God in person (per John 1). Acts and the Epistles may be thought of more as divinely inspired commentary and application.

First off, Jesus reminds us in John 14:15 of how covenants work: "If you love me, you will keep my commandments." That still leaves us with, "Which ones *are* those?" but I think we see a framework emerging with John 13:34 (NLT): "I am giving you a new commandment: Love each other. Just as I have loved you, you should love each other." How did Jesus love people? Generously, sacrificially, faithfully, servant-heartedly, and graciously.

That seems like a good start. And not least because it fits well with something Jesus said about the Old Testament commandments. When asked which was the most important, he famously answered as follows in Matt 22:35–40 (and parallels):

> "Love the Lord your God with all your heart and with all your soul and with all your mind." This is the first and greatest commandment. And the second is like it: "Love your neighbor as yourself."

---

4. Christian Assemblies International, "1,050 New Testament Commandments."
5. It wasn't legalistic, but it's typically been presumed to be.

Perhaps most relevantly is what he added as a postscript: "All the Law and the Prophets *hang on* these two commandments." Which is effectively saying that you can group all the others—every other divine expectation—under these two. *The rest of the 613 are simply contextual examples of fulfilling one or both of them.*[6] So a helpful test for us is to ask ourselves how a proposed application of any commandment in Scripture—anything we are minded to insist upon as "the Bible says"—will advance those two: loving God and loving people. Now of course this only gets us so far, in that the context in which Jesus was being asked that "Which is the most important?" question was the covenant in Torah. But it seems entirely reasonable to suppose—given that the same God who is unchanging in nature and character is the author of both old and new covenants—that he would envisage all of the New Testament commandments hanging on those two as well. Perhaps with one variation—one upgrade, if you like—which is replacing Lev 19:18 ("Love your neighbor *as yourself*") with the John 13:34 commandment that we mentioned a moment ago ("Love one another *as I have loved you*").

Why? Because, *before* the coming of Jesus, commanding a John 13:34 kind of love wasn't an option. But *with* the coming of Jesus, love for others was taken to a new level. Previously, the "as yourself" bit put a brake on the extent to which love went (the point at which love showed to others would be no longer loving yourself as well). For example, in Luke 3:11, "If you have two coats, give one away," is loving your neighbor as yourself (one coat each). But a John 13:34 kind of love would say that if Jesus had *just one* coat and his brother was in need, he would still give that away.

One final question—given that we're talking about there being 613 commandments in the Old Testament, plus 1,050, or 684, or however many it is, in the New Testament—is how those lists can possibly cover all situations and circumstances that people find themselves in, then or now. And the reality is, of course, that they can't . . . *and they were never intended to*. It is an error to insist on a universal application based on "the Bible says" without asking the why question and considering the particular circumstances. The commandments were never intended as a static list of a "Because I say so" variety, but as a dynamic frame of reference for making wise ethical decisions. The rabbis were regularly being asked that

---

6. I think the reason Jesus cited two, when he was only asked for one, is because from God's perspective they are effectively one and the same; they are two sides of the same coin. We cannot be loving God if we are not loving people.

kind of question—"What should I do?"—and would offer counsel based on relevant provisions in Torah. These served as a "test" book rather than a "textbook" to apply by rote.[7] Torah's commandments were, as the psalmist said, "a lamp to my feet and a light to my path" (Ps 119:105).

Jesus never rewrote Torah—indeed he specifically said in Matt 5:18 that "until heaven and earth pass away, not the smallest letter or stroke shall pass from the Law"—but he did interpret and apply it differently. His applications were people first, not law first.[8] He explained this memorably in Mark 2:27 (NLT): "The Sabbath was made to meet the needs of people, and not people to meet the requirements of the Sabbath." Many of Jesus' arguments with Pharisees and experts in the law were about harsh, oppressive application of Torah (plus their own add-ons), de facto weaponizing it against the ordinary people in the misguided belief that loving God was fulfilled through loving the law. In contrast, Jesus saw loving God as fulfilled through loving the people. Hence, "You have heard it said, but I say to you . . ." The intended lens for the application of commandments was compassion.

In Matt 12:7, Jesus quotes Hos 6:6: "I desire mercy, not sacrifice." It's easy to miss the significance of that statement (for both Hosea and Jesus). Commandments to do with sacrifices were at the very center of Israel's worship, a fundamental component of the law. This profound Scripture is saying that mercy *overrides* commandments, if mercy is not equally or more present. This, then, serves as another New Testament commandment: make sure that the way you apply any commandment prioritizes mercy. James 2:12–13: "Speak and act as those who are going to be judged by the law that gives freedom, because judgment without mercy will be shown to anyone who has not been merciful. Mercy triumphs over judgment." The goal of both the Word and the words is to be life enhancing,[9] not life oppressing.

---

7. For example, Exod 18:13–26.
8. For example, Matt 12:1–8.
9. John 10:10.

— 3 —

Parables

SOME OF JESUS' MOST well-known teaching, within and without church circles, comes in the form of parables. Parables were by no means unique to Jesus; they were a way of teaching used by other Jewish rabbis. They come to us in various forms (there are different views as to how one defines "a parable") ranging from simple idiomatic sayings, though metaphors, to short stories (occasionally quite a long one, such as the parable of the prodigal son). What they have in common is to be painting a picture with words—so-called "picture language"—to convey a truth or truths and by doing so engage the hearers more effectively than simply stating propositions.

For our purposes, we will focus on a central definition of parables along the following lines: a parable is a made-up story featuring archetypal characters and contexts of a kind that would be familiar to the hearers from everyday life, engaging their attention and imagination, and challenging them to reflect and act upon the underlying truth that the parable teller intends the story to convey.

The first and most important thing to grasp in the interpretation of parables—and this can hardly be stressed too much—is that the story has an obvious "surface" meaning (which is *never* the point) and a less-obvious "deeper" underlying meaning which is *actually* the point. The idea was for the hearers to figure out the deeper meaning since *that* was the teaching. The teaching is *not* in the surface features of the story; they are just the props and the stage setting. In the parable of the sower, the point is not for farmers to take care where they sow seeds (it's not teaching agricultural truths), and in the parable of the lost sheep, the point is not to offer comfort for shepherds considering abandoning their flocks on Galilean hillsides while they go off to look for a lost one (it's not teaching husbandry truths). Watch out for the tendency to misread parables by unwittingly exegeting surface features.

The extent to which the meaning of Jesus' parables was intended to be concealed from the hearers should not be overstated based on Matt 13:13–14 (and parallels). In many cases, we see the meaning and application explained. For sure, though, to really grasp Jesus' intentions requires (a) an engagement of the heart as well as the mind, and (b) locating the "message" of the parable in harmony with his other teaching. The meaning may well be concealed—in the sense of missed—by the casual hearer who can't be bothered to engage.

Does a parable have one teaching point or more than one? Yes and no! The idea of a single "point" to a parable came about as a much-needed corrective to an over-allegorization of parables in the premodern era in which a multitude of supposed equivalences were identified ("this" means "that," to warp factor ten) which could not possibly have occurred to either Jesus or his followers as anything to do with the parable's intended "meaning."

But that said, in the parable of the prodigal son, there are surely equally valid teaching points that Jesus intended in relation to the younger son, the older brother, and, perhaps most of all, the father. Our best course usually is to seek to identify "the main" point in a parable, but also to be open to additional points, while avoiding those being too abstract, far-fetched, or strained in relation to how the original hearers would have heard what it was and wasn't saying.

In terms of a parable's meaning, we start from our standard definition of the meaning of anything we read in the Bible: the meaning that was intended by the original author as that would have been understood by the original audience. To which as always we need to add a postscript: *as best we can reconstruct that*, taking account of all of the hermeneutical tools at our disposal (such as context, language, and genre). And here we come to the biggest single challenge that we have as interpreters of parables. The stories feature characters and contexts of a kind that would be familiar to the original hearers from everyday life. But we are very far removed from them. It is extremely hard for us to "hear" the references to the characters and events as they would have heard them. For example, in the parable of the good Samaritan, for us the Samaritan is obviously the hero. To speak of someone as a good Samaritan is to pay them a huge compliment: respect! But nothing could be further from how the word "Samaritan" would have been heard by Jesus' audience. Samaritans were the lowest of the low: heretical, mongrel-Jews, worse than pagan gentiles, held in utter contempt. In Luke 10:37, when Jesus asks the expert in the law to tell him who the (surely by now, obvious) hero is, the man cannot even bring himself to say, "the Samaritan" (instead he says, "The one who had mercy"). When some of Jesus' enemies are looking to find the worst insults they can throw at him in John 8:48, they say, "Aren't we right in saying that you are a Samaritan and demon-possessed?" Our lack of familiarity with the biblical world is our single biggest obstacle when it comes to reading parables well. What would it have meant (what would it have been saying, how would it have been heard) by those people, then? Quite often with a parable, if we do not find at least something in it a bit odd, or even shocking, then we may need to be working a bit harder to find it.

Speaking of the risk of reading badly, let's pause for a moment on one aspect in our working definition, "featuring archetypal characters and contexts of a kind that would be familiar to the hearers from everyday life." This does not mean that they are real or true. When a preacher uses a story or characters from, say, Star Wars to illustrate a truth, she is simply using a modern parable as a vehicle. The communicative power of the illustration relies on the fact that the congregation will be familiar with the movies. She is not teaching express or implied truths about outer space, far-flung galaxies, or space travel; it's just a stage setting.

The same is true when it comes to characters and events in Jesus' parables. For example—and this is an important example, given how influential what it *isn't* teaching has been in evangelical thinking about hell—the parable of Abraham, Lazarus, and the (unnamed) rich man in Luke 16. The parable is set in Hades, which was understood not as "hell" (as evangelicals generally understand it) but simply "the realm of the dead." However, the popularly assumed meaning is that the parable is describing what happens in hell. But that is reading the "surface." The intended "deeper" meaning of the parable is that there are consequences in the afterlife to the choices we make in this life, especially in how we treat others.

Since this life was known to be "unfair" (cheats do prosper, rich and powerful abusers do get away with it, and so on) the Jewish understanding was that at the end of life God would ensure there was a "balancing of the books" in favor of those who are life's victims, along with adverse consequences for those who are the abusers. Jesus setting a parable "in Hades" simply reflects the widespread cultural assumptions of the day about what happens after death (a bit like we might use "standing at the Pearly Gates" in a sermon—as I for one have done). Jesus is not teaching facts about hell (notice that Abraham is also there, within speaking distance) and nor is he teaching that somewhere called Hades really does exist as a kind of transit lounge on the way to heaven or hell (and these are the things that happen there). It's simply a stage setting. If we are unfamiliar with Hades in the popular imagination of that first-century world, we will miss the point, and especially if we assume that Hades = hell (as the KJV translated it, but most modern versions quite rightly no longer do).

Separating the teaching truth from the vehicle it is conveyed in is important. A further example would be the parable of the unjust steward (a rich man's business manager) in Luke 16, where the principal character is an embezzler. Though it's the parable's setting, it is not encouraging fraud against one's employer as a shrewd way of behaving; it's simply a vehicle for the truth that it *is* teaching.

Why did Jesus so often teach through parables, picture language, and metaphor? Mainly for the same reasons that the Bible is mostly narrative. Especially in an oral culture, stories are easy to remember, and therefore to pass on. They also engage the imagination in a way that facts and propositional truth statements do not. And they encourage relational dialogue in debating their meaning.

A notable feature of Jesus' parables is a focus on the kingdom of God (or as Matthew says it, the kingdom of heaven). In a sense, all of his parables are about the kingdom, insofar as his coming inaugurated the kingdom; it arrived in his person. However, several parables are explicitly introduced with "The kingdom is like . . ."—likened *to* something, in a metaphorical sense. It's therefore essential to understand what the kingdom is and isn't when reading these parables (see chapter 9 of Part I).

A few closing thoughts on parables.

The first is that we should beware not only of overinterpreting a parable but also reading into it information that isn't being offered to us. However true to life a parable may come across, we need to remember that what we know (and are supposed to know) about the characters and events is only what the parable has chosen to tell us; these are not real people or real events (they are usually stereotypes).

The second thought is that parables can include deliberate exaggeration or hyperbole as part of the art of storytelling and engaging the imagination; they entertain as well as teach, as part of being memorable (a technique that preachers also use). Some parables' story lines and characters are intentionally far-fetched or OTT. Don't misread all of a parable's features as literal.

The third is that our first aim should always be to identify the main point—the principal truth that Jesus seems to have had in mind. There may well be more than one, but beware finding too many; the more we think we are finding, the less likely it is that Jesus would recognize them.

The fourth thought is that when it comes to picture language and metaphors, the way in which they convey something that is true is by a limited correspondence ("this is a bit like that, in this way or these ways"), not a complete correspondence ("this is exactly like that, in every way"). When we press a picture or metaphor too hard, it starts to become untrue.

And my final thought is to keep an eye out for who the original audience was for a parable, where this can be determined (to do so, you may at times need to ignore paragraphing, chapter breaks, and headings—none of which were in the original). The options will usually be the ordinary people, Pharisees, and teachers of the law, or a combination. It can be helpful even when the audience can't be identified to consider how the different groups *would* have heard the parable. Keep it simple: the religious leaders (the religious elite), and the ordinary people (by which I mean the poor people).

4

Exaggeration/Hyperbole

ALREADY WE HAVE TOUCHED on exaggeration and hyperbole in the context of parables. But we see this elsewhere in Scripture, as well. There is a danger that as Bible readers we may be disinclined to believe that this would be part of the word of God, because we tend to think of exaggeration and hyperbole as "untrue." Hence, we want to "take everything literally" (if we possibly can).

Exaggeration and hyperbole are not quite the same,[1] but we'll treat them as such for the purposes of this chapter, since the main point is for us to be alert to their presence and treat them accordingly in our interpretation of "what something is saying."

It's easy to assume that a literal interpretation must always be the most faithful interpretation, wherever that seems to be not impossible. But this is a misnomer; the most faithful reading is always the one that corresponds to the writer's intentions. We need to wean ourselves off the idea that "the plain meaning of the text" is slam dunk the best way of reading everything (not least because the major flaw here is that what that really means is "the plain meaning *to me*").

Exaggeration features in types of literature that are intended to "do something" for the reader or hearer—to stir the emotions or stir

---

1. Exaggeration is overstating something that is or could be true, whereas hyperbole is extravagant overstatement to a point of literal impossibility.

to action. This is in contrast to types of literature that are intended to factually "explain something." The first of these types is the category of artists: poetry, song, and drama. The second is the category of scientists and mathematicians. If we exaggerate in science or math, we are providing wrong answers (data that is incorrect, which could be very problematic—for example, in health and safety contexts). But if we exaggerate in poetry, song, or drama, we are simply deploying the tools of the trade in creative ways, to good effect.

The particular reason for a writer to use exaggeration is to emphasize the importance of something. As Stein helpfully explains,

> The presence of exaggeration is a clear indication of the importance that the author places on what is being said. We tend to use exaggerated language to emphasize what is important. We do not exaggerate trivial matters. Rather, we use such language when we seek to convey something that we think is especially significant. As a result, we need to pay special attention when we find this literary form in the Bible. When we come across such examples, we need to ask ourselves, Why was this teaching so important in the mind of the author that he used exaggeration to express what he meant?[2]

Once we become aware of the presence of exaggeration in Scripture, we will see it far more than we might have imagined. It will become a question that we ask ourselves when we approach a text. Obviously we need also to be conscious of a natural tendency to want to limit the occasions on which we perceive it and overcome that.

Intentionally exaggerated statements are to be found throughout Scripture, beginning in the very first book, and even in statements attributed directly to God. In Gen 22, for example, speaking to Abraham, "I will . . . make your descendants as numerous as the stars in the sky and as the sand on the seashore" (cf. Gen 32:12).

Examples in the New Testament may be more helpful, especially those that suggest action on our part. In Matt 18:8–10 (ESV):

> If your hand or your foot causes you to sin, cut it off and throw it away. It is better for you to enter life crippled or lame than with two hands or two feet to be thrown into the eternal fire. And if your eye causes you to sin, tear it out and throw it away. It is better for you to enter life with one eye than with two eyes to be thrown into the hell of fire.

2. Stein, *Basic Guide*, 188.

This is what we might call "an attention grabber"—one of those "Whoo!" moments. Jesus' statement is not intended as a commandment to be implemented literally, but to alert us to something important (an underlying truth) that we need to think about more deeply. Another example would be Luke 14:26 (ESV):

> If anyone comes to me and does not hate his own father and mother and wife and children and brothers and sisters, yes, and even his own life, he cannot be my disciple.

Once again, it's the same kind of rhetorical device, deployed for the same kind of purpose: to grab our attention and to make us think, "What's the underlying point here, of which this statement is an exaggerated version for effect?" And not just to make us think, but to consider what action we should take as a result.

In that last example, we see one of the main clues as to how to recognize that a statement is deliberate exaggeration: when taken literally, it contradicts clear teachings elsewhere in Scripture. A Jesus who would say, "Love your neighbor" (Luke 10:27) is hardly likely to say, "But hate your mom and dad, wife, children, and siblings." I could have cited, "Love your enemies, do good to those who hate you" (Luke 6:27), but this too is something of an exaggeration, albeit a lesser one.

Some other interpretive clues—to help us to know when something is not to be taken literally (but not to be ignored either!)—are to be found in asking ourselves questions about the text such as:

- Would Jesus say or do such a thing, or ask his followers to? Is this consonant with the nature and character of God?
- Is this a genre of literature in which exaggeration is typically used (such as poetry, proverbs, or prophecy)?
- Is this even possible? Does this happen?
- Does a statement *suggest* universal application simply because it uses language such as "all," "everyone," or "everything," but likely *does not intend that*, since it's self-evidently *not correct* in relation to all, everyone, or everything?

5

Letters

IN SOME WAYS THE New Testaments letters (or, as they are often called, "Epistles") may seem relatively easy to understand compared to some other parts of Scripture. The most frequent mistakes that are made come down to missing two things, which is easily done but crucial to reading letters well.

The first is that they are what is known as "occasional" writings—which means they were written to particular people/churches, for particular reasons. We therefore need to take full account of "the occasion" of a letter's writing—they were "occasioned" by particular circumstances. They were not written, at least in the first instance, as timeless theology textbooks. Usually a letter was responding to particular pastoral problems, disputes, or concerns. Sometimes we know from the letters themselves something of what those were, but not always. At times there is another side to the conversation that we are missing. For example, when Paul says in 1 Cor 7:1, "Now regarding the questions you asked in your letter . . ." that's a letter we do not have.

The second mistake with letters is to be reading them as twenty-first-century Christians rather than first-century Christians. They are in the Bible *for* us, but they were not addressed *to* us. They do not speak to us directly; they speak to us secondarily. It is essential that we start by hearing them within their context, as best we can determine that, as they would have been heard in that time and place. The original author and audience shared a common worldview and cultural context; they were "on the same wavelength."

Remember that the meaning of any text is, in the first instance, what it would have meant in the minds of the original author and his audience—what it was "saying" in that context, and why.[1] Only when we have determined that can we move to the separate question of what it may be saying in our context—how their "then" relates to our "now." What we must not do is skip the first part of that process, and especially so when it comes to interpreting individual verses in isolation on their own.

"Saying" is the right word here. Letters were written to be heard publicly, not read privately (people did not have their own copies). A letter was substituting for the presence of the writer; when Paul wrote to a church, it was his voice that the church was listening to, addressing them directly, "as if" he was present.

Letters are a particularly good example of the warning that "a text taken out of its context is a pretext" for whatever someone wants to say it means; take "text" out of "context" and what's left is . . . "con." The reason that "The Bible says . . ." plus a verse quoted *out* of context is so potentially problematic is because it can be taken to mean things that it was not saying *in* its context.

Of course, this is not to say that the principles, values, and truths that a letter writer referenced are inapplicable today; often they will be. But that cannot be taken for granted *ab initio*. As with the rest of Scripture, the letters were written not only within a time and place but also within a worldview; interpretation requires that we reflect wisely on "that was then, this is now" to separate the timeless truths from the time-bound truths. This is *not*, repeat not, to say that we "pick and choose" which Scriptures we believe and act upon. It *is* to say that reading the Bible well requires more than "The Bible says . . ." plus a verse out of context. The Bible is not authoritative when it's read and applied badly.

Hopefully a simple example will suffice: "Isn't it obvious that it's disgraceful for a man to have long hair?" says Paul in 1 Cor 11:14. The first question is whether Paul would say the same thing in all contexts, or whether he had particular reasons for writing that in the Corinthian context (and if so, what those reasons were). Interestingly, Acts 18:18 tells

---

1. Coming from a slightly different direction, but in the same vein, a text *cannot* mean today something that it *could never have meant* to its original author and audience. Would that more preachers knew and practiced that!

us that Paul himself had long hair at a time when he was in Corinth, having taken a Nazarite vow.[2] The second question is whether Paul is speaking timelessly on behalf of the divine author in saying what he said. Paul's statement is in the word of God for us to read, but is it the words of God for us to obey? Was it simply a norm of the time and place in some way, or is it supposed to be normative for all times and places in every way? These are the kinds of contextual questions we need to be asking ourselves to determine the authoritative nature of what we read.

The majority of the New Testament comprises letters. The circumstances attaching to each letter can be found in a good commentary. Here we will offer a generalized overview focused on Paul and say a little more about a couple of examples.

Paul's letters were typically written to churches he had founded and/or to which he had an existing close pastoral relationship (Romans is an exception). The churches were situated in Greco-Roman urban city contexts (not Bible Belt contexts, or rural communities). Though there were unquestionably some Jewish believers, the congregations were mostly made up of gentile converts—former pagans or sympathetic gentile "Godfearers" associated with a synagogue who had not gone the whole hog to become Jewish (circumcision et al.). The makeup of a congregation is particularly important when it comes to the message of a letter—in other words, to whom it is speaking and why it says some of the things it says (Galatians is a case in point, as we will come to in a moment). These former pagans would not have had a good Jewish upbringing, steeped in traditional Jewish ethics and values. (This is comparable to pastoring people who become Christians today from no church background or prior familiarity with the Bible.) Equally importantly, these Jesus-followers would have been a tiny minority in their urban context, surrounded by a very pagan and debauched social world as "the water they were swimming in." These factors are generally significant in the background to Paul's writing.

Notwithstanding the predominantly gentile makeup of Paul's congregations—his calling was as "the apostle to the gentiles" (Rom 11:13; Gal 2:8)—Christianity as we now call it was for a long period of time (at least a century or two, if not longer) understood as a stream within Judaism. The earliest Jesus-followers were all Jewish. No doubt for Paul, Peter, and the others it was simply *authentic* Judaism, in full continuity. But this

---

2. See Num 6:5. The Hebrew word *nāzar* means "to dedicate, consecrate, or separate" oneself.

ethnic mix of Jesus-followers gave rise to the biggest single theological and pastoral question for the first-century church and its predominantly Jewish early leadership: the extent to which gentile believers in Jesus should be practicing a Jewish lifestyle centered in Torah.

You may say, "What's the big deal? Surely it's obvious?" But at the time it *was* a big deal and it was *by no means* obvious. It was the reason for calling the so-called Council of Jerusalem in Acts 15 (cf. Gal 2). The question they were grappling with was how to reconcile God's wonderful existing gift of Torah that had been the basis of their relationship for so many centuries with the wonderful new gift of God in Jesus. For Jewish Jesus-followers it might seem obvious that they would simply add on Jesus (so to speak)—but for gentile Jesus-followers, did that mean adding on some or all of Torah?[3]

This dilemma underlies Galatians in particular and to some extent Romans and Philippians. It's particularly what Galatians is all about—not so-called Jewish legalism and not human legalistic tendencies in general. The so-called Judaizers who had come down from Jerusalem were likely sincere Jewish Jesus-followers who simply took a different (more "traditional" or "conservative") view on the continuing role of Torah for gentile Jesus-followers than Paul did. For these Jesus-followers, Paul was too "progressive."

So *how* did Paul arrive at his view? Again it had nothing to do with so-called legalism, Jewish or otherwise. He was simply following what he saw as the Holy Spirit's lead. Paul's experience was that the Spirit had bypassed Torah (bypassed gentiles "becoming Jewish") in his outpouring on gentiles, which served both as a sign of the end times having begun and confirming Jesus as Israel's messiah. Paul's argument in Gal 3 is, "Did the Holy Spirit coming upon you in power have anything to do with being Torah followers? No. The Spirit did not require that of you, so why are you now listening to these traditionalists trying to 'bolt on' bits of Torah to your relationship with God as gentiles through Christ?"

---

3. This obviously pointed to a further question, of continuing Torah observance for Jewish Jesus-followers, but the pressing issue concerned the gentiles. There is no reason to think Jewish Jesus-followers would not have continued to practice Torah, as Acts indicates that Paul did. When accused of violating Torah, Paul's defense is, "I have done nothing wrong against the Jewish law or against the temple or against Caesar" (Acts 25:8). Similarly, "I have done nothing against our people or against the customs of our ancestors" (Acts 28:17).

This Holy Spirit bypassing of Torah is evident in the expansion of the people of God to include gentiles *as gentiles* in Acts. The first instance is in Acts 10, in the house of Cornelius (a "Godfearing" gentile):

> While Peter was still speaking these words, the Holy Spirit came on all who heard the message. The circumcised believers [i.e., the Jewish Torah-following Jesus believers] who had come with Peter were astonished that the gift of the Holy Spirit had been poured out even on Gentiles. For they heard them speaking in tongues and praising God. Then Peter said, "Surely no one can stand in the way of their being baptized with water. They have received the Holy Spirit just as we have." (Acts 10:44–47)

The reason they were "astonished" is because Torah had been bypassed! Reading Galatians with this background in mind is illuminating. Keep in mind that "works of the law" has nothing to do with "good works" or "works-righteousness" in a getting-to-heaven-by-one's-own-efforts-sense; it's simply the practices of Torah. Also keep in mind that when Paul speaks of "the circumcision" or "the circumcision group" he is speaking not of that one feature of the covenant alone, but of Jews who were insisting on gentile Torah keeping more broadly (it serves as a synecdoche). The predominantly gentile audience for his letter is significant; imagine how differently the meaning of "what Paul is saying" would come across had he been writing to a Jewish audience (or writing decontextualized theological teaching for all).

Let's review another example: 1 Corinthians. Here Paul's concerns for writing are rather different. Keep in mind the general background: Corinth as a Greco-Roman city, a fledgling church of mostly former pagans, and an overwhelmingly pagan cultural environment. Here Paul is addressing a number of pastoral problems, some being questions that have been raised with him ("Now for the matters you wrote about . . ." [1 Cor 7:1]; "Now about . . ." [1 Cor 7:25, 8:1, 12:1, 16:1, and 16:12]) and others that he has been told about ("It is actually reported that . . ." [1 Cor 5:1]; "I hear that when you come together as a church . . ." [1 Cor 11:18]). These matters are certainly *particular* to the Corinthian situation but are they *peculiar* to it? Does their application extend in some way to today? To which the answer is yes and no! It's easy for Christians to universalize biblical statements outside their immediate context and apply them as "principles" to matters that the biblical authors were not speaking about. But that is not being "biblical" and nor is it "what the Bible clearly teaches." That said, nor should we make the opposite mistake:

treat everything they said as relevant only to that situation, time, and culture. Rather, what is said should be applied to "genuinely comparable situations"—whenever we share "comparable life situations" with that first-century setting.[4] The challenge is that it is not necessarily "obvious" how to go about that; opinions can reasonably differ. But discernment must begin with properly understanding why the writers said what they said in *their* situation (how they understood the issue or the problem, and why they said what they said about it). Get *that* right and we have a good chance of getting any extended application right. We must always ask "why it says it" questions, not just "what it says" questions, if we are to apply Scripture thoughtfully not just legalistically.

A case in point from 1 Corinthians would be "meat sacrificed to idols," where most of us might think there is nothing comparable in our world. But first we need to know what the issues were at the time in that context.

The Greek word translated by that phrase (*eidōlothuton*) would call to mind not simply the meat but the venue in which the sacrifice took place: a pagan temple. The sacrifices were made to the pagan gods who were believed to reside there and participate in the feasts that were hosted there (the meals were taking place in their presence). Hence, as Ben Witherington III memorably puts it, "The issue is not menu, but venue."[5] The problem is not the meat but the event.

No doubt some of the former pagan gentile Christians in the church were saying, "What's the big deal? These 'gods' are not *real* gods; there is only *one* God (you've told us that). So why does it matter if we go along?" But in 1 Cor 10:20–21, Paul says that rather than false gods, it's actually demons that are present and participating in those temple meals.

Temple dining rooms were the restaurants of antiquity for big celebrations. However, these were not simply everyday meals; they were always preceded by pagan worship. The RSVP invitations were sent out in the name of the pagan gods. They began with sacrifices, followed by overindulgence of food and alcohol, and (at least by reputation in the Jewish understanding) frequently ended in sexual orgies as the "after-dinner entertainment," with the sexual abuse of slaves, male and female prostitutes, and wife-swapping.

---

4. Fee and Stuart, *How to Read the Bible*, 60 and 63.

5. Witherington, *Making a Meal*, 42. See also Witherington, *What's in the Word*, 89–101; and Dodson, "Convivial Background."

The Latin word for these depraved temple "dinner parties" was the *convivium* from which, somewhat unfortunately, we get our word "convivial." At least six of the nine behaviors that Paul condemns in 1 Cor 6:9 were things that happened there: "greed," "drunkenness," "idolatry," "sexual immorality," "adultery," and "men having sex with men."[6] It's likely what Peter had in mind in 1 Pet 4:3 when he said, "You have spent enough time in the past doing what pagans choose to do: living in debauchery, lust, drunkenness, orgies, carousing and detestable idolatry." Joseph Dodson finds evidence of some Christians turning *agape* meals into these pagan feasts in the background to Jude and 2 Pet 2:13–14.

With a *convivium* sacrifice, there was lots of meat to be eaten, so wealthy patrons would invite their friends and neighbors for a big party. And meat was expensive—a luxury item—so the gentile Christians would be minded to go (horrifying the Jewish Christians). We can easily imagine the peer pressure to be "like everyone else" in that culture, that the biblical writers were concerned about. The apostles are saying to these former pagans who are now following Jesus, "You need to turn down those invitations; you need to be different to the world around you." Which meant having nothing to do with the places and events where these things happened.[7] The "table of demons" in 1 Cor 10:21 is a reference to the dining table (not a sacrificial altar).

The question concerning purchasing meat in the marketplace that had been offered to idols follows on, but is rather different. The concern that Paul is being asked about arises from the fact that the meat being sold is likely left over from pagan temple sacrifices. In 1 Cor 10:25–28, Paul is talking about meals in homes (where the pagan gods/demons would not be understood as present). Hence, he says that in this context it is a matter of personal conscience and sensitivity to other believers. It is the idols and their worship (the events in the temple) that are the polluting factors, not the meat as such.

Understanding why the writers said what they said in *their* situation—how they understood the issue or the problem, and why they said

---

6. Paul worries that the Corinthian believers' participation in these banquets is putting them dangerously close to Israel's idolatry and promiscuity in the infamous golden calf incident (in Exod 32): "Do not be idolaters, as some of them were; as it is written: 'The people sat down to eat and drink and got up to indulge in revelry.' We should not commit sexual immorality, as some of them did. . . . Therefore, my dear friends, flee from idolatry" (1 Cor 10:7–8, 14).

7. See also Acts 15:28–29, which seems clearly to have a pagan temple *convivium* context in mind. Cf. Rev 2:14, 20.

what they said about it—helps us to see where "genuinely comparable situations" do and do not arise for us today.

Some final thoughts on the mechanics of letter writing in those days. It is wrong to assume that Paul and his fellows simply went into their studies one day and prayerfully penned their thoughts, in a similar way to me writing this.

> The involvement of a secretary or scribe in the actual writing of an ancient letter is more important than modern readers might suspect. Professional writers were used for virtually every letter written in antiquity. For those who were themselves illiterate and needed someone to write for them, a scribe usually took down notes regarding the subjects that concerned the sender and then employed a standard format and used conventional expressions to write the letter. For those who were themselves able to read and perhaps write, scribes were still often used to take down literal dictation—although the skill involved often made this prohibitively expensive—or to take notes from which they wrote a first draft, which the "author" then reviewed, altered, and approved. Two New Testament scribes are identified by name: Tertius in Romans 16:22 and Silvanus in 1 Peter 5:12. In both cases, they seem to have been fellow Christians who were competent in letter writing. . . . [Scribes'] involvement in the composition process may, in fact, help to explain the differences of style and diction between the different letters of Paul.[8]

All in all, this would have been a time-consuming, protracted (as well as expensive) process. Several drafts may well have been involved. The involvement of scribes in the New Testament letter writing is almost certain. The author would often be involved in "signing off" a letter in their own hand—adding a "postscript"—where literacy permitted. This would also serve to authenticate the writing. For example, we have instances at the end of 1 Cor 16 ("I, Paul, write this greeting in my own hand"), Gal 6:11 ("See what large letters I use as I write to you with my own hand!"), and Phlm 19 ("I, Paul, am writing this with my own hand"). Moreover, there would not be just the one copy (not even one "original" manuscript) since as well as the letter couriered to the addressee church, a scribe would have produced one for Paul to keep and perhaps one for use elsewhere.

---

8. Huntsman, "Occasional Nature," 198–99.

6

Wisdom

WISE WORDS AND SAYINGS are, not unnaturally, to be found throughout the Bible, but in this chapter we are concerned with the genre of Hebrew wisdom literature. Principally this means the Old Testament books of Proverbs, Job, and Ecclesiastes.

The easiest examples of wisdom literature are found in proverbs—the genre as well as the book which bears that name. A proverb is a shorty, pithy saying or statement that offers a truth perceived to be wise concerning something in life. That it is a *biblical* proverb suggests that the truth comes from a divine perspective or is, at least, divinely affirmed in some way.

However, not all wisdom literature is by way of proverbs, and by no means is it all entirely straightforward. For example, there are times when what something is really saying is not what it appears to be saying! The wisdom may be found in the opposite of what it's saying—another instance, perhaps, of the "plain meaning" of a text being a less than adequate way of reading something. For example, we find that the "wise" counsel of Job's friends is anything but that; in Ecclesiastes, its apparent pessimism about life comes across as dark if not depressing.

A further challenge comes from our distance from the world of the text—its social world and its cultural assumptions. This gives us some challenges in "what we are to make of it" for ourselves, in our world, today. As modern readers, our interest is unsurprisingly centered in what does this mean to me, what is it "saying" to me, in terms of potential application, but its original context is very alien.

Interestingly, much or even most wisdom literature is addressed to individuals. This is somewhat unusual in Scripture, which is usually very much concerned with the group. Moreover, we do not see much there in the way of biblical theology concerning Scripture's "big themes" or salvation history.

Since what you're reading is not so much a book *about* the Bible as a book about how to *read* the Bible—biblical interpretation—we will focus on that in relation to the wisdom literature, and especially on the mistaken (unwise?) ways of reading and applying it that Christians sometimes can make.

Let's start with proverbs (as the easiest category) and specifically on the "truth" of a proverb. The first thing we need to note is that as a short, pithy, generalized statement a proverb is intending to reflect only a general truth; not a universal or absolute truth. In other words, while what it says may be generally true—and hence, these are wise words, recommended to be taken on board—it is not being offered as a divinely attested universal guarantee. For example, the well-known proverb "Train up a child in the way he should go; even when he is old he will not depart from it" (Prov 22:6 ESV) should not be interpreted either as saying that God guarantees the outcome that the child will be a committed Christian in adult life, or, if it turns out that they are, that the credit for that is all down to the parents (nor for that matter, vice versa, in terms of attributing the blame if they're not). We must not read proverbs as written guarantees or universal cosmic laws that must come to pass, or even as divine promises to be claimed. Quoting a proverb as "God's Word" is not the equivalent of rubbing a lamp so that a genie pops out to do our bidding.

There are, of course, proverbs that can be taken to convey a timeless and universal truth, especially when they are speaking of the nature and character of God. An example would be: "The Lord detests lying lips, but he delights in people who are trustworthy" (Prov 12:22).

At the same time, there are examples where timeless universalization would be a misreading, even where on its face it appears to be offering a cause-and-effect kind of outcome for those who comply. For example, "He holds success in store for the upright, he is a shield to those whose way of life is blameless, for he guards the course of the just and protects the way of his faithful ones" (Prov 2:7–8). Does every faithful believer experience success in life? Does God always shield them from bad outcomes? No, clearly not. Not only is it not our universal experience, but it's not even true of all faithful biblical characters. See, for example, what happened to some of the "heroes of faith" in the Old Testament, per Heb 11:35–38,

> who were tortured, refusing to be released so that they might gain an even better resurrection. Some faced jeers and flogging, and even chains and imprisonment. They were put to death by stoning; they were sawn in two; they were killed by the sword. They went about in sheepskins and goatskins, destitute, persecuted and ill-treated. . . . They wandered in deserts and mountains, living in caves and in holes in the ground.

We ought not to conclude that proverbs which indicate positive outcomes for right behaviors are therefore "untrue," "unreliable," or "false promises." Simply that this is not the right way to read the genre.

A more problematic example—problematic for pastors and preachers, certainly, depending on how they teach on financial giving—is this well-known proverb: "Honor the Lord with your wealth, with the firstfruits of all your crops; then your barns will be filled to overflowing, and your vats will brim over with new wine" (Prov 3:9–10). If this is to be taken as a cosmic divine "law"—as prosperity gospel teachers would have it—then how are we to know which proverbs are in which category? The "Proverbs 3:9–10" category (*definitely* a guaranteed outcome), or the "Proverbs 2:7–8" category (definitely *not* a guaranteed outcome)? Again, the problem comes from this being a wrong way of reading, and again, it is not our experience. The only people guaranteed to get rich from a prosperity gospel way of reading these verses is the prosperity gospel teachers themselves.

One final well-known example will suffice to hopefully drive home the point: "Commit to the Lord everything you do. Then he will make your plans succeed" (Prov 16:3 NIrV). Fee and Stuart say well what needs to be said:

> [A] person might assume that Proverbs 16:3 is a direct, clear-cut, always-applicable promise from God that if one dedicates his or her plans to God, those plans *must* succeed. People who reason that way, of course, can be disappointed. They can dedicate some perfectly selfish or idiotic scheme to God, then if it happens to succeed, even briefly, they can assume that God blessed it. A hasty marriage, a rash business decision, an

ill-thought-out vocational decision—all can be dedicated to God but can eventually result in misery. Or, a person might commit a plan to God only to have it fail; then the person would wonder why God did not keep His promise, why He went back on His inspired Word. In either case they have failed to see that the proverb is not a categorical, always applicable, iron-clad promise, but a more general truth.[1]

How might we reconcile Proverbs' admonitions and encouragements with the fact that the indicated outcomes are *not* guaranteed? Firstly, we are being encouraged to pursue these actions not in order to *get* an outcome but because they're simply *the right thing to do*. The same is true of every faithful behavior that is encouraged in Scripture—where blessing comes, it comes from the grace and kindness of God, not because we've earned it in some cosmic transaction with God. Proverbs are offering inspired principles, encouraging living in ways that please the heart of God, "doing the right thing"—these are the takeaways. A personal blessing may well be the fruit, but also may not be (because that's not "how it works").

A further problematic way of reading and applying proverbs comes from the fact that—as *we* just did in those last three examples—we are inclined to extract them from their context and interpret them as if they are stand-alone truths. One of the several problems with so-called "prooftexts" (in other words, individual verses taken out of their context and quoted as supposedly "proving" a "truth") is that we lose everything to do with the context, including the genre.

As preachers and teachers, we should only cite a verse as "saying" something or "proving" something (as divine truth) if we are certain that the claims we are making for it (expressly or impliedly) are in full accord with what it was saying in its context. Too many sermons are framed around a list of extracted verses plucked from here, there, and everywhere, like a magpie filling its nest with random unrelated shiny things. A selection of decontextualized verses chosen from the results of a word-search for "faith" or "love" on biblegateway.com are not the same thing as "what the Bible clearly teaches" on those subjects.

And then, finally, proverbs are designed to be memorable rather than comprehensive. They are pithy phrases, not journal articles. Their brevity is telling us something about their limitations. Rather as a metaphor is

---

1. Fee and Stuart, *How to Read the Bible*, 198.

only true to an extent—and that if we press it too far, too literally, it soon becomes untrue—this is also the case with a proverb.

> No proverb is a complete statement of truth. No proverb is so perfectly worded that it can stand up to the unreasonable demand that it apply in every situation at every time. The more briefly and parabolically [i.e., in a parable context] a principle is stated, the more common sense and good judgment are needed to interpret it properly—but the more effective and memorable it is.[2]

So that is wisdom in Proverbs. When we move on to Job, the approach is rather different. Its wisdom teaching is framed in a story, with characters and a plot.

The first piece of critical information comes at the very start: Job is "blameless and upright" (Job 1:1), a model God-fearing man. The historical setting for the folktale is in the patriarchal age, pre-Moses; the narrator tells us of a parallel heavenly setting (unbeknown to the human characters) that is almost pantomime-like: angels and Satan presenting themselves before God in the royal court.

Satan says, in effect, "Job only serves you for what he gets out of you; take away the nice things in his life and he will turn on you." God responds, in effect, "Oh no, he won't!" (Satan: "Oh yes, he will") and God says, "OK, we'll see about that" and grants permission for Satan to take things away in stages (but within limits). The implied question is whether we are all like that—even the devout among us only serving God because life is good.

First Job's wealth, then his ten children, and then his health are all taken from him. But Satan's accusation fails: "Job did not sin by charging God with wrongdoing" (1:22). The first attempted undermining of Job's trust in God comes from his wife, "Are you still maintaining your integrity? Curse God and die!" But Job responds, "Shall we accept good from God, and not trouble?" The narrator tells us that "in all this, Job did not sin in what he said" (2:9–10).

Three friends now appear, to sympathize and "comfort" him. Their assumption—indeed, their accusation—is that Job "must have" sinned; there is some secret, hidden sin that he's not being honest about. Their wisdom is that good things happen to righteous people and bad things happen to sinful people—it's cause and effect in a moral cosmos

---

2. Fee and Stuart, *How to Read the Bible*, 201.

superintended by a moral God—so we can work backward from what happens to know whether someone is righteous or sinful. This is the second implied question: Is that right? Is that how things work? Is that what God is like?

One friend asks, "Consider now: who, being innocent, has ever perished? Where were the upright ever destroyed? As I have observed, those who plough evil and those who sow trouble reap it" (4:7–8). In other words, Job is obviously not as righteous as people thought, otherwise these things wouldn't have happened. Similarly, concerning the deaths of Job's children, a friend says, "When your children sinned against him [God], he gave them over to the penalty of their sin" (8:4).

The dialogue between Job and the three friends is lengthy: from chapter 3 through 31. As we read through, it's important to be aware that it "contains all sorts of wrong advice and incorrect conclusions as they come from the lips of Job's well-meaning 'comforters.'"[3] We shall get ourselves into trouble if we prooftext some of this "advice."

One of the tangential messages we can draw from Job is not to read even true proverbs as offering guaranteed divine outcomes in a literalist, cause-and-effect kind of way.

Job's friends are by no means unique in assuming that God blesses righteous people—the fact that they're blessed appears to prove that (even if at times we see unrighteous people prosper, too). Certainly, this was a common assumption in Jesus' day (it does after all seem logical), as evidenced by the disciples in John 9:1—when calamities happen, *someone* must have sinned, we just need to identify who. The Pharisees saw Israel's troubles (Roman occupation; the delay in the messiah's coming) as God's judgment on the sinfulness of the ordinary people (but not *their own* sinfulness, of course—the problem is never us, it's always those other people).

Depending on the time period of the composition of Job, which seems likely to have been around the time of the Babylonian exile, perhaps the nation of Israel is the "Job character" in the story. Perhaps his calamities are Israel's calamities; the questions the story asks of him are those it's asking of Israel in exile: why are these things happening to us and what will be the ultimate outcome?

The implied thinking of some Christians today is that *because* they are a Christian God will give them a better deal in life. They therefore

---

3. Fee and Stuart, *How to Read the Bible*, 193–94.

struggle when something goes wrong, when God seems to have let them down on his side of a bargain they signed up for. For other Christians, their fear of God is less a case of awe-filled respect but more one of fright—that God may punish them with calamities in life if they do not behave themselves (by avoiding notable sins, going to church fairly regularly, tithing, etc.).

How are we to read some of the elements in the Job story? In particular, the heavenly royal court scenes? In the first instance, we must remember that it presents as a folktale. That being the case, as with a proverb, we need to remember how to read it:

> The first and most important thing to grasp in the interpretation of parables—and this can hardly be stressed too much—is that the story has an obvious "surface" meaning (which is *never* the point) and a less obvious "deeper" underlying meaning which is *actually* the point. The idea was for the hearers to figure out the deeper meaning since *that* was the teaching. The teaching is *not* in the surface features of the story, they are just the props and the stage setting.[4]

In a parable-like way, the dialogue between God and Satan in Job is being presented to us as *what is popularly presumed* to happen in the heavenly royal court. The question we as hearers are being invited to ask is whether this *is in fact* what happens; clearly, it is not an eyewitness account. It offers *a way* of explaining why there is evil in the world—why bad things happen to good people—but is it *the right* way? We are invited to do midrash on that key question.[5] But we need to wait until the conclusion of the story to find out.

Taken at face value, the rather Calvinistic way of thinking that the account offers gives God full credit for being "in control" of everything that happens in the world. It sounds commendable. But that kind of "meticulous sovereignty" cannot avoid giving God the credit for every bad thing that happens, including all manner of evil, which he either causes or at least permits (which is really the same thing, linguistic niceties aside).

If we read the first two chapters literalistically, assuming them to be validating the idea that real conversations between God and Satan happen

---

4. See Part II, chapter 3, "Parables."

5. Strictly speaking, "midrash aggadah"—which is to do creative theological reflection on the meaning and application of the biblical text, even arguing and debating with it, in a group setting.

like that all the time—with the same consequences for things that happen to us—then that is a conclusion we can reach as to what it is "teaching." But if we understand it as simply a frame for the story, reflecting the popular assumptions of the day—or at least, reflecting one such assumption, that the story is actually challenging rather than affirming—then we will see it differently. How to decide? By considering the witness of Scripture as a whole, and especially that of the Gospels and the New Testament; but *not* through a fundamentalist "the Bible clearly teaches" based on a literalistic reading of Job 1–2 on its own.

The final chapter wraps things up. Job says, "I know that you can do all things; no purpose of yours can be thwarted" (42:2). In other words, "I believe and trust that everything that happens in life ultimately conforms to the goals that you have for your creation" (what we call God's "sovereign will"). Ephesians 1:11 tells us he works out everything to fit his plan and purpose; in Rom 8:28, he makes all things work together for good—even the things that are not good in themselves. But *ultimate* sovereignty—God's control over the timing and execution of the major waypoints in salvation history—is not the same as *meticulous* sovereignty—a puppet master controlling each and every movement of their puppets.

Job has not been perfect in his responses to what has happened to him—he receives a mild divine rebuke—and sensitive as always to wanting to please God, he repents of his human failings (42:6). Nonetheless, God dissociates himself from how the friends have read the situation. This was not divine wisdom, and specifically not reflecting the true nature and character of God: "You have not spoken the truth about me, as my servant Job has," he chides them (42:7). Job's standing as blameless and upright (from Job 1:1) is affirmed.

Although some of the tragedies cannot be undone (Job's ten children still lost their lives), the story does in one sense end "happily ever after." Again we must remember it is not a "true" story in which real children died. Hence, the positive conclusion, in which God restores his fortunes (42:10)—ten more children, double the possessions, and long life—must be seen in those terms.

Is this intending to tell us a normative truth about God—that whenever we suffer loss unfairly, God will restore it to us in this life (we just have to be patient)? I don't think so; to assume that would be to take us back to the flawed mechanistic ways of reading things that we've seen previously. What it should tell us, however, is that Job is right—that we should echo those faith-filled words in 42:2: "I know that you can do all things; no purpose of yours can be thwarted." As a God of justice and a God of love, he is a restorer of fortunes and a righter of wrongs (though it may not always happen in this life).

And then, finally, we need to shift gears once again when it comes to Ecclesiastes. As we saw with Job, the genre we are dealing with includes sayings and statements that are not in and of themselves divine "truths." It's another example of why in speaking of Scripture as the "inerrant" and "authoritative" word of God we need to be nuanced at times. And especially, avoid "prooftexting."

The scene is set in Eccl 1:2 for what we are mostly to encounter thereafter: "Meaningless! Meaningless!" says the Teacher. "Utterly meaningless! Everything is meaningless." I think we get the message. But what is that message, exactly, and why is it in the Bible?

To start with, there is no scholarly consensus on the identity of the Teacher (even though he is described as a "son of David" and "king over Israel in Jerusalem" in Eccl 1:1, 12). Solomon is but one suggestion. But the bigger challenge is how to read the content and its message. For sure, this is not easy, and the following thoughts are tentative, approached theologically.

On its face, the message is, "We all know that life sucks. Everything is ultimately a waste of time, so we might as well just go out and enjoy ourselves as best we can, while we can, because death will come soon enough and then that's the end of it. All our lifetime gains are canceled by death, the great leveler. There is no God, or if there is, he is remote and disinterested in human affairs, including human misery. He is capricious and unfair. We're on our own, people." Essentially, the text of Ecclesiastes is cynical, dark, and negative, if not depressing. Enough to make Leonard Cohen seem like a happy-go-lucky optimist in comparison. For a piece of wisdom literature, its counterintuitive wisdom is that living in accordance with wisdom simply doesn't work!

How then are we to understand why it's in the Bible? What role does its "wisdom" serve? The hardest purpose to affirm is that it authorizes the opinions it offers about life and God. So . . . might it actually be *the opposite* that we are supposed to glean from it? Rather like when we read the "advice" of Job's friends. Might we be supposed to argue with the "theology" presented and say, "No! That is not right!"? A midrashic approach might agree—encouraging us to ask questions of the text not just imbibing everything at face-value as if it were a textbook. Perhaps Ecclesiastes is challenging us along the lines, "Yes, that most definitely does express how life comes across, and how most people—if they are honest—think of it. But there is more to be said . . ."

Even when it comes to this well-known poetic passage in Eccl 3:1–8—memorialized for many in the Pete Seeger song—it is unclear how it is to be taken. Is it speaking divinely authorized wisdom, godless reasoning, or just the way things are?

> There is a time for everything,
> and a season for every activity under the heavens:
> a time to be born and a time to die,
> a time to plant and a time to uproot,
> a time to kill and a time to heal,
> a time to tear down and a time to build,
> a time to weep and a time to laugh,
> a time to mourn and a time to dance,
> a time to scatter stones and a time to gather them,
> a time to embrace and a time to refrain from embracing,
> a time to search and a time to give up,
> a time to keep and a time to throw away,
> a time to tear and a time to mend,
> a time to be silent and a time to speak,
> a time to love and a time to hate,
> a time for war and a time for peace.

None of this is to say that wisdom statements that accord with what one might expect to see are not occasionally to be found, but the inconsistency is awkward. For example, in Eccl 3:17, "God will bring into judgment both the righteous and the wicked, for there will be a time for every activity, a time to judge every deed." (Perhaps this serves as a commentary on vv. 1–8 preceding.) But immediately thereafter, we read, "As for humans, God tests them so that they may see that they are like the animals." And "Who knows if the human spirit rises upward and if the spirit of the animal goes down into the earth?" (Eccl 3:18, 21). Hmm . . .

What we can be more sure of is the interpretive significance in the close of the book—its epilogue or conclusion, in chapter 12. The message here may be paraphrased as, "Yes, all of this is what someone would think. But while you are still young, before you start to think like this—as one day you will be tempted to, by what life throws at you—remember your Creator. Remember him now, before it's too late."

The ending, in chapter 12, is answering the charge at the beginning, in chapter 1—"Meaningless! Everything is meaningless" (repeated for reference in 12:8).

> Remember your Creator in the days of your youth, before the days of trouble come and the years approach when you will say ... [all these things]. (Eccl 12:1)

> Now all has been heard; here is the conclusion of the matter: fear God and keep his commandments,[6] for this is the duty of all mankind. For God will bring every deed into judgment, including every hidden thing, whether it is good or evil. (Eccl 12:13–14)

Ecclesiastes presents a view of life that conforms to what someone would conclude if there were no God, or if he is not a good God—if how he is presented elsewhere in Scripture is untrue. It's a well-reasoned, starkly honest, and logical way of thinking about life in the absence of a plausible God-framework. The role of the rest of Scripture, read well, is to present the perspective that there is indeed a God, and this is what he is like (which, at best, Ecclesiastes only hints toward).

---

6. "Fear" in the sense of "to hold in deep awe and respect" (not "to be terrorized by the very thought of him," which is an unhealthy fear).

7

Poetry, Song, and Lament

WHEN WE THINK OF poetry and song in the Bible, our thoughts are likely to turn to the psalms. In contrast to much of the Old Testament, the psalms seem relatively easy to relate to; they could almost have been written yesterday. Indeed, many are the basis for Christian hymns and worship songs. They convey easily recognizable truths about the God that we know. In part, this ease of association comes from the poetic and picture language that the psalms often employ, which tends to translate well across cultures. No wonder that if there is one book from the Old Testament that regularly gets added to printed New Testaments, it's the psalms.

And yet, to some extent this sense of familiarity can be misleading. There are times that we need to adjust what it actually says to something we would say. For example, "Oh, how I love your law! I meditate on it all day long" (Ps 119:97) is not something most self-respecting Reformed evangelicals would be likely to sing about, but I guess it would be fine if we tweak it to say, "I love your Bible" (though to make it popular it would certainly need a catchy tune—and Catholics might struggle to fit in "I love your Bible and your Apocrypha").

Sometimes the cultural gap between the twenty-first-century Western world and first-century Israel seems easy to bridge, but sometimes it does not, even within the same psalm. Let's take the seemingly straightforward and ever-popular Ps 23. We all know how it starts off: "The Lord is my shepherd; I shall not want." Lovely. Not that we really know much about shepherds in the first century, of course, but we can easily conjure up mental pictures. And if in doubt, we can Google "The Lord is my shepherd," which will deliver inspiring images of an exceedingly handsome, blue-eyed, long-haired, lightly bearded, fair-skinned Jesus-like character in white robes with a crook (and probably a faraway look in his eyes). Perfect. Well, not really. But what about "Your rod and your staff protect and comfort me"? How does *that* work? What is *that* saying?

Far less straightforward—and even less likely to be something we Google—is a verse like Ps 137:9, "Happy is the one who takes your babies and smashes them against the rocks!" Still less is that likely to end up in a worship song. The psalm is set in the context of the Babylonian exile and addressed to Israel's captors; it serves as a lament.

The shock factor of reading a verse like this causes us to reflect on the nature of the word of God as we have it in the Bible. When we read the nice bits in the psalms, the lovely verses that get copied and pasted into Facebook and Instagram, it's easy to see the divinity coming to the fore as "words of God." But when we encounter something like this, we're seeing the humanity coming to the fore—"words of people" that are still part of the word of God. We might wonder how something like this can be "inspired"; and, frankly, it isn't, in the "inspiring" sense of Ps 23. But it is part of the humanity of the Bible that God has intentionally permitted to be there. Second Timothy 3:16 tells us that Scripture was "God-breathed," but that doesn't mean "God-dictated," nor even "God-redacted," in terms of filtering out the more starkly human elements. Those are there for us to read, learn from, question, and debate—not simply to imbibe and parrot. Not everything we read is "God speaking." Not every verse is stating a truth as such (as we have seen, in the previous chapter).

This leads on to something else about the psalms: as well as poetry, worship, and praise they include prayers, lament, and cries of the heart. We see humanity to the fore in a way that we might not expect in something called the word of God.

When we consider that variety of genre in the psalms—along with the challenges of placing ourselves in the psalmists' world, with the very different points of reference that come with the psalmists' worldview, and we read the psalms accordingly—it's no wonder that we end up being rather selective, focusing on the content that seems consonant with Christian faith in our place and time, while quietly dropping that which doesn't.

With that in mind, how do psalms "teach"? We're used to thinking that everything in the Bible is there to teach us something. Grasping how psalms teach begins from being aware of some of their features, so that we can read them accordingly, in what they are and are not saying.

The first thing to remember is that psalms are poetry and song; they appeal, in the first instance, to the heart and the emotions, rather than to the mind. Or perhaps one might say, they speak to the mind *through* the heart. As with all poetry and song, their stock-in-trade is picture language and metaphor. The thing about a metaphor is that it is likening something to something else as true in *one* sense, as a helpful way of picturing *that* aspect, but it is *never* saying that the two are alike in *every* sense. Metaphors that picture something should not be pressed too hard, with reference to too many presumed points of comparison, because they soon then become untrue. There is a sense in which Jesus wants us to become like little children (Matt 18:3), but it's not in every sense—there's *also* a sense in which we need to grow up (Heb 5:12–13). God is our Father in one sense, but not in every sense. Meditating on psalms can be a helpful spiritual discipline, but overinterpreting a psalm by reading too much into its poetic features—meanings that could never have been known or intended by the writer at the time—is a risk to be aware of.

We all know that songbooks and poetry books do not teach in the same way that textbooks and encyclopedias teach. In some ways, then, to speak in terms of what the psalms teach is a misnomer. We certainly need to read them from within their genre. The psalms "are not propositions, or imperatives, or stories that illustrate doctrines, they do not function primarily for the teaching of doctrine or moral behavior."[1] In that sense, psalms do not "teach"! To read them as if they did teach in any of those ways is a category error. This does not for one moment mean they are any less the word of God, but (as always) we need to be clear on what we mean by that—and especially, what those two little words ("of God") are intending.

Perhaps a helpful way to characterize the value we find in the psalms is that they function *relationally* more than *informationally*. They inspire and encourage us in our relationship with God. They encourage a relationship with him that is characterized by both intimacy and honesty. It is perhaps no surprise that Jesus should quote from the psalms in the agony of the cross (Mark 15:34), identifying with King David in

---

1. Fee and Stuart, *How to Read the Bible*, 169.

Ps 22:1: "My God, my God, why have you abandoned me? Why are you so far away when I groan for help?" The rest of Ps 22 is notable in this context, too, insofar as a shorthand reference (or allusion) in the New Testament to an Old Testament text is often intended to call to mind (that we are to "read in") the whole of the longer passage from which it comes—in this case, the rest of Ps 22.[2]

A risk that comes with focusing only on the psalms we like best is similar to the risk in wisdom proverbs: reading them selectively as a compendium of sure and certain promises of a happy life. Surprisingly, perhaps, it is laments that comprise the largest category of psalms. Despite how Christians commonly think of them, by no means are the psalms all celebratory praise and worship, thanking God that life is good and enjoyable; many are anguished, crying out that life is hard and distressing. We can and should be familiar with both types, since both reflect human experience at times and, indeed, Christian experience, too. To expect otherwise is to have wrong expectations of being a Christian. Both types can be profitable, devotionally. Laments are telling us that God understands; that he is OK with us expressing our hurts and fears and anxieties about life, even at times with anger and distress to the fore; that he encourages us to come to him "as we are," not as a sanitized, Sunday-best, version of who we are; to bring prayers of lament as well as prayers of praise. A feature that we do see in the psalms is both lament *and* praise, in the same psalm; by no means need they be mutually exclusive for us.

Christians often think that the psalms were written by King David, but of the 150 psalms in the Psalter, only seventy-three are directly attributed to him, while two more are attributed via the New Testament: Ps 2 (in Acts 4:25) and Ps 95 (in Heb 4:7). That's only 50 percent. The psalms are not numbered in the chronological order of their composition or writing, and they span a number of centuries.[3]

Though we find lament in the psalms, we do not only find it there; in particular, we should say a few words about the Old Testament book of Lamentations. The things we have said about lament elsewhere in Scripture apply equally here. Both Jewish and Christian interpretive traditions connected this book with Jeremiah, the so-called "weeping

---

2. This is known as "allusory intertextuality."

3. The Blue Letter Bible website offers a potential timeline for when each psalm was composed, ranging from 1489–444 BCE. It is perhaps best thought of illustratively rather than definitively: Blue Letter Bible, "Probable Occasion."

prophet" (Jer 9:1), though the scholarly consensus today sees its authorship as anonymous.

> The book of Lamentations offers a window into the struggle of the people of God in the wake of the fall of Jerusalem and demise of the kingdom of Judah. The book presents a series of poems that express the grief of the community using language, imagery, forms and theology in line with Hebrew traditions of mourning and suffering. The struggle expressed in these poems is communicated through contrasting voices: female and male, individual and corporate, bitter and penitent, suppliant and prophetic.[4]

As Whitney Woollard puts it, this is the book of grief in the Bible: 2 Kgs 24–25 and Jer 52 give us the facts; Lamentations gives us the emotions, emotions that are raw, honest, dark, and even volatile at times.[5]

It is fair to say that corporate lament is a rare feature in Western societies today. Examples, however, may be found in the periods following the sudden and tragic death of Diana, Princess of Wales, in a Parisian car crash in the early hours of August 31, 1997, and the al-Qaeda terrorist attacks on the World Trade Center complex and other US targets on September 11, 2001. The outpouring of grief to a level that touched nations is comparable to that reflected in biblical corporate lament. In television news reports, we perhaps see it more regularly in nonwestern cultures.

As poetry, we should read lament within its genre. All that has previously been said about poetry applies to lament as well. It is unsurprising that—being mostly funereal dirges of sorrow, mourning, and sadness—Lamentations is not often read or cited by Christians; when we do read it, it's unmistakably painful. And yet there has been little or no dispute about its place in the Hebrew or Christian canon. It is Scripture, but not in the sense in which we usually like to think about Scripture (perhaps we might say that it's not our favorite kind of Scripture). And yet, Lamentations so often cries out about the painful realities of our own human experience and "gives voice to our grief."

> Although we can't draw a one-to-one application from Israel's circumstances to ours, Lamentations can teach us to hear and speak the biblical language of lament, which is crucial to dealing with grief. Lament allows us to fully face and name our pain,

---

4. Boda, "Lamentations I," 399.
5. Woollard, "Lamentations."

and it creates space for future resolution and hope without glossing over our trauma. It gives us permission to protest life's difficulties, to scream, cry, vent, plead, and complain in the presence of God and others. It lets us ask the hard questions without condemnation: Why did this have to happen? How could you allow it? Where are you in the midst of it? It allows weeping without explanation. It might be messy and uncomfortable, but it's the first step towards healing.[6]

---

6. Woollard, "Lamentations," para. 9.

8

Prophecy and Apocalyptic

Prophecy

FOR MANY PENTECOSTAL/CHARISMATIC CHRISTIANS, prophecy would seem to bring us back to more familiar territory compared to some of the stranger genres we encountered in the last chapter. For one thing, most of us will have heard teaching about prophecy; people characterized as prophets; and even, perhaps, words delivered to us or to others as modern-day prophecies. In this chapter, it will therefore be difficult to put all that to one side as we consider *the biblical genre* of prophecy. When we think we know something about a subject at the outset (and especially when the information has been drawn from popular sources, where there is always the danger of some "folk theology" getting blended in), this can mean rather a lot of presuppositions come with us into the chapter.

Ask a person in the street (churchgoer or otherwise) what prophecy means and they will likely respond along the lines of "predicting future events"—rather like a Christianized version of horoscopes. Certainly that is one of if not the main thing that dictionary definitions focus on. I am writing this chapter over the Christmas season, when nativity Bible readings tell us, "All this took place to fulfill what the Lord had said through the prophet" (in the angel of the Lord's conversation with Joseph, in Matt 1); there are half a dozen instances of such a phrase in the first four chapters of Matthew alone. When Jesus begins his public ministry in Luke 4, in his first recorded sermon in the synagogue at Nazareth, he closes with, "Today this scripture [Isa 61:1–2] is fulfilled in your hearing." New Testament writers frequently speak of the fulfillment of messianic promises in the coming of Jesus.

And yet, surprisingly when set against this background,

> Less than 2 percent of Old Testament prophecy is messianic.
> Less than 5 percent specifically describes the New Covenant age.
> Less than 1 percent describes events yet to come.[1]

It may be worth reading those rather unexpected statistics again. It's very easy (though wrong) to assume that the biblical prophecies that were not about Jesus are "all about us," and/or all about the end times (a subject in which contemporary Christians tend to be disproportionately interested). If we ask our standard question concerning "the meaning" of a text of the prophetic texts—what did this mean to the person who spoke/wrote it and the people who first heard it?—we find that in the overwhelming majority of cases they were speaking of future events for Israel, Judah, and the surrounding nations; God speaking about *their* future, not *our* future. Moreover, this was not some dim, distant future, but an immediate future within the hearers' times. What this means is that what was at the time of its speaking/writing talking of the future, is now, with the passage of time, something in the past. For example, the hope of a promised return for the Jewish people from exile in Babylon.

Another element we need to be aware of is that though we tend to think of prophecy as "foretelling" in the sense of predicting events, more often than not prophecy is "forthtelling" concerning the purposes of God, such as divine warnings to God's people that they were getting things wrong and that if they did not wake up to that and change their ways, this was inevitably leading to bad consequences.

By no means were they always negative messages; we also see messages of hope, promise, and encouragement concerning who God is and what he is like. And often, even when the messages are negative warnings (if people *don't* change), the prophet is speaking from God in the hope that they *will* change and those bad consequences will be averted (in other words, what is "prophesied" to happen will *not* then happen)—see Jer 18:7–10.

---

1. Fee and Stuart, *How to Read the Bible*, 150.

This was precisely the prophet Jonah's experience concerning Nineveh: he prophesied God's coming judgment, as God asked him, but because they repented, God relented and it didn't come to pass. Jonah's speech in Jonah 4:1–2 could be paraphrased, "Oh great! That's typical of you, God! It's exactly what I said would happen and why I didn't want to go there in the first place: I *knew* you would go and forgive them instead of judging them. And now my prophetic credentials are shot. This is *so* embarrassing. Thanks a lot!"

Jonah was, in one sense, completely right in foreseeing that this was something that was likely to happen: "I knew that you are a gracious and compassionate God, slow to anger and abounding in love, a God who relents from sending calamity" (Jonah 4:2).

This phrase—"you are a gracious and compassionate God, slow to anger and abounding in love"—is one that we see over and over again in the Old Testament, and echoed in the New; so much so that we could almost say it is presented as a principal defining divine characteristic (for example, Exod 34:6; Num 14:18; Neh 9:17; Pss 86:15, 103:8, 145:8; Joel 2:13; cf. Jas 5:11). This would also make it a defining characteristic underlying the prophets' message.

Before we turn to prophecy for today, we need to say a little something about the *sensus plenior*—a Latin phrase referring to a "fuller" or "deeper" meaning of a prophetic text. We see this kind of interpretation taking place on a number of occasions in the New Testament in relation to Old Testament texts: for example, "So was fulfilled what the Lord had said through the prophet: 'Out of Egypt I called my son'" in Matt 2:15.

Sensus plenior is a somewhat controversial idea insofar as it stretches a text's "meaning" beyond that of which the original writer and audience would have been aware and therefore breaks the "first rule" of interpretation. And yet it's something we see the New Testament writers doing when it comes to messianic prophecies, in particular. So what does this mean for us?

The first thing to say is that just because the New Testament writers do this it does not give us license to—they were themselves writing inspired Scripture in their *sensus plenior* interpretations, we would not be. Once we lose the anchor of the original meaning of a text, the sky is the limit when it comes to finding "meaning" in something. The more creative a proposed reading is, the more potentially error prone it will be.

The second thing to say is that because a *sensus plenior* reading can only be identified in hindsight adds to its riskiness. Losing our mooring in the original meaning means we are into the realms of speculation.

That said, it somewhat depends on what we mean by "meaning"! We know that at a personal, devotional level, the Holy Spirit can and does *speak meaningfully to* us through texts outside their original meaning. But this is *never the same thing* as that text's "meaning." Whether something is the Holy Spirit speaking (or not) is to be discerned through its consonance with Scripture as a whole, and specifically whether it sounds like something Jesus would say: whether it accords with the nature and character of God.

Tangential to *sensus plenior* is seeing an implication that can be *derived* from a text though not present *within* it as such. Stein cites a helpful example—outside of a messianic context—in 1 Cor 9:9, where Paul quotes Deut 25:4 ("You shall not muzzle the ox when it is treading out the grain") in justification of ministers of the gospel receiving financial support for what they do; if oxen are allowed to share in the benefits of their work, how much more so ministers? The point here, however, is not so much a fuller or deeper meaning, but an inference that may reasonably be drawn by analogy.[2]

A further possibility may be a second meaning in a subsequent event (the prophetic words being fulfilled more than once). For example, a prophecy that was first fulfilled in concrete events in an earlier time being fulfilled once again in a messianic event in New Testament times.

When we turn to prophecy as presented in the New Testament (beyond Old Testament prophecies seen as fulfilled in the New), our context changes. It moves beyond the relationship of God to the Jewish people in the context of the nation of Israel. John the Baptist is the last of the "Old Testament–style" prophets. Along with the style of the prophets, the style of the prophecies themselves shifts. We no longer see lengthy, prophetic discourses addressed to a nation. This difference is framed by the opening to the book of Hebrews:

> In the past God spoke to our ancestors through the prophets at many times and in various ways, but in these last days he has spoken to us by his Son, whom he appointed heir of all things, and through whom also he made the universe. The Son is the radiance of God's glory and the exact representation of his being, sustaining all things by his powerful word. (Heb 1:1–3)

2. Stein, *Basic Guide*, 148.

Jesus, the Word of John 1, reframes the manner of God's interaction with humanity away from reliance on the words of human prophets. Prophecy now takes on a decidedly Christocentric (Jesus-centered) character. In other words, the characteristics of prophecy in this new era will visibly conform to Jesus and his presence—as the image of God, he is also the image of the Father and the Spirit, since they are one in nature and character.

In 1 Cor 12-14, Paul provides a theological and pastoral framework for understanding and practicing the gifts of the Holy Spirit, including prophecy. In describing them as gifts of the Holy Spirit, their Christ-reflective character does not change (he is, after all, the Spirit of Jesus, per Acts 16:7, and our doctrine of the Trinity tells us that whenever one of the persons is active, all three persons are present and involved).

As the exact image of the invisible God (Col 1:15), Jesus reveals to us in a new and clearer way God's plans, purposes, and ways, to which the moving of the Spirit of God naturally corresponds. The focus of the prophetic gift shifts from divinely inspired messages to the nation(s) to divinely inspired messages to the church and those within it.

The overarching goal of prophecy in the post–New Testament era is, as Paul tells us, "the common good" (1 Cor 12:7). Sandwiched between chapters 12 and 14, we see Paul explaining that the greatest gift of the Spirit is actually love (in the absence of which, the other gifts are simply "a resounding gong or a clanging cymbal"—1 Cor 13:1; without love, prophecy "is nothing"—v. 2). First Corinthians 13 is not in the first instance an excursus for marriage ceremonies, it's the framework and goal for the spiritual gifts.

Rather than prophecy being seen as a foretelling kind of "predictions competition," the validity of which is to be judged by whether something comes true (enhancing the prophet's reputation), "the one who prophesies speaks to people for their strengthening, encouraging and comfort" (1 Cor 14:3). *That* is the criterion on which prophecy today should be judged and evaluated—is it strengthening, encouraging, and comforting for people? "The one who prophesies edifies the church" (v. 4), which *is* the people. In 1 Thess 5:21, Paul says, "Test everything" and "hold on to what's good." If it isn't good—if it hasn't done good, if it didn't strengthen, encourage, and comfort—then ignore it. If the message is really important, God is more than capable of finding another way or another person to communicate it better another time. The test of whether a prophecy is "right" is less whether it comes true than whether it does good in the life of the person receiving it; in *their* opinion, no one else's.

Against this background, there is no merit in delivering prophecies that mimic an Old Testament prophet, especially one speaking in "King James language." There is no need for "Thus saith the Lord," or "I say to you my children" introductions. Still less are prophets today being asked to speak to the nation(s). The style and the purpose of prophecy has changed in the light of Jesus and the new covenantal era. It would be helpful if more Pentecostal/charismatic Christians were aware of that.

Apocalyptic

Our final biblical genre, apocalyptic literature, is arguably one of the strangest of all, certainly for today's reader. We really have no modern equivalent. Perhaps for that reason, along with its association with prophecy concerning the end times (or more particularly, its association with highly speculative, fanciful "interpretations" of that), for many Christians it holds a strange kind of fascination. Who doesn't like the idea of a book full of insights into what's going to happen in the future, where all we need to do is simply decode it (or so it is supposed)?

To the extent they have come across the term, most Christians' awareness of apocalyptic literature will center on the book of Revelation. This is unsurprising; other than the odd snippet here and there embedded in a Gospel or a letter, Revelation is the only apocalyptic literature in the New Testament; the only other instance in the whole Bible is in Dan 7–12, in the Old Testament.

Apocalyptic derives from a Greek word, *apokalypsis*, meaning "revelation" or "disclosure," which appears in the very first verse of the book of Revelation: "The revelation [*apokalypsis*] from Jesus Christ, which God gave him to show his servants what must soon take place. He made it known by sending his angel to his servant John." Its defining characteristics—distinguishing it from prophecy more generally—are the combination of (i) revelation by God to a human prophet, (ii) through the medium of a vision or dream, (iii) via an otherworldly mediator, (iv) concerning future events, (v) for a present-day audience (community) undergoing struggles and challenges (such as persecution), and (vi) for its strengthening and encouragement (though times are tough right now, it will end well: God is in control of history). The content is supernatural and its imagery otherworldly. Though there is some apparently familiar imagery of people and animals, there is also lots of symbolism and fantasy characters (such as beasts with seven heads) mixed in.

To begin, we must be blunt and say that virtually all "popular-level" (nonscholarly) Christian books and videos offering to make Revelation easy to understand, with a simple direct correspondence to contemporary (or soon-to-unfold) events—even naming individuals or nation-states in our own times—are complete nonsense. They are simply fanciful speculation, promising an ease of interpretation and literal correspondence ("*this* is referring to *that*") which is totally misplaced.

We have said before, and it bears repeating, that the most faithful interpretation is not a literal interpretation. A literal reading is not automatically the same thing as "the plain meaning" of a text. The big problem with defaulting to a literal interpretation as presumed best practice is that it ignores both the genre and the author's intentions (in fact, it overrides them and imposes the reader's own instead). In contrast, the most faithful reading respects both. Its primary concern is what did this mean to its original author and audience; what was it saying, then, through the genre that the author used in order to convey it? Simply because a piece of biblical literature is apocalyptic in genre does not change this "first rule." It is almost inevitably the case that whatever distant-future meaning there might be in a passage, the author's original audience would have perceived a present-day meaning and application in the first instance. When we are looking for original meaning, this is to be derived (in the case of Revelation) from the contexts in which John found himself and into which he was writing—pay particular attention to that in good recent commentaries.

Our two biggest dangers as modern readers and interpreters—we are always both; there is no reading without interpretation—are to think that Revelation is (a) too hard to understand (and so ignore it), or (b) too easy to understand (provided we read the right popular books that promise that).[3] Footnoted below are a few scholarly works that are worth consulting.[4] In the absence of help from such sources, there is no chance of understanding what is going on most of the time.

---

3. If you *do* want to read them, which I don't recommend, at least borrow them from a library rather than waste money buying them.

4. McKnight and Matchett, *Revelation*; Witherington, *Revelation*; and Keener, *Revelation*.

The genre of Revelation is primarily prophetic-apocalyptic, but set within the framework of a letter: "This letter is from John to the seven churches in the province of Asia" (Rev 1:4 NLT). Chapter 1 sets the scene for the rest of the book. In his apocalyptic vision, the writer John is instructed in v. 13 by "someone like a son of man" (whom the context indicates to be the resurrected and ascended Jesus) to "write . . . what you have seen, what is now and what will take place later" (v. 19). We see here the two components of what John will see in his vision: things taking place now, in his audience's present experience, and things to come. Guided by good commentaries, we particularly need to be aware of that first element, too often ignored by the casual reader. The context is clear in v. 9: "I, John, am your brother and your partner in suffering and in God's kingdom and in the patient endurance to which Jesus calls us. I was exiled to the island of Patmos for preaching the word of God and for my testimony about Jesus" (NLT).

Chapters 2 and 3 comprise short messages to churches located in seven identifiable cities within the Roman Empire. These are prophetic, but in the sense we've already mentioned: "forthtelling" words from God for their present situations more than "foretelling" future events. Already we have seen that the genre of letters is what's known as "occasional" writings—to particular people/churches, for particular reasons. Letters were "occasioned" by local circumstances, usually responding to pastoral problems or concerns. In this case, the backdrop is suffering under persecution, into which John's prophetic words from Jesus speak a combination of encouragement and admonition.

The next several chapters, 4 through 20, comprise a lengthy discourse of John's apocalyptic vision, and the book concludes with chapters 21 and 22, in which we see pictured an eschatological ("end-time") new creation—a new heavens and earth.

How, then, to sum up reading the book of Revelation "with its writer," in an appropriate way? Here's a suggested checklist of ten Dos and Don'ts, in all of which be guided and informed by good, scholarly resources:

1. Remember that the apocalyptic content is set within a letter context that was, in the first instance, within a real, historical situation: *their present*. Be aware, for example, of John speaking cryptically ("in code") concerning the Roman Empire ("Babylon") and the Roman emperor;

2. Rather than focusing on the detail, look for the big picture and the big themes—for example, that God ultimately reigns over human affairs and will be victorious against his (and his audience's) enemies who will face judgment for their actions, while the saints will be rewarded for their faithfulness even in martyrdom;

3. Pay special attention to "heaven" as Rev 21–22 pictures it—see Part I, chapter 1, "Reimagining What We Mean by 'Heaven'";

4. Beware reading-in a literal intention to certain elements that you read, especially those that feel like they should be taken literally because they appear to tie in with ideas acquired from elsewhere—for example, that the "lake of fire" (Rev 20:15) "must be" a reference to eternal conscious torment in hell;

5. Keep in mind that "the pictures express a reality but they are not themselves to be confused with the reality, nor are the details of every picture necessarily to be 'fulfilled' in some specific way";[5]

6. Remember that although this kind of literature is "painting a picture," its artistic genre is not realist (paintings that are photo-like, such as Leonardo da Vinci's *Mona Lisa*) but impressionist (Monet and Van Gogh) and expressionist (such as Edvard Munch's *The Scream*)—read it accordingly;

7. Notice the structure of "sets of seven" through the book;

8. Do not treat the events portrayed as being in chronological order—many are parallel accounts (otherwise, the end of the world occurs several times);

9. Remember that even where the text was speaking prophetically of events still to come, it meant still to come *from the original audience and author's perspective*, not necessarily from our perspective today (it's not "all about us")—there is every reason to think of many of the events having occurred in *their* lifetimes and no reason to assume they will occur in our lifetimes; and

10. Finally, have nothing to do with so-called prophetic timelines, date charts, or the supposed identification within Revelation of references to present-day countries or individuals (Christians have spent two millennia, including most of the twentieth century, getting all that wrong). If Jesus himself didn't have access to a timeline or date

---

5. Fee and Stuart, *How to Read the Bible*, 216.

chart (Matt 24:36), it's unlikely that today's hyperimaginative readers of Revelation do. By all means keep an eye out for "signs of the times" in a thematic sense when reading apocalyptic-style passages in the New Testament, but hold things lightly, not rigidly.

Bibliography

Barker, Paul A. "Sabbath, Sabbatical Year, Jubilee." In *Dictionary of the Old Testament: Pentateuch*, edited by T. Desmond Alexander and David W. Baker, 695–706. Downers Grove, IL: InterVarsity, 2003.

Bebbington, David W. *Evangelicalism in Modern Britain: A History from the 1730s to the 1980s.* London: Unwin Hyman, 1989.

Belousek, Darrin W. Snyder. *Marriage, Scripture, and the Church: Theological Discernment on the Question of Same-Sex Union.* Grand Rapids: Baker Academic, 2021.

Blue Letter Bible. "Probable Occasion When Each Psalm Was Composed." https://www.blueletterbible.org/study/parallel/paral18.cfm.

Boda, Mark J. "Lamentations I: Book of." In *Dictionary of the Old Testament: Wisdom, Poetry and Writings*, edited by Tremper Longman III and Peter Enns, 399–410. Downers Grove, IL: InterVarsity, 2008.

Burnhope, Stephen. *How to Read the Bible Well: What It Is, What It Isn't, and How to Love It (Again).* Eugene, OR: Cascade, 2021.

———. *Telling the Old, Old Story in a Postmodern World.* Great Missenden, UK: Adiaphora, 2022.

Carey, Holly J. *Women Who Do: Female Disciples in the Gospels.* Grand Rapids: Eerdmans, 2023.

Christian Assemblies International. "1,050 New Testament Commandments." https://www.abc.net.au/reslib/201407/r1308729_17984331.pdf.

Dawkins, Richard. *The God Delusion.* London: Bantam, 2006.

De Jonge, Marinus. "Messiah." In *The Anchor Yale Bible Dictionary*, edited by David Noel Freedman, 4:777–88. New Haven: Yale University Press, 2007.

Dodson, Joseph R. "The Convivial Background of Romans 1:26–27." *Lexington Theology Quarterly* 47 (2017) 105–21.

Erickson, Millard J. *Christian Theology.* Grand Rapids: Baker, 1987.

Evangelical Alliance. "Basis of Faith." https://www.eauk.org/about-us/how-we-work/basis-of-faith.

Fee, Gordon D. *The Disease of the Health and Wealth Gospels*. Vancouver: Regent College, 2006.
Fee, Gordon D., and Douglas Stuart. *How to Read the Bible for All Its Worth: A Guide to Understanding the Bible*. Grand Rapids: Zondervan, 1982.
Grenz, Stanley J. *Theology for the Community of God*. Grand Rapids: Eerdmans, 1994.
Grudem, Wayne. *Systematic Theology: An Introduction to Biblical Doctrine*. Leicester: InterVarsity, 1994.
Hiebert, Paul G. "The Flaw of the Excluded Middle." *Missiology: An International Review* 10:1 (1982) 35–47.
Huntsman, Eric D. "The Occasional Nature, Composition, and Structure of Paul's Letters." In *How the New Testament Came to Be*, edited by Kent P. Jackson and Frank F. Judd Jr., 190–207. Salt Lake City: Deseret, 2006.
Keener, Craig S. *The NIV Application Commentary: Revelation*. Grand Rapids: Zondervan, 2000.
Kika, Thomas. "US Faces New 'Axis of Evil' in Iran, China and Russia: Mitch McConnell." *Newsweek*, Oct. 22, 2023. https://www.newsweek.com/us-faces-new-axis-evil-iran-china-russia-mitch-mcconnell-1836775.
Kuiper, Kathleen. "Tanakh." Britannica.com. https://www.britannica.com/topic/Tanakh.
Ladd, George Eldon. *The Gospel of the Kingdom: Scriptural Studies in the Kingdom of God*. Grand Rapids: Eerdmans, 1990.
———. *The Presence of the Future: The Eschatology of Biblical Realism*. Grand Rapids: Eerdmans, 1996.
Mafico, Temba L. J. "Just, Justice." In *The Anchor Yale Bible Dictionary*, edited by David Noel Freedman, 3:1127–29. New Haven: Yale University Press, 2007.
Major, John. "Sir John Major's Statement on Treaties and Agreements Signed by the UK, 9 September 2020." https://johnmajorarchive.org.uk/2020/09/10/sir-john-majors-statement-on-treaties-and-agreements-signed-by-the-uk-9-september-2020/.
McGrath, Alister. *Evangelicalism and the Future of Christianity*. Leicester: InterVarsity, 1995.
McKnight, Scot. *Jesus and His Death: Historiography, the Historical Jesus and Atonement Theology*. Waco, TX: Baylor University Press, 2005.
———. "Women Who Do." *Scot's Newsletter*, Oct. 26, 2023. https://scotmcknight.substack.com/p/women-who-do.
McKnight, Scot, with Cody Matchett. *Revelation for the Rest of Us*. Grand Rapids: Zondervan, 2023.
Noll, Mark A., et al. *Evangelicals: Who They Have Been, Are Now, and Could Be*. Grand Rapids: Eerdmans, 2019.
Reumann, John. "Righteousness (Early Judaism)." In *The Anchor Yale Bible Dictionary*, edited by David Noel Freedman, 5:737–42. New Haven: Yale University Press, 2009.
———. "Righteousness (NT)." In *The Anchor Yale Bible Dictionary*, edited by David Noel Freedman, 5:745–73. New Haven: Yale University Press, 2009.
Schaff, Philip. *The Creeds of Christendom*. Vol. 3: *The Evangelical Protestant Creeds*. Grand Rapids: Baker, 1998.
Scullion, John J. "Righteousness (OT)." In *The Anchor Yale Bible Dictionary*, edited by David Noel Freedman, 5:724–36. New Haven: Yale University Press, 2009.
Stein, Robert H. *A Basic Guide to Interpreting the Bible: Playing by the Rules*. Grand Rapids: Baker Academic, 2011.

Walton, John H. *The NIV Application Commentary: Genesis*. Grand Rapids: Zondervan, 2001.

Witherington, Ben, III. *Making a Meal of It: Rethinking the Theology of the Lord's Supper*. Waco, TX: Baylor University Press, 2007.

———. *Revelation*. Cambridge: Cambridge University Press, 2003.

———. *What's in the Word: Rethinking the Socio-Rhetorical Character of the New Testament*. Waco, TX: Baylor University Press, 2009.

Wong, Kate. "Tiny Genetic Differences Between Humans and Other Primates Pervade the Genome: Genome Comparisons Reveals the DNA That Distinguishes *Homo sapiens* from Its Kin." *Scientific American*, Sept. 1, 2014. https://www.scientificamerican.com/article/tiny-genetic-differences-between-humans-and-other-primates-pervade-the-genome/.

Woollard, Whitney. "Lamentations: The Volatile Voice of Grief; A Voice We Need to Hear." BibleProject, June 25, 2018. bibleproject.com/articles/lamentations-voice-of-grief/.

World Vision UK. *The UK Church in Action: Perceptions of Social Justice and Mission in a Changing World*. 2018. https://www.worldvision.org.uk/media/gu5mdp1i/the_uk_church_in_action_report.pdf.

Wright, Christopher J. H. "Atonement in the Old Testament." In *The Atonement Debate: Papers from the London Symposium on the Theology of Atonement*, edited by Derek Tidball et al., 69–82. Grand Rapids: Zondervan, 2008.

Wright, N. T. "The New Testament Doesn't Say What Most People Think It Does About Heaven." *Time*, Dec. 16, 2019. https://time.com/5743505/new-testament-heaven/.

www.ingramcontent.com/pod-product-compliance
Lightning Source LLC
Chambersburg PA
CBHW020408230426
43664CB00009B/1237